THE
MILLENNIAL
MANUAL

{ The Complete How-To Guide to Manage, Develop, and Engage Millennials at Work }

RYAN JENKINS

The Millennial Manual: The Complete How-To Guide To Manage, Develop, and Engage Millennials At Work

...

Ryan Jenkins

ISBN-13: 9780998891903
ISBN-10: 0998891908
Library of Congress Control Number: 2017905807
Ryan Jenkins LLC, Atlanta, GA

Dedication

• • •

- *To Ashley: may this serve as a stark reminder of our journey together, your ceaseless sacrifices, and your endless pursuit to serve others.*
- *To Ella: may this inspire you to boldly share your talent with the world someday.*
- *To you: may this satisfy your thirst for continuous learning, your itch to remain relevant in a workplace in flux, and your hunger to compound your influence by leading the next generation well.*

Contents

How to Read This Book

• • •

As the title suggests, this is a manual. A manual is a book of instructions to help you learn about a specific subject, which in this case is Millennials. The book is meant as a quick reference guide for solving (nearly) all of the challenges managers face when leading Millennials. Keep it handy.

You don't have to read this book straight through, cover to cover, but if you do, you'll be a master of Millennials. However, the chapters each stand alone, so you can jump between them and choose the ones that are most useful to you and use the book as your Swiss Army knife for leading, developing, and engaging Millennials. (Note: I recommend that you read the "Generations Overview" section through first to get a helpful foundation and useful context for the rest of the book and then read the chapters that are most pertinent for you.)

Happy reading and leading.

Introduction

• • •

THE MILLENNIAL GENERATION IS THE most scrutinized of all time. You can't attend a conference, scroll through a news feed, or watch a movie without seeing the mention of Millennials.

Millennials are heavily scrutinized because…

- They are the largest generation on the planet.
- They make up a majority of the labor force.
- They approach work much differently than did previous generations.
- They have different buying habits.
- They represent future change and disruption.
- They have skills and knowledge that previous generations don't possess.
- They have begun to step into decision-making roles.
- They have been largely misunderstood and mislabeled.
- They are underprepared in fundamental workplace behavior and etiquette.

Because Millennials are so highly scrutinized, it's likely that you have some understanding of who Millennials are and the challenges they bring to the workplace.

The Millennial Manual will build on that knowledge (or deconstruct any misconceptions) to provide you with a clear, fresh, and forward-thinking understanding of Millennials. Then you'll be equipped with forty-seven proven how-tos that will enable you to increase productivity, improve retention, and accelerate the development of your Millennial workforce.

This book is the culmination of five years of research gathered from hundreds of companies and thousands of leaders sharing their best practices for managing and working with Millennials.

Over the years of speaking to thousands of people who manage Millennials, I've learned firsthand the specific challenges they face. As those challenges became more and more glaring and urgent, I decided to write this book to give leaders a manual for effectively managing, developing, and engaging Millennials at work.

Simon Sinek, the *New York Times* best-selling author of *Start With Why: How Great Leaders Inspire Everyone to Take Action*, recently stated in the viral YouTube video titled "Millennials in the Workplace," it's a "total lack of good leadership" that contributes to Millennials' inadequacies in the workplace. He opines that "it's the company's responsibility" to help Millennials overcome this problem. And so, it is the responsibility of a leader to change, adapt, and prepare the Millennial workforce.

As more and more Millennials enter the workplace, they need well-equipped leaders who are committed to Millennials' professional growth and who can help them become high-performing workers in the twenty-first century. *The Millennial Manual* will give you a glimpse of the future of work that Millennials are ushering in. At times, it may sound or feel like you must change for the sake of Millennials, but the bigger picture is about adapting to the new world of work.

How we work is changing fast—faster than ever before. Millennials are a big contributor to this acceleration, so learning how to manage, develop, and engage them will positively position you and your organization in tomorrow's in-flux workplace.

American author Eric Hoffer said it best: "In times of change, learners inherit the earth, while the learned find themselves beautifully equipped to deal with a world that no longer exists." *The Millennial Manual* will equip you to thrive in the new world of work and powerfully influence the next generation of workers.

Section 1
Generations Overview

• • •

CHAPTER 1

The Creation, Differences, and Growing Gaps of the Generations

• • •

THE TRADITIONAL MEASURE OF GENERATIONS is a familial one, defined by a single step in the line of descent from an ancestor.

The idea of generations defined socially was introduced in the nineteenth century. Social generations are cohorts of people who were born within a particular date range, share similar cultural experiences, and have been shaped by significant events or societal trends while coming of age.

William Strauss and Neil Howe, influential authors on American generations, define a social generation as the aggregate of all people born over a span of roughly twenty years or about the length of one phase of life: childhood, young adulthood, midlife, and old age.

Strauss and Howe's generations are identified by age cohorts sharing three criteria:

1   Age location in history. Members of a generation encounter key historical events (the world wars, the moon landing, terrorist attacks, etc.) and social trends (the Internet, technology, etc.) while occupying the same phase of life.

2   Beliefs and behaviors. Members of a generation are shaped in lasting ways by the eras they encounter as children and young adults, and they share common beliefs and behaviors.

3   Perceived membership. Members of a generation are aware of the experiences and traits that they share with their peers, and they share a common perceived membership in that generation.

NAMING THE GENERATIONS

In 1945, following World War II, economists, businesses, and policy makers began labeling generations as a new way to measure and study demographics. The Baby Boomers—those born between 1946 and 1964—were the first generation to accept a widely used label. They were so named because they represented a spike in birth rates following the war that had a clear end date with the introduction of hormonal birth control for women.

The Census Bureau first referred to the years between 1946 and 1964 as the *post war baby boom*. As the people born in this boom started to age, ad agencies began using the term "Baby Boomers" to help them target the demographic. This was the first and last time a generation's "official" name had its origin in a government agency.

The generations before the Baby Boomers were named retroactively.

In 1991, Douglas Coupland wrote *Generation X: Talents for an Accelerated Culture* about the anonymity he and his contemporaries felt growing up in the shadow of Baby Boomers. The letter *X* was meant to signify this generation's desire not to be defined.

The term "Millennials" simply refers to the generation who came of age during the recent turn of the millennium. *Advertising Age* has been credited with creating the term "Generation Y" in 1993, but Strauss and Howe used "Millennials" instead because the members of that generation did not want to be associated with their predecessors, Generation X. Soon after, *Advertising Age* conceded that "Millennials" was a better name and insisted that "Generation Y" was only a placeholder until more was discovered about them.

Similarly, the name of the post-Millennial generation, Generation Z, will likely change as more is discovered about the youngest generation.

As we see, the naming of generations can be tentative and typically takes time to evolve before becoming "official."

Do Generations Differ Across the World?

As generations come of age, the moods of their society have impacts on them. For example, Baby Boomers were born post–World War II, a time with a high social mood and in which expansion and growth were prevalent. This provided Baby Boomers with a heightened sense of confidence.

However, in other parts of the world, like Japan, the post–World War II times were not of a high social mood. Thus, its equivalent generation had characteristics more like those of our Silent Generation, the US generation that grew up during World War II.

To relate to international generations, it's important to be aware of the unique social moods and cycles that each generation has experienced in that area of the world.

However, Millennials are the first generation to collapse the locational divides between generations. Because Millennials have been in communication (visually, audibly, and/or in person) with their global peers as they've come of age, Millennials' communications and characteristics are very similar across the world.

The Growing Generational Gap

An individual's age is one of the most common predictors of differences in attitudes and behaviors. Generational differences lead to disengagement in the workplace that can lead to poor communication, decreased productivity, leadership miscues, and more. In fact, 52 percent of workers say they're least likely to get along with someone from another generation, according to a recent poll by research-and-consulting firm Frank N. Magid Associates, Inc.

According to a number of generational studies recently compiled by MidAmerica Nazarene University, such generational gaps can clearly be wide...

- 75 percent of managers agree that managing multigenerational teams is a challenge.
- 55 percent of Millennials describe their generation as "most productive," yet only 16 percent of Generation X and 6 percent of Baby Boomers would describe Millennials that way.
- 49 percent of Generation X describe their generation as "most creative," yet only 15 percent of Millennials would describe Generation X that way.
- 61 percent of Baby Boomers describe their generation as "most friendly/helpful," yet only 22 percent of Generation X and 12 percent of Millennials would describe Baby Boomers that way.

To create a cohesive team and avoid conflict, it's important for workers to understand how different generations see themselves and each other. It can be beneficial to blend experience and youthful energy in today's workplace, but it's also difficult to manage across the various generations.

Specifically in this book, we will cover the the steep challenges managers face when managing the Millennial generation, who have very distinct strengths, skills, and approaches to work, communication, leadership, and more.

CHAPTER 2

Who Are the Generations?

• • •

GEORGE ORWELL SAID, "EVERY GENERATION imagines itself to be more intelligent than the one that went before it, and wiser than the one that comes after it." Does his statement describe your feelings toward other generations? People tend to feel that their generation is the best one, but no generation is better than another—just different.

A firm understanding of just how different the generations are is important in today's multigenerational workplace and marketplace. Understanding the generations allows you to appreciate those who went before you by comprehending some of their struggles and triumphs, and it can prepare you for the changes and opportunities that will inevitably come with the next generation.

Below is a chart of the Western social generations. We've already seen that other areas of the world (such as Japan, other parts of Asia, and portions of Europe) have generation definitions based on their own cultural, political, and economic influences. However, more so than previous generations, the emerging generations (Millennials and Generation Z) have characteristics and behaviors that match those of their global peers.

Also note that these are generalizations. Many variations within generations can exist, especially between geographically and culturally different milieus.

Generation	Birth Years (approximate)	US Population
Generation Z	1998<	50+ million
Millennials	1981–1997	76 million
Generation X	1965–1980	51 million
Baby Boomers	1946–1964	75 million
Silent Generation	1928–1945	56 million*
GI Generation	1900–1927	60 million*

*These are peak numbers. The older generations are not this large anymore as their members pass away.

GI Generation (~1900–1927)

Age range as of 2017: 90+

Alternate name: the Greatest Generation

Shaped by: Great Depression, World Wars

Traits: hardworking, patriotic, respect authority, save conservatively

Silent Generation (~1928–1945)

Age range as of 2017: ~72–89

Alternate names: Builders, Traditionalists, Lucky Few, Postwar Cohort

Shaped by: World War II, Vietnam War, Korean War

Traits: military veteran, conformist, loyal, follow rules, nonprotestors

Baby Boomers (~1946–1964)

Age range as of 2017: ~53–71

Alternate names: Me Generation, Generation Jones

Shaped by: Woodstock, civil rights, economic prosperity, Kennedy assassinations, rock 'n' roll

Traits: driven, question authority, optimistic, efficient, team players, consumerist

Generation X (~1965–1980)
Age range as of 2017: ~37–52
Alternate names: Baby Busters, Gen Bust, the Lost Generation, Latchkey Generation
Shaped by: Watergate, layoffs, family instability, the *Challenger* explosion, MTV
Traits: latchkey kids, self-reliant, skeptical, independent

Millennials (~1981–1997)
Age range as of 2017: ~20–36
Alternate names: Generation Y, Echo Boomers, Generation Me
Shaped by: 9/11, the Columbine High School shooting, Y2K, the Internet, the Great Recession, technology
Traits: ask why, creative, optimistic, collaborative, entrepreneurial

Generation Z (~1998<)
Age range as of 2017: <19
Alternate names: iGen, Centennials, Globals, Homelanders, post-Millennials, Founders
Shaped by: terrorism, mobile technology, social media, cyberbullying
Traits: pragmatic, cautious, tech-dependent, Individualistic

Generational spans are likely to shrink to five to ten years (from fifteen-to-twenty-year spans) because of the increased level of exposure to innovations in technology and to significant events (thanks to our hyperconnected world) that mold one's early experiences.

CHAPTER 3

Who Millennials Are and Five Monumental Reasons That They Matter

• • •

As I'VE NOTED, THE MOST highly scrutinized generation of all time is the Millennial generation. They have been called tech-savvy, lazy, optimistic, entitled, overachieving, innovative, impatient, selfish, world-changers, social-media addicts, coddled, and influential, just to name a few epithets. But the one word I think best describes Millennials is...unprecedented.

It's not so much about Millennials themselves as it is about the innovations and other external factors that have converged to make this time in history and this generation truly unprecedented. It's an unprecedented time with unprecedented opportunity for companies and leaders who are positioned to capitalize on the culture and work shifts being ushered in by Millennials. (In chapter 4, we'll take a deep dive into the innovations and external factors that have shaped the Millennial generation.)

A MILLENNIAL OVERVIEW

- Millennials are on the verge of entering their prime working and spending years.

- Millennials have grown up in a time of rapid change, giving them a set of priorities and expectations sharply different from those of previous generations.
- Technology, a turbulent economic climate, and globalization have given the Millennials a new set of perspectives, experiences, and behaviors related to work and life.
- Millennials are waiting to get married and move out on their own. They have a new approach to ownership, which has birthed the "sharing economy."
- Being raised in a digital age, Millennials' affinity for technology has influenced how they shop. They value instant access to product information, peer reviews, and price comparisons.

MILLENNIALS BY THE NUMBERS

- Millennials are the largest US and global generation.
- Millennials are the largest generation in the US labor force.
- 63 percent of Millennials have bachelor's degrees, making them the most educated generation ever.
- 70 percent of Millennials across the globe may reject traditional business and work independently.
- 66 percent of Millennials expect to leave their organizations by the end of 2020.
- $15,000 to $25,000 is the average cost to replace a Millennial employee.
- 70 percent of the 2025 global workforce will be Millennials and Generation Z.
- $1.4 trillion annually is the estimated spending power of US Millennials by 2020.

WHY MILLENNIALS MATTER

Beyond being the largest generation on the planet and being on the verge of entering their prime working and spending years, there are other reasons Millennials matter that warrant your consideration.

1. CONNECTIVITY CONVERGENCE

Technology and the Internet are arguably the biggest social disruptors in history. They've changed how we live, work, and play. No individual or industry is immune to this disruptive power.

To make matters more disruptive...the Internet, mobile technology, and social media all converged on the largest generation on the planet during their influential years and during a phase of life when they could experiment with innovations.

Being connected to an Internet-enabled supercomputer throughout childhood and early adulthood has changed everything for Millennials and anyone who leads, communicates, or markets to them. The x factor is not Millennials themselves but rather the ubiquitous connectivity made possible by the Internet and mobile technology, coupled with those who have grown up with it, that has and will continue to be the recipe for massive change and disruption for years to come.

Connectivity has been a complete game changer for this generation. Millennials' values and behaviors are fundamentally different because they have been connected to the world's information and the world's largest amassed network of humans, all the while being empowered and encouraged to contribute.

Millennials can efficiently and effortlessly job hop, learn anything, build a personal brand, work anywhere and anytime, shop on the go, launch a business or "side hustle," have a voice, crowdsource major decisions, instantly price compare, build a global network, and more, all thanks to connectivity.

2. TOPICAL TALENT

For the first time in history, there is an emerging generation that has knowledge and skills that previous generations don't possess. Millennials grew up teaching Mom and Dad how to troubleshoot a computer, how to download apps, or how to use Facebook. They are the first generation that has entered the workplace ready to contribute using their unique skill sets. (This is also one of the main reasons there is so much workplace friction surrounding Millennials.)

Their talents are topical. In fact, 68 percent of hiring managers agree that Millennials have skills that previous generations don't.

Now, more than ever, there is high risk if you ask Millennials to sit the bench and wait their turn, because your competitors will leverage their Millennial talent and propel their business further into the twenty-first century.

Millennials still have plenty to learn (don't we all?), but not leveraging the unique talents of your organization's future leaders is a mistake.

3. IMPORTANT INDICATORS

A sound strategy for predicting what's next for your market or business is understanding Millennial behaviors and trends.

The goal should not be to change for Millennials but rather to change so you can lead, communicate, market, and run a business like it's the twenty-first century. Millennials offer the appropriate data points to powerfully influence future decisions.

One example of current technology is Snapchat. Seventy percent of US Snapchat users are Millennials. Do you think the generation who uses the image-messaging and multimedia mobile application on a daily basis is going to be satisfied with using e-mail at work? Probably not. That's why the office-productivity app positioned to "kill e-mail," Slack, has gained massive appeal with Millennials, and now 77 percent of Fortune 100 companies use the service.

Become a student of Millennials and be rewarded with important indicators of the future of work and/or the marketplace.

4. VAST VALUE

Because Millennials are young consumers and professionals, they inevitably carry a high lifetime value. Whether you're trying to market to Millennial consumers, sell to Millennial B2B buyers, or attract and retain Millennial workers, there is tremendous benefit in the long-term value they carry.

It's up for debate how loyal Millennials truly are. What is certain is that Millennials' loyalty is up for grabs more frequently than ever before. There is always more competing for their time, attention, and wallets, so it's important that you consistently and compellingly stay in front of your Millennial prospects.

Benefit from vast value by nurturing Millennial relationships so that their customer and company loyalty deepens over time.

5. ELEVATED EXPECTATIONS

Today's hyperconnected world and never-ending streams of information have instilled a never-ending appetite in Millennials for more, better, faster. The effortless and seamless experiences Millennials have routinely encountered throughout their lives has become the new lens of expectation they carry into every brand and employer interaction.

Here are a few examples of the internal dialogue of Millennials when they encounter friction-filled experiences:

- "Why do I need to wait in line for a hotel key when I can skip the front desk at Marriott by securing a digital room key with my mobile device?"
- "Why do I have to sit through this hour-long classroom training when I could have learned the same content on 21Mill.com's mobile learning platform in a fraction of the time?"
- "Why do I have to interact with a cashier when Amazon Go stores allow for 'just walk out' technology with no lines and no checkout?"
- "Why should I remain at this company when I can find companies and salaries on Glassdoor.com that are a better fit for me?"

Every time technology makes a process or procedure more frictionless, it becomes the new expectation or standard for the generations who never experienced what it was like before the innovation. Many might argue that this is entitlement, but it's not when it's your only frame of reference. The world is shifting, and Millennials' expectations have shifted with it.

CHAPTER 4

The Life of Millennials: A Timeline That Reveals How the Digital Age Shaped Them

• • •

MATURITY IS THE ABILITY TO see and act on the behalf of others. Immaturity is not being able to see things from someone else's point of view.

It's natural for Millennials to exude immaturity in the workplace because they lack the necessary context and experience. But unfortunately, it's all too common for leaders of Millennials to also be immature.

Leaders of Millennials aren't immature in their experience, knowledge, or skills but rather in seeing the world from the perspective of Millennials. As you will learn in this chapter, the digital age has fundamentally rewired Millennials.

Millennials' unprecedented digital upbringing has made it difficult for experienced leaders to see the world from their point of view. This results in leaders becoming frustrated and defaulting to correcting instead of connecting.

Correcting positions the leader as a nitpicking and authority-hungry parent figure. Connecting positions the leader as a wise coach.

Which would you prefer to be?

This chapter will provide you with the abbreviated story of the Millennial generation. The goal is to give you a better understanding of who this generation really is so that you are better equipped to connect and lead them.

Millennials aren't trying to be difficult or frustrate you on purpose. They have just had a very different upbringing (one the world has never seen before), and this has created a new breed of worker. Thus, a new breed of leader is needed to effectively and influentially lead them.

A MILLENNIAL'S TIMELINE

For you to more clearly see the world from the Millennial perspective, let's look at a fictitious example...we'll call him Millennial Mike.

The timeline covers pivotal innovations in the life of Millennials and how they have shaped their view of life and work. Each section is highlighted with an example of how companies are adapting to the unique Millennial mind-set.

1990: MILLENNIAL MIKE IS BORN.

1997: MILLENNIAL MIKE GROWS UP GAMING.

At age seven, Millennial Mike is enamored with the Nintendo 64. The Millennial generation grew up gaming, and it has fundamentally rewired how this generation approaches work, teams, and communication. Gaming offers constant feedback loops, opportunities to make a difference by saving the world, and global collaboration as Millennials put on headsets and gamed alongside peers halfway around the world. All of these qualities are now expectations that Millennials pull into the workplace.

Millennial mind-set: Millennials desire feedback, to make a difference, and diverse collaboration thanks to gaming.

Innovation influencer: Nintendo

Company example: Applebee's, a national chain of casual-dining restaurants, used a game called Bee Block to have employees collaborate and compete on metrics like getting to work on time, selling special menu items, and completing quizzes about company rules. The game led to a 20 percent reduction in staff turnover and larger average tickets.

2000: MILLENNIAL MIKE IS INTRODUCED TO THE WORLD WIDE WEB.

At age ten, Millennial Mike first hears about online chat rooms. Mike and his friends deal with the sluggish and bizarre sounds of dial-up modems to create an AOL (originally known as America Online) username and begin chatting with the world. Millennials become the first generation in history for whom digital-technology platforms are the essential mediators of social life and information acquisition. Millennials have not had to adapt to technology, because it's all they've ever known. They have a knack for technological adaptability.

Digital technology has fundamentally shaped their friendships, perspective on the world, structure of their social networks, how they learn, how they interact with brands and institutions, and how they allocate their time. Millennial Mike has become a digital native and will soon carry his new disruptive perspectives and values into the workplace.

Millennial mind-set: Millennials approach differently how they learn, work, socialize, buy, communicate, and play due to technology.

Innovation influencer: AOL

Company example: Airbnb, an online marketplace and hospitality service, has a "chief employee experience officer" whose job it is to rethink how employees learn, work, socialize, communicate, and play. Other companies, like Cisco and Pandora, have similar job functions. (Learn more about "employee experience" in chapter 32.)

2004: MILLENNIAL MIKE USES THE INTERNET WITH EASE.

At age fourteen, Millennial Mike has access to Google while in high school and leverages the Internet to do the legwork for major projects. The world's information is now at his fingertips and aggregated by Google. Libraries become ghost towns as online resources such as SparkNotes and Wikipedia become shortcuts for learning material. Mike also joins one of the first social networks, MySpace, but begins to hear rumblings about another, college-only, social network.

Millennial mind-set: Millennials are the first generation that didn't consider parents or teachers as their authorities but rather the Internet. They treat the Internet as their external brain and approach problems in a whole new way from previous generations.

Innovation influencer: Google

Company example: Angela Ahrendts, a past CEO of Burberry, saw an opportunity to leverage the different thinking and resourcefulness of Millennials and created a "Strategic Innovation Council" where Millennials came together once a month with company leaders with the single goal to innovate Burberry's future.

2005: MILLENNIAL MIKE GOES SOCIAL.

At age fifteen, Millennial Mike joins Facebook (which launched in 2004 but was not open to high-school students until 2005), and he quickly amasses thousands of "friends." Millennials leverage social media to consume, collaborate, and contribute.

Also this year, Mike's parents decide to give him a cell phone for two primary reasons: safety and logistics. It takes Mike's parents only a month to regret their decision: Mike discovers texting (T9 style), and the phone bill skyrockets.

Millennial mind-set: Millennials are early adopters (of social media, cell phones, texting, and so on) and seek opportunities to innovate, especially as they enter the workforce.

Innovation influencer: Facebook

Company example: LinkedIn has an internal incubator where employees are encouraged to innovate. Once a quarter, employees with a new idea can put a team together for it and pitch it to the executive team. If their idea is approved, they may dedicate up to three months to turn the idea into something that benefits the company.

2007: MILLENNIAL MIKE PARTICIPATES IN THE MOBILE REVOLUTION.

At age seventeen, Millennial Mike is fortunate enough to have his parents buy him the first-generation iPhone. A big part of the phone's success is that it caters to Millennials with its multitouch interface, virtual keyboard with automatic spell check and correction, predictive text technology, and the ability to learn new words.

On the heels of the iPhone launch, 2007 is the first year that Americans send and receive more text messages per month than phone calls. Millennials channel their previous AOL instant-messaging days into mainstream texting and usher in a dominate new communication medium.

Millennial mind-set: Millennials' (and every other generation's) communication has and will continue to be shaped by technology.

Innovation influencers: iPhone and texting

Company example: A nonprofit organization that provides clean and safe drinking water to people in developing nations, Charity: Water, has changed how it communicates internally by eliminating e-mail and instead using Slack, an easy-to-use messaging platform, to make workplace communications more dynamic, modern, and next-generation ready.

2008: MILLENNIAL MIKE ESTABLISHES HIMSELF ONLINE.
At age eighteen, Millennial Mike joins Twitter as it gains traction with its adoption of the limited-character format and as a microblogging platform. Twitter opens Mike's eyes to the power of blogging, so he starts a blog on Tumblr, sharing his passions on a public and global platform. Growing up with access to the Internet has empowered Millennials to contribute and have a voice.

Millennial mind-set: Millennials are contributors (not passive consumers or employees) looking for an active role and immediate impact.

Innovation influencers: Twitter and blogging

Company example: AT&T recently charged a Millennial team with producing and hosting a company podcast (titled *Life at AT&T*) that provides a behind-the-scenes look at what it's like to be an employee there. AT&T launched the podcast to empower Millennials as contributors.

2011: MILLENNIAL MIKE LEVERAGES HIS NETWORK.

At age twenty-one and as a senior in college, Millennial Mike sets his sights on getting a job and begins cleaning up his online reputation. First, he leverages his robust social networks (on Facebook, Twitter, and LinkedIn) to crowdsource answers for his major life decisions. He asks his network where to live, what to eat, what to buy, and where to apply for work. Millennials value lifestyle and relationships over career, which is why it's not unusual for Millennials to choose a city before securing a job.

Millennial mind-set: Millennials are heavily persuaded by their peers, constantly turning to their networks for new opportunities, to stay in touch, connect with brands, and to acquire news.

Innovation influencers: LinkedIn and crowdsourcing

Company Example: Zendesk, an HR software company, created a recruiting video that not only highlighted its workplace and actual employees but showcased the city in which the employee would work. It focused on coffee shops, bars, public transportation, and such, which appeal to Millennials' lifestyle value.

2014: MILLENNIAL MIKE OWNS HIS CAREER.

At age twenty-four, Millennial Mike is a young professional who has already had two or three different jobs. Glassdoor.com, a website that gives people the inside scoop on companies with employee reviews and information on salaries, benefits, and more, has created complete transparency in the job market. This is how Mike knows which companies can offer him a better fit and salary.

Facebook friends and YouTube videos offer exposure into what it's like to work at other companies, and LinkedIn provides the platform to connect with anyone at them. Today's connected and transparent culture no longer allows companies to pull the wool over the eyes of their employees. Instead, it keeps them accountable for delivering exceptional employee experiences so they can retain top talent.

Millennial mind-set: Millennials demand transparency from leaders, employers, and brands.

Innovation influencer: Glassdoor

Company example: Mastercard, a multinational financial-services company, allows Millennial new hires to choose the leaders they want to work for. Transparency and accountability is created with leader profiles that include reviews and ratings.

2016: MILLENNIAL MIKE DISRUPTS ROUTINELY AND UNKNOWINGLY.
At age twenty-six, Millennial Mike is beginning to settle in as a professional, and technology continues to influence his life at work and home. For example, Netflix and Amazon have created an generation of on-demand consumers, Snapchat has disrupted the way an entire generation communicates (much like the intro of the iPhone did), Uber and Airbnb have created a generation that appreciates the sharing economy (*Why own when I can rent or share?*), and Slack—a messaging app for teams whose provider Inc.com rated as its 2016

Company of the Year—has enabled collaborative and real-time workplace communications that Millennials have come to expect.

Technology has and will continue to create new behaviors and values that have never existed before. Technology, coupled with Millennials, will usher in unparalleled and unavoidable disruption into every industry and workplace.

Millennial mind-set: Millennials' work and life behavior and values continue to be shaped by technology.

Innovation influencers: Netflix, Amazon, Uber, Snapchat, Airbnb, Slack

Company example: Taco Bell, an American chain of fast-food restaurants, is considering Uber-izing its front-line employee experience. Taco Bell employees not scheduled to work would use an app to see which restaurants in their area might need extra help during the peak lunchtime hours. Employees would check in via the app and get paid a premium for helping out for a few hours. This approach mirrors how Uber drivers can turn the app on or off based on their availability.

2017: MILLENNIAL MIKE BECOMES A DECISION-MAKER.
At age twenty-seven, Millennial Mike has been working for several years and is on the verge of accepting his first leadership role. In fact, according to *The Atlantic*, 30 percent of twenty-one-to-thirty-two-year-olds have already achieved management positions. How will your organization or industry change when these high-tech and hyperconnected Millennials begin making leadership decisions?

Millennial mind-set: Millennials' high-tech and hyperconnected upbringing have made them disruption-prone leaders.

Innovation influencer: (Yet to be determined.)

Company example: Bacardi recently created the Bacardi Rising Stars program, where emerging Millennial leaders will be equipped with the knowledge, expertise, and experiences to prepare them to be future leaders, all the while being encouraged to innovate and disrupt the organization from the inside out (more on this in chapter 27).

Millennials are a new breed of employee because they had an upbringing like no other in history. Use this new understanding of the Millennial journey and evolution to influence how you lead, connect, and communicate with this next-generation workforce.

CHAPTER 5

The Competitive Advantage of Generational and Cognitive Diversity

• • •

LIKE-MINDED TEAMS MAINTAIN; DIVERSE TEAMS innovate.

It's nearly impossible to learn something new from someone who shares your views or thinks like you. Why is diversity so challenging for many organizations and leaders? Because it's more comfortable to be with people who think and act similarly. The confrontational aspect of different viewpoints is complicated and harder to manage.

Organizations that hire and promote the same kind of thinkers are capping their potential.

More perspectives on a team leads to better decision-making. Perspective diversity can come in many forms: through different backgrounds, personalities, genders, races and ethnicities, experiences, thinking patterns, locations, skills, leadership styles, and ages.

A diverse workforce is better equipped to respond to today's high-flux and disruption-prone twenty-first-century marketplace.

Research shows that nondiverse teams are likely to apply a more uniform approach to problem solving, which ultimately dampens creativity and limits the solutions the team will try. A diverse team is better equipped to approach a problem from every angle, resulting in a better, more thought-through solution. Testing ideas against opposing points of view are how the best ideas get developed.

According to Anka Wittenberg, senior vice-president and chief diversity and inclusion officer at SAP, 85 percent of enterprises agree that diversity results in the most innovative ideas. In addition, external organizations, across industries, rated highly for diversity and inclusiveness report 57 percent better team collaboration, 19 percent greater retention, 45 percent more likelihood of improving market share, and 70 percent more likelihood of achieving success in new markets.

A diverse team provides the opportunity for the unique strengths of each team member to be leveraged. The greater the diversity, the greater the breadth of strengths available. Each diverse team member has strengths that can compensate for the shortcomings or blind spots of other team members.

Cognitive diversity is where a team of people has distinctly varied ways of thinking (experimental, analytical, logical, creative, etc.). Cognitive diversity fuels innovation, enhances employee engagement, boosts customer satisfaction (because diverse customers are represented internally), and drives business success in today's rapidly changing workplace.

Diversity of thought spurs innovation.

One of the most valued forms of cognitive diversity in today's changeable world can be found in a multigenerational workplace. Because Millennials fundamentally think and approach problem solving differently than previous generations, generational diversity is a very powerful version of cognitive diversity.

Generational differences have never been wider than they are today. Most workers—52 percent—say they are least likely to get along with someone from another generation compared to 30 percent with a different racial background and 19 percent with the opposite sex, according to a recent poll by research-and-consulting firm Frank N. Magid Associates. "Generational understanding is the new diversity training," says Sharalyn Orr, its executive director.

Friction across generations is likely to continue into the future: 45 percent of Generation Z (the post-Millennial generation) anticipates potential challenges working with Baby Boomers, 17 percent with Generation X—but only 5 percent with Millennials.

With generations being one of the greatest diversities that divides employees, leaders must act intentionally to unite generations in order to reap the benefits of generational diversity.

Fostering an environment of respect, inclusion, open communication, and freedom to create and implement ideas will help organizations capitalize on their generations' diverse cognitive power. Marrying previous generations' experience with Millennials' fresh perspectives and innovation will help future-proof organizations in the twenty-first century.

For example, a team that benefits from generational diversity will be able to communicate with the confidence of a Baby Boomer, the experience of Generation X, and the velocity of a Millennial.

Dennis Kennedy, founder and CEO of the National Diversity Council, says, "Managing generational diversity is key for organizations to gain a competitive advantage and make a positive impact on employee morale, productivity, and retention." He adds, "Organizations that want to thrive in the future will need to have employees and managers who are skilled in dealing with differences along these and other dimensions, including generational diversity."

Up until now, companies have asked employees to adjust to the corporate culture, but Wittenberg encourages corporate cultures to "open up to being inclusive" and allow the uniqueness of each generation and the individual to influence the company culture.

Achieving cognitive diversity through a multigenerational team enables workers to ask better questions, be more effective, and deliver improved experiences for employees and customers of all ages.

Section 2
Manage Millennials

. . .

CHAPTER 6

How to Motivate Millennials at Work

• • •

WHERE THERE ARE UNMOTIVATED MILLENNIAL employees, you will find unin-spired leaders who lead teams of anxious, job-hop-in-a-heartbeat Millennials. For leaders eager to spark change and energy in their organizations, there are specific Millennial motivators that can be leveraged to ignite Millennial hustle and extend Millennial retention.

1. INFUSE INNOVATION

- 78 percent of Millennials were strongly influenced by how innovative a company was when deciding if they wanted to work there (The 2014 Millennial Study).
- 66 percent of Millennials work in organizations that actively encourage and reward its people for innovative ideas (Deloitte).
- 42 percent of Millennials are likely to leave a job with substandard tech (Dell/Intel).
- 82 percent of Millennials say workplace tech is an influence on the deci-sion to take a new job (Dell/Intel).

Innovation is a catalyst for Millennials to perform more efficiently and effectively in the workplace. Millennials lean into their high-tech and hyperconnected up-bringing to make the workplace more collaborative, productive, and innovative.

According to the *2016 Dell & Intel Future-Ready Workforce Study U.S. Report,* a majority of Millennial workers look forward to higher levels of virtual sharing (73 percent) that allows them to collaborate with colleagues remotely, smart offices (70 percent) that recognize an employee and knows his or her ideal workspace environment, and virtual/augmented reality (67 percent) equipment to use in meetings, product development, and so on.

For example, Adobe, a computer-software company, recently launched a program called Kickbox to help employees develop and test ideas. Employees get $1,000 and lots of encouragement to submit and refine their ideas. They also introduced "experience-a-thons" where employees can dig in to new Adobe products and provide feedback ahead of launch.

Watch Millennial motivation soar when they have the tools and permission to innovate.

2. Favor Flexibility

- 72 percent of Millennials expect to be able to modify and customize their work computers; 63 percent will go around IT to find the solutions they need (Mobile Enterprise).
- 69 percent of Millennials believe that regular office attendance is unnecessary (Cisco).
- 88 percent of Millennials wish they could have greater opportunity to start and finish work at the times they choose.

Millennials are interested in flexibility regarding what they work on, how they work, and where they work. More and more research reveals that employees (especially Millennials) get more done and have a better impression of their employer when they have workplace flexibility.

Millennials are interested in customizing their career tracks and the work that they do. Millennials grew up in an age of customization enabled by the Internet. They now expect a similar level of customization and flexibility at work.

Rigor, rated one of the best places to work in Atlanta, has a "work from any-where, anytime" policy and a "take vacation whenever you want" policy. This flexibility builds trust with employees. The average Rigor employee only takes ten to twenty days off a year.

Deloitte injects flexibility into its career tracks. It has a Mass Career Customization program that allows employees to change their work preferences.

PricewaterhouseCoopers has been flexible with its incentives. Starting in 2016, PwC pays up to $1,200 a year toward school loans for qualified employees. Leaders at the firm have stated that this student-loan paydown program was created specifically to motivate Millennials.

Millennial motivation mounts where flexibility is present.

3. Deliver Development

- Millennials rate "professional growth and career development" as the number-one driver of engagement and retention at work.
- 50 percent of Millennials believe their organization could do more to develop future leaders (Deloitte Millennial Study).
- 71 percent of Millennials likely to leave a company in the next two years are unhappy with how their leadership skills are being developed.
- Only 20 percent of Millennials say that their employers provide ade-quate training opportunities to keep up with needed job skills.

Millennials want a clear picture of what is expected of them in the workplace coupled with the necessary training and development to upgrade their skills.

Zappos, an online retailer, provides all the training and mentorship necessary for any employee to have the opportunity to become a senior leader within five to seven years. It also offers a system that allows employees to get certified and receive a pay bump with each new skill set acquired.

Another example of a company that delivers development opportunity is DreamWorks Animation, a two-thousand-person-plus company with motion-picture hits like *Shrek, Rise of the Guardians, Antz,* and others. It allows any employee to pitch a movie idea to members of the executive team. More important, DreamWorks offers workshops and mentoring on how to make the movie pitches successful.

Delivering development opportunities will spark Millennial motivation.

4. FURNISH FEEDBACK

- Millennials want feedback 50 percent more often than other generations.
- 42 percent of Millennials want feedback every week—twice the percentage of every other generation.
- Only 23 percent of Millennials say they are getting enough feedback.
- 72 percent of Millennials whose managers provide accurate and consistent feedback find their jobs fulfilling.

Millennials grew up in an on-demand world where they have received instant feedback (likes, retweets, views, etc.) on anything they choose to share online. They now pull the expectation of frequent feedback into the workplace.

Thanks to collaborative technologies, it's easier than ever before to deliver frequent and fast feedback.

General Electric recently changed from its thirty-year-old annual performance-review process to an app that provides employees with frequent, fast, and mobile-enabled feedback. According to GE's head of human resources, Millennials were a big reason for the switch, and the new approach is aligned with how they are used to working and getting feedback.

Gain Millennial motivation momentum by furnishing more feedback.

5. EXTEND EXPERIENCES

- 78 percent of Millennials would choose to spend money on a desirable experience or event over buying a physical item.
- 82 percent of Millennials attended or participated in a variety of live experiences (parties, concerts, festivals, races, sports, etc.) in the past year.
- 77 percent of Millennials say some of their best memories are from an event or live experience they attended or participated in.

For a generation that grew up with everything at their fingertips, they are looking for unique experiences that they can't get online. Millennials are on a never-ending quest to discover experiences that are one-of-a-kind.

Catalyst Conference is a series of leadership conferences focused on a new generation of leaders. At each event, it breaks an obscure world record, such as the largest pillow fight, most people to sit on a whoopie cushion, highest belly flop, and more. It creates a unique circumstance that can only be experienced at the event.

After five years with New Belgium Brewing Company, its employees receive a one-week trip to Belgium. Yahoo provides employees with corporate outings like concerts and backyard barbecues. Freeborn & Peters, a full-service law firm headquartered in Chicago, has an annual "luggage party" where four employees are randomly chosen for an all-expense paid trip to Las Vegas.

Experiences power Millennial motivation.

6. PROMOTE PURPOSE

- 77 percent of Millennials said part of the reason they chose to work where they do is the company's sense of purpose.
- 84 percent of Millennials say making a difference is more important than professional recognition (Bentley University's Center for Women and Business).
- 92 percent of Millennials believe businesses should be measured by more than their profits (Deloitte).
- 75 percent of Millennials say they feel businesses are focused on their own agendas, not on improving society.

Millennials define career success by how meaningful the work is and/or how much impact they can have. They are attracted to organizations with heavy impact and to leaders who can communicate the purposeful vision of the organization.

At Warby Parker, an innovative eyeglass retailer, for every pair of glasses purchased, a pair is distributed to someone in need. It's a one-for-one model much like that of TOMS Shoes. So far, the firm has distributed over a million pairs of free glasses. There is a clear purpose for every pair sold, and the purpose of every employee's job is bigger than themselves.

Purpose prompts Millennial motivation.

POWER OF COMMUNICATING THE "WHY" (OR PURPOSE) WITH MILLENNIALS

German philosopher Friedrich Nietzsche once said, "He who has a why can endure any how." Viktor Frankl, Holocaust survivor and the author of *Man's Search for Meaning*, would agree that having a strong sense of meaning is the key to rising above adversity. Millennial motivation in the workplace has a similar origin.

According to the Career Advisory Board, the number-one factor that Millennials (ages twenty-one to thirty-one) wanted in a successful career was a sense of meaning. And nearly three-quarters of Millennials surveyed said that "meaningful work was among the three most important factors defining career success."

By now, it should be no surprise that Millennials value meaningful work and want to have an impact in the workplace. However, what is surprising is how many leaders fail to deliver on this Millennial value. Leaders of Millennials fall short in communicating the "why"—the why behind the organization, the why behind tasks or procedures, and the why behind an employee's work.

Don Charlton, founder and CEO of JazzHR, provides a great example of communicating the why when it comes to workplace focus:

> Explain why they [Millennials] should change their behavior in a way that resonates. For example, let's say you're tired of seeing your Millennial's phone light up with *another* Facebook notification. You can't just say, "Facebook is for home." Instead, say something like, "People who advance quickly here avoid unnecessary distractions at work, and all those phone notifications could easily distract you from your goal of being successful at this company." If you can keep a dialogue of "If you want to be successful...do this...," Millennials are more apt to listen.

Disengaged employees are the fault of the leader. Great leaders establish a vision of "why." Great leaders also know that vision leaks, so they communicate the why over and over and over again. Jim Collins, the best-selling author of *Good to Great*, says, "Teams should be sick of hearing the organization's why." Collins suggests that leaders ingrain the "why" into every single employee so that they have a meaningful lens through which to view work.

Millennials may be a different breed of worker, but they are human. And humans have hopes, dreams, and a longing for meaning.

Communicate the "why" to win the head, heart, and hustle of the Millennial worker.

CHAPTER 7

How to Adapt Your Leadership for Millennials

• • •

THERE MAY BE NO INDUSTRY plagued with more generational chasms and clashes than professional sports. In the National Football League, for example, every year, new and eager Millennial rookies join teams with established cultures, playbooks, veteran players, and seasoned coaches who are separated by a generation or even two.

When Jim Tomsula was coaching the San Francisco 49ers, he was asked about his stance on social media. His response was, "I don't like it at all. I don't know anything about it. I don't do it. I don't use it." With a team that has an average age of just over twenty-five years, it only took Coach Tomsula a month to change his perspective on social media once he realized it was a crucial component to connecting with his new players and leading Millennials.

Here are a few items that the San Francisco 49ers are doing differently to lead Millennials:

- **Reverse mentoring.** Coach Tomsula held weekly meetings to learn the new apps and technology his players are using.
- **Shorter meetings.** Meetings last thirty minutes instead of two hours. The team strives for more visuals and interactivity in each meeting.

- **Going digital.** Instead of the traditional printed schedule, the 49ers now send digital alerts that players can access on their mobile devices.

Many fans and 49ers staff are skeptical of all of the changes and of any need to give in to tech-dependent Millennials. They think, *Why should we cater to them?* Leaders and employers shouldn't cater to Millennials. Rather, they need to lead and work like it's the present day. Technology and the Internet have forever changed (and continue to change) how we work. Millennials are simply the signposts of change.

Tim Elmore, the founder and president of Growing Leaders and best-selling author of more than twenty-five books, offers a different angle on Coach Tomsula and the 49ers' Millennial approach. Elmore suggests we "coach as a missionary." Be a pioneer who leaves your comfort zone, enters a different culture, and learns the language and customs in order to reach people with your message. First, study the culture and learn its values so that you can add value to it.

It's not just coaches who have to make adjustments. Recently I had the pleasure to see five-time NFL MVP Peyton Manning deliver a keynote presentation at a conference, where he spoke about the constant need to "adapt his leadership to the next generation [of players]" by refreshing his expectations, perspectives, and vocabulary. Manning embraces a missionary approach by first learning and then earning the right to lead.

World-renowned leadership expert and author John C. Maxwell recently taught that to achieve posterity and legacy, leaders must pass the baton. But, more important, as Maxwell states, leaders must pass the baton at "full speed." They shouldn't be out of touch with today's tech, just viewing from the sidelines, but rather in a full sprint, fully aware of the exponential speed of the times we live and work in.

Coach Tomsula is taking his leadership to the next gear, achieving the speed that is now necessary to take Millennials and the entire team to a new level.

Isn't it time you gear up?

CHAPTER 8

How to Bridge the Communication Gap with Millennials

• • •

WORKPLACE COMMUNICATIONS TODAY ARE A tangled web of varying preferences. Some call, some e-mail, and others text while sitting right next to you.

Evolving technologies have wreaked havoc on our communication choices. There has never been a greater divide between preferred communication channels than there is today. When is face-to-face better than a call? When is a text better than an e-mail? When is Slack better than Skype?

The way people communicate varies by generation. According to Gallup:

Sending and receiving text messages is the most prevalent form of communication for Americans younger than 50. More than two-thirds of 18-to-29-year-olds say they sent and received text messages "a lot" the previous day, as did nearly half of Americans between 30 and 49. Young Americans are also well above average in their use of email and social media on a daily basis.

Recent RealityMine research shows similar trends, with e-mailing and calling increasing and texting decreasing with age. The data is clear that the younger the individual, the more likely he or she is to communicate using newer technologies.

With such disparity, how are you to find communication cohesion in today's multigenerational workplace?

Defer.

Consider the communication preference of the individual you wish to communicate with, and defer to their likely communication preference. We often communicate with others in the way we prefer to be communicated with, but the countless options for communication that now exist force us to be adaptive.

Since age has a strong correlation with an individual's communication preference, generations can be useful as clues to which form of communication would be most efficient and impactful.

For example, if a Millennial employee wants to get in touch with a Baby Boomer manager, the Millennial should consider deferring to a phone call or face-to-face meeting. If that Baby Boomer manager wants to get in touch with the Millennial employee, deferring to texting or instant messaging may prove most effective—certainly not a phone call. Once a connection is made, ask how the individual would prefer to communicate moving forward, and then stay with that form.

Adjusting our communications for each generation can be exhausting, but it's a new reality we must face. What's more exhausting is the constant miscommunication that occurs when you try to communicate with others using your own communication preference.

This simple strategy will also help generations become more versed in communication skills that they lack. Millennials can become stronger offline communicators, and older generations can become stronger digital communicators.

Considering one's generation, while not fail proof, can be a quick and effective way to decide what communication method to use.

If you don't know the generation of the individual you're going to communicate with, default to e-mail. While texting is the dominant communication function on mobile, it can be too personal for a first communication. E-mail (at the moment) is the most generation-neutral form of communication.

With their front-row seat for today's communication challenges, I anticipate that Generation Z—the post-Millennial generation—will begin to finally streamline the workplace communications as they come of age.

But until then...prefer to defer.

CHAPTER 9

How to Use Reverse Mentoring to Retain and Engage Millennials

• • •

It produced...an inversion of expertise because we had so many changes at the lower levels in technology and tactics and whatnot that suddenly the things we grew up doing weren't what the force was doing anymore. So how does a leader stay credible and legitimate when you haven't done what the people you're leading are doing? It's a brand-new leadership challenge, and it forced me to become a lot more transparent, a lot more willing to listen, and a lot more willing to be reverse-mentored.

RETIRED FOUR-STAR GENERAL STANLEY MCCHRYSTAL made this bold statement in his "Learn, listen...then lead" TED talk. Today's exponentially fast times and the rise of Millennials forced McChrystal into adopting a new perspective on mentorship—specifically reverse mentoring.

Reverse mentoring has become a powerful strategy for leaders and organizations to close the generational gap at work and to retain and engage Millennials.

Millennials place a premium on mentorship. In fact, Millennials intending to stay with their organizations for more than five years are twice as likely to have a mentor (68 percent) than not (32 percent). And over 90 percent of Millennials with mentors describe the quality of advice and the level of interest shown in their development as "good." A company culture of mentorship promotes Millennial loyalty and, as we'll see, reverse mentoring engages Millennial talent.

WHAT IS REVERSE MENTORING?

Reverse mentoring is a learning relationship where the mentor is younger than the mentee. Senior executives or veteran employees are paired with younger employees, who then share their insights and perspectives on various topics such as technology, social media, leadership, workplace trends, and more.

Unlike traditional mentoring, in which the mentor is always a senior individual who can pass on experience without much risk of pushback from the mentee, reverse mentoring provides an environment where information and insights can freely flow and where the organizational hierarchy is flattened.

Each generation brings with it strengths shaped by its members' unique circumstances. Today's younger generations carry a very unique and high-demand skill set and knowledge that previous generations have not had at that age. In fact, 68 percent of hiring managers agree that Millennials have skills that previous generations don't.

Millennials are familiar and comfortable with reverse mentoring because they grew up doing it. Millennials were the "household CTOs," helping Mom and Dad troubleshoot computers, set up Facebook, and embrace texting.

WHO USES REVERSE MENTORING?

Jack Welch, while CEO at General Electric, was credited for being one of the first adopters of reverse mentoring. Welch selected a junior employee to mentor him and then encouraged five hundred other organizational leaders to find reverse mentors. Since then, other companies including Hewlett-Packard, The Hartford, Power Home Remodeling (a *Fortune* top ten of the "100 Best Workplaces for Millennials"), PayPal, Cisco, and Coca-Cola have initiated reverse-mentoring programs.

According to Thomas Koulopoulos and Dan Keldsen, authors of *The Gen Z Effect: The Six Forces Shaping the Future of Business*, mentoring is used in 56 percent of a six-hundred-company sample polled by Delphi Group. Yet, of those six hundred companies, only 14 percent had a reverse-mentoring program in place, even though 51 percent of the companies have cross-generational teams.

Reverse mentoring is underutilized and isn't widely used because leaders...

- are unaware of the benefits
- are already engaged in peer-to-peer mentoring
- feel pressured to focus on tasks with clear ROI
- lack the time
- are prideful

Yet, reverse mentoring is becoming increasingly important to consider as more and more Millennials and Generation Z members pour into the workplace.

In their book, Koulopoulos and Keldsen highlight how Carlos Dominguez, a senior vice-president at Cisco, is retaining Millennials and sharing their behaviors across generations by leveraging a formal approach to reverse mentoring.

Cisco hires many Millennials into their associate programs. After speaking with some of the new hires, Dominguez realized many might leave after a relatively short period despite the large investments Cisco made in their training and education.

This realization led Dominguez to ask what can the company do differently to keep Millennials engaged and onboard.

The answer was reverse mentoring. Reverse mentoring provided Millennials with a voice, encouraged participation and contribution, and got them engaged. It also allowed the company to learn more about how Millennials see the world and approach their career.

Cisco piloted the program with a small group and made it voluntary. Eventually they created an app that matched mentors with mentees.

According to Dominguez, "In reverse mentoring, if it's done right, I'm not sure who's the bigger recipient of value because they're both getting something really vital. The younger person is, in some cases, mentoring some of the most powerful executives in the world. What they [the mentor] can get as an ally and as a coach is just immense. In turn, the executive is getting an invaluable education through the eyes of someone on the front lines of technology and behavior."

MORE EXAMPLES OF REVERSE MENTORING

BURBERRY

Angela Ahrendts, the former CEO of the English fashion company Burberry, saw an opportunity to leverage the unique and modern approach that Millennials take to problem solving. She created a Strategic Innovation Council where Millennials come together once a month to "innovate Burberry's future" by collaborating with Burberry's leadership.

BABSON COLLEGE

This private business school in Wellesley, Massachusetts, held a five-week series of seminars that were developed and taught by students instead of faculty. The college was interested in offering courses that were more relevant to the real world, because faculty didn't have expertise in topics ranging from app development to the food-truck industry. The college stresses the importance of achieving "cognitively ambidextrous" or "effortlessly bilingual" skills, and with 96 percent of Babson graduates finding jobs, the strategy seems to be working.

WARBY PARKER

During the early stages of the prescription eyeglass-and-sunglass company, Warby Parker had planned to move aggressively into brick-and-mortar until younger employees suggested going digital first and selling the product online. Reverse mentoring was a key reason that Fast Company named Warby Parker the Most Innovative Company of 2015.

NATIONAL FOOTBALL LEAGUE

When Jim Tomsula was the head coach of the San Francisco 49ers, he held weekly meetings with players to learn about "new apps and technology," which he used to create digital reminders for the team. Tomsula also shortened the two-hour team meetings to thirty minutes and injected more visuals and interactivity based on his reverse-mentoring learnings.

TARGET

The second-largest discount retailer in the United States recently partnered with Techstars—a group that teams tech start-ups up with large corporations—to teach their leaders how start-up employees (many of whom are Millennials) work in a fast-paced environment and "scrappily to get things done." This practice has also helped diminish the negative stereotypes that can plague Millennial employees within their companies.

SLOVENIA

The small European country of Slovenia is using reverse mentoring to combat ageism. The Simbioza project was created with the goal to improve e-literacy in seniors through young people volunteering to teach computer skills. The project put technology into the hands of older adults but also instilled social responsibility into Millennials, thereby giving hope to both age cohorts. The project has been a success in bridging the country's generation gaps.

BENEFITS OF REVERSE MENTORING

A diverse workforce is required to stimulate innovation, cultivate creativity, and steer business strategies. Reverse mentoring empowers a diverse range of employees to share their opinions, ideas, knowledge, and experiences on a level playing field. Reverse mentoring creates an environment of trust, belonging, understanding, support, and encouragement.

Here are a few other benefits of reverse mentoring:

- **Transfers knowledge.** Cross-generational relationships allow specific knowledge and experience to be passed on to other generations.
- **Increases Millennial retention.** Reverse mentoring provides the opportunity to contribute and make an impact that Millennials desire.

- **Demonstrates value.** Reverse mentoring provides an opportunity for Millennials to understand the value they can bring to the organization, ultimately keeping them engaged at work.
- **Compounds growth.** Both parties get equally equipped. Millennials want insights that Google can't give them. Other generations benefit by understanding what's next.
- **Brings fresh perspectives.** Young mentors can offer insights into their target market, help define a brand voice via social media, or provide advice on digital best practices.
- **Diminishes stereotypes.** Varying viewpoints and assumptions across generations can transform into awareness and appreciation.
- **Coheres communication.** Clear and focused communications are the result when generations are intentional about connecting.
- **Shares Satisfaction.** Individuals gain satisfaction when sharing helpful and valuable information.
- **Includes diversity.** Diversity initiatives help employees learn cultural awareness to create inclusive corporate culture and to understand their importance to the organization.

It's essential that any organization help its employees acquire knowledge, skills, and expertise. Reverse mentoring is an exceptional way to organize, create, and distribute knowledge. It supports topical learning between individuals and groups.

HIDDEN BENEFITS OF REVERSE MENTORING

When leaders decide to engage in reverse mentoring, they have a golden opportunity to model the communication skills that Millennials desperately need and provide the leadership development they want.

Leaders can display firsthand the power of a firm handshake, the benefits of strong eye contact, appropriate body language, how to craft inquisitive questions, the importance of continuous learning, and much more.

Reverse mentoring is a win-win. It creates opportunities for Millennials to improve their communication skills and develop professionally while leaders get the added benefit of learning from the next generation.

HOW TO BEGIN REVERSE MENTORING?

1. Make a list of five things you don't know but need to know.
2. Identify one or two items from the list that you are least likely to learn on your own or during work.
3. Identify a junior colleague who has the expertise you need.
4. Ask the junior colleague to mentor you.
5. Clarify where to meet, frequency, expectations, etc.
6. Prepare by identifying a set of questions before the first meeting (don't be afraid to ask naive questions).
7. Meet and mentor.

CREATE REVERSE MENTORING AT A LARGER SCALE

To create reverse mentoring opportunities at a larger scale, consider creating an "employee-resource group" or "affinity group" for young professionals. Employee-resource groups are voluntary, employee-led groups that serve as a resource for members and organizations by fostering a diverse, inclusive workplace aligned with organizational mission, values, goals, business practices, and objectives.

These groups make it easier for Millennial employees to host events or training where they can share their knowledge and expertise to a larger audience. Also, since the groups are inclusive, there is opportunity for other generations to engage in reverse mentoring (directly or indirectly) with the younger members of the group.

IMPORTANT REMINDERS WHEN REVERSE MENTORING

- **Avoid reciprocal learning.** To get the full benefit of reverse mentoring, ensure you are receiving insights, instead of imparting insights, 75-100 percent of the time.
- **Go beyond technology and social media.** It's natural and easy to ask Millennials to teach you about technology or social media, but consider having them teach you something you think you already know, such as leadership or communication. While you likely have more experience in these areas, you will get to learn how Millennials approach these topics and what leadership or communication styles resonate with them. All of these are invaluable insights that reflect your consumer base or employee population and can be used to deepen the connection with your Millennial market or teams.
- **Create a safe place for discussion.** This hinges on the posture of the leader and the culture of the organization. Well-crafted questions can make the most closed-off person open up. The work rests on the shoulders of the leader to create thought-provoking questions that lead to productive discussions. Approaching the discussion from a true development/learning perspective for the leader instead of treating it like a review or traditional mentoring role is important.

- **Have a defined end point.** A stale mentoring relationship can breed resentment on both sides. Start with a short time frame (two to four meetings) and then reevaluate to see if both sides want to extend the relationship.

Conclusion

In today's ever-changing business world, it's important for leaders to stay grounded in what's next for their teams, industry, and workplace. Reverse mentoring offers the chance to disrupt and expand one's perspective as well as retain Millennials and provide them a heightened sense of engagement and ownership.

Everybody has something to learn from somebody. Mentorship will never be the same, and nor will your organization, should you choose to reverse.

CHAPTER 10

How to Give Feedback to Millennials

• • •

ONE OF THE TOP OBJECTIONS I hear after speaking to an audience about Millennials is how overly sensitive they are when receiving criticism from their managers. Many Millennials have had childhoods chock full of successes, and often the first failure they encounter is at work, which leaves the responsibility on managers to deliver the appropriate feedback.

Even the classic "feedback sandwich"—constructive or negative feedback sandwiched between positive feedback—is hard to swallow for many Millennials...which is ironic, since they are the foodie generation.

So, what's a manager of Millennials to do? Especially since Millennials want feedback 50 percent more often than other employees?

Mark Elliott, the president of Hodges Ward Elliott—a leading real-estate firm specializing in hotel mergers and acquisitions—has adjusted its organization to make delivering feedback to Millennials a breeze. When asked how it does this for its "Millennial-ized" workforce, Elliott stated, "We have Millennials do their own reviews." Millennials first spend time evaluating their own performance and then bring their own feedback to a meeting with their manager. This transforms the manager into a coach.

Simple, yet powerful.

Millennials respond better to coaching than they do to managing. Executive coach Ed Batista defines coaching as a "style of management characterized by asking questions." Purposeful and poignant questions cultivate a dynamic learning session that enables a direct report to grow through self-reflection. Coaching questions ultimately empower someone to look internally for solutions on his or her own and to change actions in the moment.

Effective coaches ask the right questions that allow the coached person to reflect and discover answers independently, ultimately empowering him or her to look internally for the solutions in a future similar situation.

Elliott discovered three benefits as a result of allowing Millennials to perform their own reviews:

1. **Millennials are more critical.** When evaluating their own results, Millennials are more critical of their performance than a manager would be. This behavior surprises many managers, as it demonstrates Millennials' deep desire to succeed and work hard.
2. **Millennials take ownership.** After spending time reflecting upon their past performance, Millennials are likely to take ownership of their mistakes and shortcomings. The organization and manager benefit as the Millennial begins to develop the self-evaluation muscle that can be flexed in real time to create a more productive and dependable worker.
3. **Managers become encouragers.** Since Millennials bring their own assessment to the table at reviews, the manager can affirm the positives and offer encouragement in the areas where a Millennial highlights a

weakness. This makes the review process a much more pleasant experience for both parties—not to mention that it saves time for the manager—and positions the manager as an inspiring coach instead of a nitpicking boss.

CHAPTER 11

How to Manage the Mobile-Centric Millennial Employee

• • •

IN THE NOT-SO-DISTANT PAST, WORK was confined to a building and executed at a desk bound by a physical location. If you asked someone who was on the road between 7:00 and 9:00 a.m., "Where are you going?" he or she would likely respond, "I'm going to work." Work once was at a specific place.

The tech shift from fixed to mobile communications has redefined where and how we work. Work has shifted from a place to a space.

According to a 2015 study by Adobe, 87 percent of respondents said that they check their work e-mail at home. The study found that Millennials are more likely to check work e-mail outside of normal work hours, with 70 percent checking it while in bed. And now, mobile represents 49 percent of all e-mail opens.

More and more, we are squeezing work into the cracks of life...when we're in line for coffee, on our way to a meeting, or on vacation.

Since we are now enabled to work anywhere and anytime, it has become in-sufficient to manage people based on input—i.e., measured by employees' time at their desks, in the office. Instead, today's managers must manage outputs— i.e., an employee's results of a task or project.

Millennials specifically don't view work as bound by time or space. In fact, 69 percent of Millennials believe that regular office attendance is unnecessary. Previous generations have defined company loyalty by tenure—how much time is put in—but Millennials define company loyalty by impact: how meaningful their output is.

I recently spoke with a manager of a remote team who explained his shift from input to output management. He had recently hired his first Millennial employee. The team would routinely log in at 9:00 a.m. to start the workday, but the manager was frustrated to notice the new Millennial employee consistently starting his day at 12:00 p.m.

The manager perceived the Millennial's input as lazy, but upon confronting the him, he learned that the employee was working well beyond the conventional 5:00 p.m. end time, sometimes working as late as 2:00 a.m.

The manager had not considered alternate work hours and decided to allow the Millennial to work wherever and whenever he could produce the best work. The manager made the crucial shift from managing inputs (time logged in) to managing outputs (quality of work).

The manager in this example is not alone. Seventy-two percent of global businesses report that increased productivity is a direct result of flexible working practices.

For managers ready to make the shift from managing input to managing output, here are a few tips:

- Clearly communicate the desired output. Provide real examples whenever possible.
- Consistently communicate time frames for deliverables.
- Frequently deliver relevant feedback via collaborative technologies, such as Slack.
- If necessary, schedule a recurring time when your team can collaborate in real time (online or offline).

The twenty-first century demands management skills that can transcend generations, time zones, and cyberspace.

Work has shifted, and so should your leadership.

CHAPTER 12

How to Effectively Delegate to Millennials

• • •

SAVE TIME, BUILD TRUST, AND develop future leaders by delegating in these five simple steps.

Delegation is the catalyst behind the growth of any business or team. Entrepreneurs and leaders must choose control or growth. They can't have both. If growth is your choice, then you must delegate.

To delegate means to entrust (a task or responsibility) to another person, typically one who is less senior than oneself.

When delegating, leaders must delegate authority, not just the task. Delegating only tasks creates followers. Delegating authority creates leaders. Empower your team to make it better.

Perhaps the generation most interested in being on the receiving end of delegation are Millennials. Seventy-one percent of Millennials likely to leave a company in the next two years are unhappy with how their leadership skills are being developed. Seventy-five percent of Millennials believe their organizations could do more to develop future leaders.

Besides building trust and saving time, the other benefit of delegation is the opportunity it provides to develop future leaders.

How to Delegate to Millennials Effectively:

1. **Select strategically.** Choose the right person for the project. If you're having difficulty finding the right person, you may have a hiring problem.
2. **Clarify expectations.** Explain the results you are looking for and what success will look like. Delegation without details is a disaster.
3. **Grant full authority.** Provide ownership that breeds new leaders.
4. **Provide feedback.** Inspect what you expect by scheduling check-ins and checkpoints. Offer input but avoid interference.
5. **Evaluate the outcome.** Correct or celebrate based on the results.

Delegation is a two-way street. The delegating leader must set the tone of the team with integrity and a good work ethic, and the team needs to deliver for the leader.

If growth is your goal, make delegation a priority.

CHAPTER 13

How to Succeed as a Leader of Millennials

• • •

HE IS THE WINNINGEST DIVISION I basketball coach of all time with over 1,020 wins as a head coach. He's won five national championships, second only to the great UCLA coach John Wooden. He has won two Olympic gold medals and two other international tournament golds as head coach of USA Basketball. Perhaps most impressive, however, is this coach's relevant perspective on leading Millennials in today's turbulent times.

Mike Krzyzewski, better known as Coach K, is considered by many as the world's greatest living coach. is the head coach of men's basketball at Duke University. In a recent interview with *SUCCESS* magazine, Coach K shared a powerful view on leadership: "The most incredibly interesting thing about a leader is what adjustments you make and how you make them while keeping your core principles alive and well."

This is the relevant tension every leader has to manage today. How do you adjust to the changing expectations, technology, and communications plus the flood of Millennials into the workforce while not compromising your core principles as a leader?

"A lot of things are easier to do if you are a willing learner," explains Coach K. "You have to be willing to learn what's best and then adjust because every year is different, every team is different. If you believe what you've done in the past is the only way to do it with a new group, time will prove you wrong. So you should want to be in a constant state of making adjustments."

Today's leaders must be agile, making relevant adjustments and not relying on legacy thinking, which is viewing the present and future through thoughts or a lens from the past.

Coach K understands better than most the balance between the pain of change and the power of adjustment. As a college coach, he has a guaranteed 100 percent turnover rate every four years. And in today's fast times, it's often shorter as players leave school early to play professionally. Days after winning the 2015 title, Coach K lost three freshman players to the NBA draft.

Coach K offers the following advice on adapting as a leader, "Get to know those you're leading and learn to communicate in a way they can understand." He says, "It is up to you as the communicator to know who you are addressing. It is not like some special science. It's wanting to learn more about people and really knowing the people you are leading at that point. And not making those people fit into something that you did in the past."

Too often, leaders expect Millennials to get to know them as leaders, but as Coach K states, it's the leader's responsibility to first invest in those that they lead. Leaders cannot control the actions of their team; however, they can influence its actions by setting the right example.

Coach K has also adjusted his leadership when it comes to recruiting new talent.

Early in Coach K's career, he was determined to recruit players who intended to stay four years at Duke. He explained, "When players started coming into college for one year and then leaving, my first reaction was to not recruit those guys. Then we had to play against them because our competitors recruited them. So we decided to adjust but to do so in pursuit of players who fit here not just because they were good players, but because they could fit our culture."

Are you still trying to hire lifers? Do you still view job-hopping as a negative? Or will you take a page from Coach K's playbook and make the necessary adjustments to hire and lead in today's competitive work environment?

When asked what the key to success is, Coach K said, "To coach and lead others is a great opportunity, but to be successful over the long haul, you have to adapt and adjust."

A leadership...swish.

CHAPTER 14

How to Manage Remote Millennial Workers

• • •

IN CHAPTER 37, WE HIGHLIGHT why Millennials seek flexible work and the benefits of delivering it to them. In this chapter, we'll discuss how you can successfully manage remote Millennial workers.

THE DEMAND FOR REMOTE WORKING

According to the 2016 Global Workplace Analytics Telecommuting Statistics...

- 50 percent of the US workforce holds a job that is compatible with at least partial telework. Approximately 20 to 25 percent of the workforce teleworks at some frequency.
- 80 to 90 percent of the US workforce says it would like to telework at least part time.
- 50 to 60 percent of the time, workers are not at their desks. Fortune 1000 companies are entirely revamping their spaces for mobile employees.
- 75 percent of employees who work from home earn over $65,000 per year, putting them in the upper 80th percentile of all employees, home or office based.

According to a 2016 FlexJobs survey, Millennials show a stronger preference for working at a coffee shop, coworking space, library, or other place besides the office than other generations. Yet, Millennials report having to stay at the office to do work at a much higher rate.

It's abundantly clear that there is a shift toward more remote-based work, especially with Millennials. Are you prepared to manage across time zones, generations, and cyberspace?

ELEVEN TIPS FOR MANAGING REMOTE MILLENNIAL WORKERS

1. Hire right. The best way to set yourself up for success when it comes to managing a remote team is to hire the right and best talent for the job. In chapter 18, we cover how to improve your Millennial hiring.

2. Outline expectations. One of the benefits of a remote team is that employees can be reviewed and rewarded based on performance (output) rather than attendance (input). This dynamic makes the buy-in of the expectations easier for the remote team.

Because remote work is less structured than on-site work, clear expectations are critical. Make the following clear with your remote Millennial team:

- Company mission and vision
- Expected number of working hours per day and week
- Key performance indicators (KPIs)
- Weekly, monthly, and yearly goals
- Communication cadence (how often communication needs to happen)
- Tools and resources to be used
- Which tasks or projects they own
- Whom to contact for help or support, and when

- Management availability (when, where, and how to be reached)
- Team availability (when, where, and how to be reached)

Remote working works best when there are clear expectations and trust. Clearly outline the expectations and offer the necessary autonomy and trust for Millennials to execute.

3. Connect consistently. When working with remote teams, if you're not connecting consistently, days will turn into weeks and weeks into months, and before you know it, you have an isolated team that is disconnected from the organization's goals and mission.

Research shows that Millennials react more negatively in the absence of consistent communication than previous generations.

Schedule predictable, reoccurring, and agreed-upon meetings. It's also important to make check-ins more conversational than the daily project updates or briefings you might conduct over e-mail or chat. This will help to build rapport and keep communication open.

In the *Harvard Business Review* article "How to Manage Remote Direct Reports," Mark Mortensen, an associate professor of organizational behavior at INSEAD, a business school, recommends visiting remote employees regularly, especially in the early stages. "If you can get yourself to their location when you first start working together, that's invaluable," he says. "Seeing people one-on-one, face-to-face sets the tone and gives people a sense of comfort." As the arrangement stabilizes, "predictability is more important than a particular frequency. If your direct report knows you're there every six months, it helps build trust."

Consider having a designated hour each day or once a week where the whole team is expected to be online, working at the same time, regardless of time zones (if possible). This allows the team to collaborate or help each other out in a unified and predictable way.

Last, an "open-door policy" doesn't work for a remote team. Instead, remote managers might consider an "open-status policy" where they keep their online status (busy, away, available, etc.) accurate so that remote employees know when they can connect with them.

4. Communicate strategically and transparently. When communicating with remote Millennial employees, every communication has to be used strategically, delivered transparently, and sent via the right channel.

Here is a quick guide for how to use today's primary communication channels.

- E-mail: for exchanging objective and brief information.
- Chat: for announcements, general news, team conversation, informal conversing, and socializing.
- Skype (video): for detailed, focused, feedback-rich, long, emotional, or difficult conversations.
- Phone: for detailed, long, emotional, or difficult conversations. (Phone should be the last resort if video chat is unavailable.)

Ensure transparency throughout your communications. The more informed the remote Millennial team is, the easier it is for its members to be productive and autonomous.

Create transparency with how and where information can be accessed. Making the same information available and easily accessible allows the team to function as a single unit. Google Docs, Dropbox, or other file-sharing services can be leverage to streamline and consolidate the consumption and sharing of important information across the remote team.

5. Track proactively. As remote workers, Millennials seek autonomy and independence, so giving them the responsibility to track and measure progress is empowering for them.

Invest in the right software and technology to track progress effectively. Time trackers (such as HubStaff, When I Work, or Time Doctor) help to boost accountability and allow for easy tracking of the time worked. Employees can also share screencasts (image or video recordings of a computer screen) of their completed or pending projects for managers to review. It's often easier to communicate this way than in writing. Also consider task-management and activity-tracking tools IDoneThis and Asana to review what the team and individuals are accomplishing.

Be sure to apply the same metrics to the entire team. Remote Millennial workers want to know they are not being treated or tracked differently than others.

6. Monitor Well-Being. Remote workers can have a harder time setting boundaries between work and personal life. Many managers fear that the independence of remote workers leads to laziness and slacking off. David Heinemeier Hansson, *New York Times* best-selling author of *Remote: Office Not Required,* says, "the greater danger is for [remote] employees to overwork themselves and burn out. It's the manager's responsibility to guard against this outcome."

Ensure that employees maintain work-life harmony and are taking the appropriate time for themselves. Consider using a tool like Culture Amp to stay ahead of employee satisfaction and engagement. Culture Amp enables new-hire surveys, onboarding, employee engagement surveys, single-question polls, and more, all delivered via web or mobile to satisfy the savvy Millennial worker.

7. Cast vision. Remote managers who fail to connect remote workers' efforts with the big picture risk employees feeling unimportant and isolated.

Consistently map the work of remote employees with the organization's objectives. Vision leaks inside every organization, so make it a priority to routinely communicate the "why" of the organization and team. A compelling and clearly defined vision also helps a remote team's members to establish common ground with each other over the shared vision.

Mapping the business progress to individual tasks and team effort is key to motivating remote Millennial workers.

8. Prioritize face-to-face meet-ups. KISSmetrics holds an annual summit for its remote workers, Buffer's remote employees get together for retreats every five months, and Automattic gets its entire four-hundred-person company together every year for a "grand meet-up" in a beautiful location.

These companies have discovered a secret to cultivating culture among remote workers…face-to-face meet-ups. These meetings create opportunities for employees to bond, build trust and relationship, and have fun. All of these are core to building enduring company culture.

Use the money you save on office space and prioritize face-to-face meet-ups, because putting a face to the name at the end of an e-mail or a personality behind the Slack/Skype profile goes a long way.

9. Cultivate culture remotely. Face-to-face meet-ups are a great way to jump-start company culture among remote workers. But to maintain that culture the rest of year takes some intentional planning. Here are three ways to cultivate culture remotely:

1. **Create a digital watercooler.** Watercooler talk (random and nonwork-related conversation) is nonexistent with a remote team. However, there are ways to cultivate the healthy aspects of such talk (spreading of ideas, team camaraderie and bonding, fun [nongossipy] chatter, etc.) with a remote team.

   Chat services like Slack, HipChat, or Basecamp are ideal for creating "channels" where watercooler talk can happen. Create a fun channel—essentially a chat room focused on a specific topic—such as #random, #LOL, #Netflix-binge-watchers, or #watercooler—where the team can let off steam while bonding and building rapport with one another.

2. **Share knowledge.** Encouraging remote employees to share their knowledge is a great way to cultivate culture. Knowledge-sharing sessions could be work related or not...the more personal or abstract the knowledge, the more fun for Millennials.

   Leaders should also consider hosting a recurring "town-hall" meeting where the status of the company, pending and upcoming decisions, recent changes, financial updates, and so forth are discussed. Some organizations have had success cultivating company culture remotely by hosting monthly "no question is off limits" Q&As where remote workers can ask anything and get honest, transparent answers.

3. **Send recognition.** Consider using gifs (short looping videos from giphy.com, for example) when using a chat service like Slack to celebrate wins and convey greater emotion and excitement among your remote Millennial workers. If a picture is worth a thousand words, then a gif must be worth two thousand. It's powerful, productive, and great for cultivating culture remotely.

   Tango Card is a Slack integration that allows employees to send e-gift cards (such as for Amazon.com) to teammates directly within

Slack. (Per-reward maximums and other parameters can be set to ensure the tool isn't abused.) Overall, it's a sleek and innovative way to boost morale and cultivate culture with your remote Millennial workers.

10. Share company swag. Because remote workers aren't walking through a building whose lobby and hallways are decked out with company logos and motivational company tag lines, it's easier for remote workers to feel disconnected from the company brand.

Sending company swag (t-shirts, phone cases, coffee cups, etc.) to your remote team can help to keep them connected to the company brand. Consider sending the swag to the remote worker's entire family, since they are essentially sharing the same "office" at times.

11. Leverage technology. Today's tech tools have made it easier than ever before to collaborate and communicate with a remote team. It's highly likely that if you're managing a remote Millennial team, it will be very digitally savvy and highly interested in leveraging technology to work smarter, faster, and better. Below are some powerful tools to leverage with your Millennial team.

16 Tools for Managing Remote Millennial Workers

It's important that everyone on a remote team uses the same tools so that productivity and collaboration are streamlined and bottlenecks minimized. A good rule of thumb is to make the tools a policy instead of a suggestion.

Be open to integrating new technology, as Millennials will be interested in finding new and improved ways to lean into technology to work smarter.

These tools will empower a remote team to stay on task, increase productivity, and effortlessly collaborate.

- Slack (www.slack.com) is a cloud-based team-collaboration tool. It's an open chat environment that offers real-time, one-on-one or group messaging. It is perhaps the premier solution for any remote team.
- Asana (www.asana.com) is a cloud-based communication tool that includes task management, conversation tracking, team assignments, and project archives.
- Basecamp (www.basecamp.com) is a project-management system (more robust than Asana) that offers task monitoring, discussions, documents, scheduling, milestones, collaboration, and more.
- Zoom (www.zoom.us) or Skype (www.skype.com) are videoconferencing services that enable online meetings and cross-platform group chat.
- Dropbox (www.dropbox.com) and Google Drive (www.google.com/drive) are file-sharing services that make it easy to sync files, organize, and collaborate.
- LastPass (www.lastpass.com) is a cloud-based tool that securely remembers passwords and allows teams to easily access necessary tools and services.
- Screenhero (www.screenhero.com) is a collaborative screen-sharing app that lets remote teams work together as if they were sitting at the same desk. It also has an integration option that connects directly to Slack.
- ToneCheck (www.tonecheck.com) is an emotional spell check for e-mail. Run messages through a tone analysis to ensure your content doesn't come across as rude.
- Trello (www.trello.com) or Cove (www.talentcove.com) offer easy and beautifully designed ways to set objectives, organize and prioritize projects, and track progress. Trello can also integrate with Slack.

- SnagIt (www.snagit.com) or Screencast (www.screencast.com) lets users share videos and images and has markup tools like blur, spotlight, magnify, and stamps.
- Hubstaff (www.hubstaff.com) or When I Work (www.wheniwork.com) are time trackers that make it easy for employees and managers to track time, boost accountability, invoice clients, distribute pay, and access in-depth reporting.
- Mural (www.mural.co) can be used for remote brainstorming and idea mapping.
- IDoneThis (www.idonethis.com) is an online tool that gathers team members' e-mail replies to the question "What did you get done today?" and puts them in a handy report for the manager or team to review. It also has an integration option for Slack.
- Buffer (www.buffer.com) allows teams to schedule, publish, and analyze all social-media posts.
- Tango Card (www.tangocard.com) makes it easy to send digital rewards (e-gift cards) to your team. Can also integrate with Slack.
- Officevibe (www.officevibe.com), Culture Amp (www.cultureamp.com), and TINYpulse (www.tinypulse.com) are effective tools for monitoring employee morale and engagement. Officevibe can integrate directly with Slack.

These eleven tips and sixteen tools will not only help you manage Millennial remote workers but any generation of remote employees. In fact, FlexJobs discovered that only 7 percent of workers say the office is their choice if they need to be most productive on important work-related projects, and 51 percent say that their home is their preferred place to work.

Ubiquitous connectivity has made places beside the office efficient to work in. It's clear that every generation will increasingly share Millennials' desire for remote working.

CHAPTER 15

How to Recruit Millennial Workers in Two Simple Steps

• • •

FOLLOW THESE TWO SIMPLE STEPS to scale your recruiting efforts and turn your company into a Millennial magnet.

A recent LinkedIn survey of over thirteen thousand Millennials explored how Millennials approach job seeking and how companies must adapt to attract Millennial talent.

WHAT ARE MILLENNIALS LOOKING FOR IN A JOB?

- The number-one thing Millennials that want to know about a company is its "culture and values," followed by "perks and benefits" and "employee perspectives of the company."
- 64 percent of Millennials care about company perks and benefits (compared to 54 percent of Generation X and 51 percent of Baby Boomers).
- The top obstacle to Millennials accepting a job is "not knowing what the company is like."

How do Millennials learn more about a company and job opportunities?

- 24 percent of Millennials report they didn't know about a company when they heard about a job opportunity (compared to 18 percent of Generation X and 16 percent of Baby Boomers).
- 22 percent of Millennials are likely to follow a company on social media to find out more about it.
- One out of three Millennials say they have used social media to find a job.

Considering the above data, how to attract Millennial workers becomes clear.

Step #1: Authentically showcase what your company is like.

Help Millennials experience what it's like to work at your company by having employees share their authentic perspectives on the company.

Matthew Jeffery, vice-president and head of global sourcing and employment branding at SAP, recently hired a videographer and created forty compelling videos of real employees sharing their perspectives on the company's culture, values, perks, benefits, and some of the unique hobbies employees enjoy outside of work, like surfing, ice hockey, and building bamboo bicycles. "The true authentic voice is the employee," says Jeffery. "They don't speak to a marketing script, and that's what makes them the best advertisement your company could ever have."

This approach satisfies the top three things Millennials want to know about a company—its culture and values, perks and benefits, and employee perspectives on it—and eliminates the top obstacle Millennials have to accepting a job, which is "not knowing what the company is like."

STEP #2: STRATEGICALLY POSITION YOUR COMPANY ON SOCIAL MEDIA.

Use social media to consistently and broadly communicate your company's values, perks, and so on. Since Millennials are most likely to turn to social media to find a job and learn more about a company, it's imperative that yours has a strong social-media presence. "[SAP is] predominantly a business to business company, but we're competing for talent with companies like Apple, Facebook and Google. So we have to work harder to get our information out," says Jeffery.

"#SAPCulture," "Life at SAP," "What can you do at SAP?," "Work...anywhere," and "All work and no play? Not here!" are all SAP YouTube playlist titles that satisfy Millennials' job-seeking questions while being accessible and searchable on the Internet's second-largest search engine. SAP even has a video specifically for Millennials.

@LifeatSAP is the social-media handle that SAP uses to showcase company culture, values, perks, and benefits via employee perspectives on Twitter, Facebook, and Instagram.

SAP also has a lively and informative LinkedIn page, where it is one of the top-followed companies with over 834,800 followers. This is an important community to have a presence in, because 65 percent of Millennials say that LinkedIn has had a positive impact on their careers.

25 Additional Tips to Effectively Recruit Millennials

1. Focus on the channels Millennials use to get your job opportunities in front of them. (Creating a Glassdoor.com profile is a must.)
2. Use authentic messaging that is native to the social-media platform you are using.
3. Use existing employees (ideally other Millennials) as a resource for referrals—they can also help you reach Millennial prospects on social media.
4. Leverage LinkedIn to post your job opportunities as well as a source for Millennial talent.
5. Make your career website and application process mobile friendly.
6. Create an entertaining video intro to your company. (Chapter 17 explores the specific elements needed to create a recruiting video that appeals to Millennials.)
7. Be simple. Don't use overcomplicated job descriptions, operational diagrams, or compensation plans.
8. Use images of real employees in all company collateral (website, marketing, etc.). Kill all stock photos and clip art.
9. Showcase young leaders in your business via a blog post, podcast, or video.
10. Define the professional-development opportunities that your company offers, and communicate two to four potential career paths beyond their entry position.
11. Specify how your company supports a work-life balance and/or flexible schedules.
12. Post your company mission and vision. Millennials will be eager to learn the "why" behind your organization.

13. Where possible, leverage your young professionals at recruiting events. Millennials get Millennials.

14. Ditch the career fair. Instead, post jobs online through a university's career center and attend niche recruiting events. Promote via social media or through relevant student clubs.

15. Highlight company culture, innovation, and professional development if you cannot compete on salary.

16. Make Millennials' first day epic. They just might return the next day with their roommates.

17. Showcase the innovative technology that will be available to them in the workplace.

18. Highlight how new hires can get creative, contribute, and innovate on day one.

19. Highlight the company social perks (happy hours, beer cart on Fridays, kickball team, etc.).

20. Get involved in young-professional associations within the community.

21. Consider creating a project-based co-op or internship program.

22. Emphasize your community as a cool place to live. Millennials pick a city first before looking for a job.

23. Provide a calendar of fun upcoming activities to do in the community (festivals, shopping, outdoor competitions, etc.), further highlighting the perks of working in your city.

24. Throw a family-and-friends work party. Make it fun, quirky, and off-the-wall enough that their friends want to join the team.

25. Communicate the volunteer and outreach opportunities available.

CHAPTER 16

How to Retain Millennials with Better Onboarding

• • •

USE THESE TIPS TO TURN your company onboarding into the differentiator needed to engage and retain Millennial talent.

These days, company loyalty from a Millennial is as rare as getting a phone call from one. However, your organization's onboarding process could be the differentiator needed to solidify Millennial loyalty once and for all.

When a guest walks into a hotel for the first time, the atmosphere, attention to detail, efficiency, and attitude of the staff all play a crucial first-impression role that determines the long-term loyalty of that guest.

In the same way, a company's onboarding process offers fertile ground to instill the excitement and passion needed for a Millennial to settle in for a long-term career. The first couple weeks of a Millennial's employment experience largely determines his or her career trajectory with the company.

There is no doubt that the below onboarding tips will take time and effort to implement, but they will ultimately save you time on the back end in recruiting and interviewing for the positions Millennials leave because they don't feel welcomed and accepted at the organization.

8 Ways to Retain Millennials with Better Onboarding

1. Tactful timing. Send a pre-first-day e-mail or text to the new Millennial hire that highlights the organization's excitement and what to expect when it comes to attire, parking, and the day's agenda.

Since employee energy levels are typically higher later in the week, consider starting the new hire on a Wednesday, Thursday, or Friday. Start the new hire's day after 10:00 a.m. This allows ample time for the new hire to find his or her way to work and the current employees to address urgent items before the new hire arrives.

2. Engage employees. Ask current employees who have worked for the organization for less than two years what they wish they had been told or had done during the onboarding process and integrate it. Stress to existing employees the importance of a warm welcome to new hires. In addition, schedule a time for the new hire to connect with at least one company leader.

3. Give gear. Nothing communicates "we forgot you were starting today" than not having the new hire's gear ready. Ensure all company-issued hardware and devices are live and preloaded with the new hire's favorite utility applications.

Surprise the new hire with company-branded swag—the quirkier and more unusual the better. This can help the new hire to begin identifying with the company.

4. Create customization. Thanks to the Internet, Millennials grew up in an age of customization. They have personalized their shoes, shirts, and cars. Lean into this expectation and allow the new hire to customize his or her workspace, devices, and/or work applications. You can learn a lot about the new hire during this customization process.

In addition, provide preprinted business cards with the new hire's name on it. This will help the Millennial see and feel that he or she is a part of the team.

5. Explain expectations. Millennials need and want to know exactly how you want them to perform. Providing a clear introduction to and overview of the job will go a long way. Provide dos and don'ts when it comes to communication, leadership, work hours, vacation, and so on.

After onboarding, the Millennial should have a basic understanding of the following: culture, values and vision, roles and responsibilities, opportunities and promotions, training and safety, and ethics/accountability.

6. Accent advancement. One of the top reasons that Millennials leave organizations is a lack of career opportunities. Get an early jump on this issue by highlighting the necessary steps for advancement within the organization. Clearly identify the employee's options and the necessary timelines for promotions.

One company in particular provides new hires with live plants to symbolize their growth with the organization. The perceived growth of existing employees' plants is a literally living example of the organization's commitment to advancement.

7. Communicate culture. Provide a "new-hire handbook" that includes insights from employees, places to eat or grab a beer close by, transit options, attire no-nos, recreation options, and so on. Consider a new-hire scavenger hunt as a way to get to know the office, people, and the culture. Keep in mind that Millennials get Millennials, so use recent Millennial hires when possible to provide these tours.

Having the company values and vision embodied by the employees and displayed throughout the physical workspace will help to clearly communicate the company culture.

8. End energetically. Many onboarding processes can drag on and on and lead to a new hire's burnout—not a good first impression. Instead, end with energy.

Use a social event or activity to signify the completion of the process. Or provide a tangible reward that can serve as a rite of passage into the organization. Oddly, Zappos offers $2,000 after orientation for folks *not* to take the job.

Infuse a few of these onboarding tips, and not only will your Millennial new hires show up eager to work, but they might recruit their roommates for you.

CHAPTER 17

How to Create a Recruiting Video That Appeals to Millennials

• • •

FINDING TALENT FOR YOUR ORGANIZATION is an ongoing process. It's even "on-going-er" today as Baby Boomers retire and Millennials change jobs in record numbers.

In chapter 15, we explored what Millennials are looking for in a job, how they learn more about a company and job opportunities, and two steps to recruit Millennials effectively. We also highlighted how SAP uses video to recruit Millennials.

This chapter covers fifteen elements to include in your recruiting video to attract the right Millennial talent effectively.

1. **Don't tell, show.** Video is the preferred method of consumption for the Millennial generation. Showcase what it looks like to work at your company.
2. **Infuse authenticity.** Give the viewer a genuine sense of the workspace, company culture, and employee perspectives.
3. **Showcase your growth.** Millennials are interested in becoming integral parts of something that's going somewhere. Use interesting visuals or comparisons to showcase your company's recent growth.

4. **Expose your culture.** Spend more time emphasizing the company culture than explaining your product or service. Millennials put a premium on culture.

5. **Flaunt your employees.** Millennials want to see who they'd be working alongside. The more diverse and creative the team...the better. Ditch any clip art and stock video and just use your real employees.

6. **Unveil the lifestyle.** As I noted earlier, Millennials often choose a city before they choose a job. Show the community amenities of your hiring city. Highlight the eateries, coffee shops, bars, public transportation, venues, etc.

7. **Reveal the office.** Highlight your innovative workspaces and work perks (pets at work, adjustable desks, cafeterias, game rooms, etc.).

8. **Depict an actual day.** Show what going to work looks like—whom your hires will meet there, a typical desk, the elevator they will use, where they will park, how they will collaborate, and where meetings are held. The easier they can visualize themselves at your organization, the easier their decision to work there.

9. **Show off technology.** Millennials desire an innovative environment to quench their tech dependence. Show employees interacting with the various pieces of technology through the office.

10. **Exhibit social perks.** Millennials are looking for community as much as they are a job. Highlight your community outreach, office sports teams, and parties.

11. **Feature your leaders.** Allow Millennials to see or hear from senior leaders inside the organization. Highly visible leaders give Millennials the impression of a flatter organization, which they prefer.

12. **Get quirky.** No Millennial dreams of working for a stuffy organization. Do not make the video too corporate and robotic. Find ways to inject some quirkiness.

13. **Keep it short.** Attention spans are shortening at alarming rates. Create a one to one-and-a-half-minute recruiting intro video and then serve

up other, longer videos (if necessary) for those interested in learning more about your organization.

14. **Use compelling music.** Your video's music can make or break the video. Music can demonstrate your relevance, innovation, and the pace of your organization.

15. **Include a visible call to action.** Make sure viewers know exactly what their next step should be (i.e., "Visit www.xyz.com/hiring to apply," or "Text *apply* to 12121"). Make it clear and visible. Place it at the end of the video and in the video description.

CHAPTER 18

How to Hire the Best Millennial Talent with Improved Interviewing

• • •

LEGENDARY COACH LOU HOLTZ ONCE said, "I've had good players, and I've had bad players. I'm a better coach with good players." The performance of an organization is elevated by the quality of its talent. Assessing the quality of talent starts in the interview.

In chapters 15 and 17, strategies and tips for recruiting Millennials were given. This chapter will provide the steps for interviewing Millennials effectively (including some key questions to ask) and the attributes and characteristics to look for in a Millennial candidate.

The steps for interviewing Millennials aren't much different from those you'd use in interviewing other generations, but there are a few nuances that could be the difference between success and failure.

9 STEPS TO SUCCESSFULLY INTERVIEW MILLENNIALS

1. Prepare yourself. Review the job description (make a list of the requirements, responsibilities, and skills needed for the job). Review the applicant's resume. Dig into the candidate's social presence (which for Millennials could be very robust and revealing, positively or negatively).

2. Prepare the candidate. An unprepared candidate can waste both parties' time. Send recommendations and details about the interview a couple of days before the interview. Include items such as interview tips, what to wear, what to bring, suggested reading, etc.

Also, reinforce that the interview process is a two-way street and that candidates are evaluating the company as much as you are evaluating them. Encourage them to prepare their own questions.

If a candidate still shows up unprepared, then disqualify him or her. The candidate won't be a fit if he or she cannot put in the necessary effort during the interview process.

Want to take this one step further? At the end of the e-mail or info packet, mention a specific action for the candidate to take, such as "please bring a red pen to the interview." If the candidate brings the red pen, you can be sure that he or she is thorough, follows directions, and follows through.

3. Relax the candidate. Chances are high that the Millennial you are considering won't have much experience interviewing, and nerves will likely show during the interview. It's important to get candidates to relax so that their true selves can come through and they can best communicate why they are the best fit for the job.

Put the candidate at ease with a smile, nonjob-related questions, and/or a tour of the office before the interview begins. Highlighting the flow and structure of the interview can also help to relax a candidate.

Evaluate how the candidate handles nerves, as it can be a strong indicator of his or her level of self-awareness and adaptability.

4. Streamline the process. Leverage technology to make the interview process seamless. Tools like Skype, Zoom, or InterviewStream can streamline interviewing with video. Other tools like Calendly, Doodle, or Vyte can streamline the scheduling of interviews. Make the interview process as digitally native as Millennials are.

Discovering ways to streamline and systemize the interviewing process (externally for candidates and internally for teams) should be a constant quest for hiring managers.

5. Evaluate quickly. In a world of endless streams of info, succinct communication is highly valuable. If a candidate cannot make a compelling case as to why he or she should be hired in thirty minutes or less, that person might not be the best fit.

Start the hiring process with a quick (fifteen- or thirty-minute) intro interview. Ask four to six questions to cover the requirements and get to know the candidate.

Following this interview, simply ask yourself, "Do I like this person?" Your answer must be yes, since you'll probably be working closely with him or her. The second question to ask yourself is, "Is this person lit up about working here?" If the candidate lacks the necessary passion for the position, he or she might just be chasing a paycheck and won't be a long-term high performer. Passion is caught, not taught, so keep looking if passion is absent.

Before concluding the first interview, address…

- Next steps in the hiring process.
- What to expect for timelines.
- Appropriate contact for additional questions.
- How the candidate would prefer to communicate moving forward. (Chapter 8 discusses the power and necessity of deferring to other generations' communication preferences.)

6. Follow up swiftly. As soon as a decision is made on the candidate (a few days max), inform the him or her (either way) and what to expect for next steps.

You cannot overcommunicate in this stage of the interview process.

7. Repeat the steps. After the initial interview, repeat steps 1 through 6, but change the interview(s) to be more behavioral ("Tell me about a time when you...") or performance-based (ask about the knowledge, skills, abilities, and other characteristics needed to perform well). Consider extending these interviews to an hour if necessary.

Depending on the job, consider having the candidate submit work samples, partake in a skill test, or solve a real problem during the interview process. Delivering real solutions to real problems equals real talent.

8. Extend the offer.

When extending a job offer to a Millennial...

- Emphasize why the person was chosen and what makes him or her a strong fit for the organization.
- Make it personal by linking the candidate's goals or previous experience with the new job.

- Mention the short-term and long-term development and career opportunities.
- Highlight the company's mission, vision, and core values.
- Describe the immediate impact the new hire will make.
- Be excited. (Accepting and starting a new job are typically top-ten life moments for people. Stoke the candidate's excitement to create positive momentum.)

9. Involve the candidate. Too often, especially for organizations hiring Millennials out of college, once the candidate formally accepts a job offer, the company vanishes. Months can go by without any communication, and the candidate begins to question if he or she actually got hired.

Keep the new hire warm and involved by inviting him or her to team meetings, social outings, or a tour of the office. Send a list of recommended books, podcasts, or videos to prepare the candidate for the industry or type of work.

OTHER MILLENNIAL INTERVIEWING ITEMS TO CONSIDER

Don't oversell. It's critical that the job, perks, and company culture match what you explained throughout the interviewing process. If they don't match, a Millennial will experience buyer's remorse and find another job before you have time to correct the misstep.

Expect feedback. Being new to interviewing and having a desire for feedback, Millennials are likely to follow up, asking for feedback on their interview performance. If you decide to give feedback, make it clear, genuine, and constructive. Then observe the next interviews to see if the candidate improves or takes the advice.

Overcome biases. Many organizations' efforts to create greater diversity are falling short due to unconscious bias.

Unconscious biases happen automatically and are triggered by our brain, making a quick decision. They are biases that we are unaware of and happen outside of our control. Unconscious bias may be preventing you from hiring the best person.

Consider these tools to eliminate unconscious bias from the interview process.

- GapJumpers (www.gapjumpers.me) is a technology platform for employers to conduct blind auditions in hiring.
- Interviewing.io (www.interviewing.io) is for anonymous interviewing that helps companies hire engineers based on what they can do, not how they look on paper.
- Blendoor (www.blendoor.com) is a "blind" recruiting app that facilitates job matching based on merit, not molds.

Prioritize transparency. Millennial candidates can connect with past employees online, review a company's reputation via Glassdoor, or double-check an employer's facts and answers. It's natural for Millennials to want employers to be as transparent as the culture in which they grew up.

A lack of company transparency (especially during the interviewing process) will cause Millennials to view the organization as unapproachable, dishonest, and difficult to work with.

TIPS FOR INTERVIEWING MILLENNIALS

The goal of interview questions is to elicit information not found on candidates' resumes and that will inform about their fit for the role. Here are a few general interview tips.

- Ask open-ended questions that elicit an informative response. Do not ask leading or closed-ended ("yes or no") questions.

- Behavioral and performance-based questions are ideal because they encourage the candidate to share past performance and behavior, which can be a good indicator of future performance.
- Hiring managers should only talk about 30 percent of the time (or less).
- In general, ask about past experiences and performances, explore candidates' short- and long-term career goals, and discuss their preferences for leadership.
- Ask each candidate the same questions. This allows for consistency in the interview process and ensures a proper basis to compare candidates.

INTERVIEW QUESTIONS FOR MILLENNIALS

Because Millennials are a different type of employee with unique skill gaps, asking specific questions to address their top weaknesses (as we'll highlight in chapter 24) are helpful to identify the best talent. Try these questions:

- What have you done in the past that will help you do this job? (Addresses a lack of experience)
- Have you ever had to wear a uniform, cover up a tattoo, or work at a time that was difficult for you, like early in the morning or late at night? How did you handle that? (Addresses capacity for compliance)
- Tell me about a time you were passed up for an award or promotion you felt you deserved. How did you react? (Addresses an entitlement weakness)
- How do you like to receive feedback, and how often? (Addresses a dependency on feedback)
- What kind of relationship do you expect to have with your boss? (Addresses lack of experience and entitlement)
- Describe a good day in the office. How do you spend your time? Where are you? (Addresses a fixation on flexibility)

- Would you rather work at home, in a traditional office, or in an office with an open floor plan? (Addresses a fixation on flexibility)
- Tell me about a time you had to handle a difficult situation with a colleague or customer. (Addresses a devaluation of face-to-face communication)
- Tell me about a time that a project took longer to complete than planned. How did you adjust? (Addresses capacity for patience)
- Tell me about a time when you put in overtime to accomplish a difficult goal. What was driving you? (Addresses a possible poor work ethic)
- What do you read or listen to every day to get your news? (Addresses a lack of experience)
- Tell me about a time when you failed. How did you handle it? (Addresses capacity to fail and/or innovate.)
- Tell me about your last employer's policy on cell phone use and visiting personal websites during the workday. Did you find any aspects of the policy challenging? (Addresses devaluation of face-to-face communication)
- What role do you expect to have in five years? (Addresses career impatience, frequent job-hopping)

4 CHARACTERISTICS TO LOOK FOR IN A MILLENNIAL HIRE

This excerpt from the John Maxwell Company's October 2016 article "4 Things to Look for When Recruiting Millennials," hiring managers have the most success spotting difference-makers when looking for the "Four C's of Recruiting":

- **Chemistry:** It doesn't take long to figure out if you like a person applying for a job. Is liking them important? Absolutely. When someone hides behind technology, for example, rather than engaging in conversation in the recruiting process, that could be a bad sign. If that person struggles to connect with other people, the entire team will likely struggle to connect with him or her. And if your managers don't like the person, they won't be effective guides. They'll be reluctant to invest time into the relationship. In addition to evaluating the personal connection, pay attention to how well that person might mesh with your organizational culture. Often you can innately sense whether a person will connect with the culture of your organization, even if you can't initially give a specific reason why. Bottom line: *chemistry matters.*

- **Character:** Good character makes trust possible. Trust makes strong relationships possible. Strong relationships make growth possible. You won't be able to develop someone who can't be trusted. And if you're expecting to instill character into a new hire, you'll be disappointed. Millennials are often mislabeled as lacking character or a "work ethic" as a group, but the truth is they place a high value on doing work that matters. You should not assume someone lacks character because of his or her age. When you dig deeper, you'll discover what make each person tick.

- **Capacity:** It can be deeply fulfilling to invest in Millennial employees to help them bring out their best. But leaders will become frustrated trying to bring out what isn't there. If you want to recruit Millennials with the capacity to be developed into good leaders, you must not ask for what the Millennial recruit could give, but evaluate what he or she actually has the potential to give. You can try to access their capacity in the following areas:
  - *Stress management*—their ability to withstand and overcome pressure, failure, deadlines, and obstacles
  - *Skill*—their ability to get specific tasks done
  - *Thinking*—their ability to be creative, develop strategy, solve problems, and adapt
  - *Leadership*—their ability to gather followers and build a team

- *Attitude*—their ability to remain positive and tenacious amidst negative circumstances
- **Contribution:** Some people possess an X factor. They are winners. They contribute beyond their job responsibilities, and they lift the performance of everyone on their team. When you discover people with these characteristics, you should aggressively recruit them. Such people who possess this intangible drive can be a joy to develop, and whatever you put into them get a terrific return on the investment. But a word of caution: Millennial employees are often multiskilled, having come of age in a high-tech era that values efficiency. It's easy to presume that hard skill capacity also means soft skill success. But not everyone who knows social media has a high emotional intelligence (EQ). Invest effort into assessing how a potential Millennial hire would *contribute* to their team before they invest time and money into training them.

CHAPTER 19

How to Terminate a Millennial (Voluntary or Involuntary)

• • •

EMPLOYEE TERMINATION, WHETHER VOLUNTARY OR involuntary, is a part of business. When it comes to terminating Millennial employees, a slightly different approach is needed to ensure a successful transition.

INVOLUNTARY TERMINATION OF MILLENNIALS

The most common involuntary terminations are for poor performance or negative behavior and layoffs for nondisciplinary reasons (such as an overall reduction in workforce). This chapter focuses on firing.

BEFORE FIRING A MILLENNIAL, ASK YOURSELF: "WOULD I EAGERLY REHIRE HIM OR HER TODAY?"

- If yes, then don't fire the employee. The urge to do so is likely an isolated circumstance.
- If no, can the Millennial meet expectations by being coached? Does the employee show evidence of the skills needed to perform in the role, and does he or she have the capacity and willingness to learn?

- If yes, set up a detailed plan to coach the person on the needed skills and expected behaviors.
- If no, then it's time to part ways.

You are likely to encounter two types of Millennials in the workplace: rich in potential rich and poor in potential. Considering whether there is evidence of the skills needed to perform and if the person is willing to learn is crucial, because it reveals which of the two types of Millennial you have.

Since Millennials are early in their careers and whose adulthoods have been delayed longer than those of previous generations (their extended schooling means relatively less job experience and later marriage, household establishment, and children), Millennials potentially lack the experience and direction needed to self-motivate at work or guide themselves in their careers.

If a Millennial shows evidence of the skills needed and is willing to learn, he or she is rich in potential. These Millennials require more coaching, but their long-term output and performance are worth the investment.

If the Millennial shows little to no evidence of the skills needed and is unwilling to learn, he or she is poor in potential. Be clear and honest about their performance and let them go. If you allow employees like this to slide, they will set a terrible example for the other Millennials and damage their careers and the company's reputation. Potential-poor Millennials likely need to get fired a couple of times before becoming potential-rich workers.

6 STEPS FOR FIRING A MILLENNIAL

Terminating a Millennial is much like terminating anyone else, but there are a few areas that you should pay closer attention to.

1. Check yourself. Before taking any action, evaluate your performance as a leader. Have you been harboring any generational preferences? Have you clearly and consistently communicated the right behaviors and standards? Have you modeled them? Have you explained the "why" behind the behaviors and standards? Have you been able to coach others into meeting the standards and performing well? If any of your answers here are no, consider self-adjusting before moving forward with the termination.

2. Check with HR. Inform HR of your termination intentions so that it can provide any necessary guidance. Ensure that there is a trail of paperwork throughout the process.

3. Provide a warning. Meet with the employee to discuss the low performance or negative behavior. Inform him or her what specific changes need to be made and provide a time frame (thirty to ninety days) to turn it around.

When firing Millennials, consider a "coaching out" approach. Have a conversation where you ask questions like:

- "If you could create a position for yourself, what would it be?"
- "If you could work anywhere or on anything in the company, where or what would it be?"

In an ideal situation, the Millennial employee describes a role that does not exist at the company. This not only confirms that the employee should move on but also should now have a better idea of what he or she would like to do, putting the manager in a position to help the employee transition to a better fit. Millennials will appreciate the candor and coaching.

4. Create a plan. Plan for reassigning the terminated employee's job duties before the position is vacated. The potential firing represents a diminished team and likely more work for its other members. Have a plan to continue projects, satisfy clients, and put the rest of the team at ease once the termination is finalized.

5. Fire the employee. If the employee has made no changes since the warning, it's time to fire him or her.

- **Get final buy-in.** To confirm that terminating the employee is the best decision, consider consulting (again) with HR or your leadership team.
- **Involve HR.** When questions arise and/or to help manage the process, make sure HR is involved.
- **Pick a day and time.** Earlier in the week is ideal. The time of day is subjective. Morning gets the tough conversation out of the way early and allows the employee time to pack up and start the search for a new job. Afternoon allows the manager to walk out with the employee like it's a normal day, limiting the potential for making a scene.
- **Have HR represented.** For legal reasons, ensure that an HR rep is able to attend the termination meeting. This is also helpful in case the employee threatens retaliation.
- **Be straightforward.** At the termination meeting, avoid small talk. Consider starting directly with, "I've got some bad news for you. Your employment has been terminated." Using the past tense is important. Then, in one or two short sentences, state the reason for the termination.
- **Provide next steps.** Inform the terminated when he or she is expected to leave (ideally immediately after gathering personal belongings). Explain how much severance pay (if any) will be provided, what benefits are available, what happens with unused vacation time, how ongoing projects will be handled, etc.
- **Field any questions.** Instead of handing over the conversation to HR, stay and answer any questions the employee has. If the employee

objects or retaliates, answer with "I'm sorry, but my mind is made up" or "I'm sorry that the situation has gotten to this point."

- **Sign a release.** Ask HR or legal if a "release of liability" is recommended for the termination. If so, consider incentivizing the employee with extending his or her severance pay if they sign the release, for example.
- **Involve IT.** Millennials are likely to have many company applications on their personal devices that need to be migrated or closed.
- **Escort out**. Depending on how the conversation went, consider escorting the employee out to ensure that no damage or stealing occurs.
- **End graciously.** Show compassion. Offer to serve as a reference, write a recommendation, or provide other help.
  - Based on the coaching or meetings leading up to the firing, provide suggestions about what industries or jobs would be a fit for the Millennial employee. Consider writing a recommendation or referring the person to a company that would be a better fit.
  - Millennials will turn to their robust social networks to either smear or praise their employers. Ending your relationship graciously helps limit any blowback.

6. Tell the team. Before the rumor mill gets a chance to start, promptly communicate the news to the rest of the colleagues affected by the termination. Don't divulge the details, because they're confidential and you want to ensure the individual's privacy. It may be appropriate to assure people that the organization is not eliminating more roles and that this is an isolated case. Highlight the steps you are taking to replace the employee to ensure minimum negative impact.

VOLUNTARY TERMINATION OF MILLENNIALS

The most common types of voluntary termination are resignation, which is initiated solely by the employee, and retirement. Since we're dealing with Millennials here, we'll focus on resignation.

11 STEPS FOR A MILLENNIAL RESIGNATION

- **Involve HR.** Once you're aware of an employee's intention to terminate employment, notify Human Resources.
- **Get it in writing.** Have the employee write a resignation letter that states a termination date. A two-week notice is ideal.
- **Involve a network administrator.** Have IT terminate the employee's access to computers and any other applications or systems on the termination date. Be sure to check Millennials' personal devices and any access they may have to company social-media accounts.
- **Revoke building access.** If applicable, terminate the employee's access to the building (swipe card, entry code, keys, etc.).
- **Collect company property.** Have the employee return all company materials, badges, technology, and any other company-owned items.
- **Collect passwords.** Manager should be provided any company passwords the employee used.
- **Provide next steps.** Explain to the employee what benefits are available, what happens with unused vacation time, how ongoing projects will be handled, how unpaid company expenses will be handled, etc.
- **Review confidentiality.** Review any confidentiality or noncompete agreements that might be applicable to the exiting employee. Or review the company rules surrounding not sharing company confidential information or trade secrets.
- **Confirm contact info.** Ensure that the employee's personal-contact and emergency-contact info are up to date should you need to communicate with this former associate.
- **End graciously.** Similarly to firing a Millennial, treat the departing employee with respect and gratitude and ensure that he or she leaves on good terms and is satisfied with the process. Because Millennials are early in their careers, they won't have a context for a healthy workplace,

and if they go elsewhere and have a terrible experience, they may boomerang back to your company.

- Ensure that you leave the door open for this possibility, because these boomerang Millennials are your strongest company ambassadors. Leaving on good terms also encourages Millennials to refer future employment candidates, recommend the company's products and services, and to create business partnerships between their former and new employers. Because of Millennials' robust social networks, it's critical that they leave your organization as a customer and ambassador.

- **Perform exit interviews**. Encourage the exiting employee to participate in a confidential exit interview with his or her manager or an HR representative. This important process will reveal what Millennials are looking for in an employer.

HOW TO EXIT-INTERVIEW A MILLENNIAL

Performing exit interviews is a great way to gain relevant information for organizational improvement. Exit interviews are opportunities to receive candid feedback from current employees.

Exit interviews executed well can to uncover problems in the organization, inform success-planning and talent-management processes, shed light on the competitive landscape, expose managers' leadership effectiveness, foster innovation by soliciting new ideas, and expose employee perceptions of the working conditions, company culture, and job design.

They can also promote engagement and enhance retention by signaling to the other employees that their views matter...that is, if the responses or feedback are implemented and taken seriously.

Before beginning the exit interview, assure the employee that no negative consequences will result from his or her responses.

EXIT INTERVIEW QUESTIONS:

- Describe your experience working here.
- Why are you leaving?
- How could the situation causing you to leave be improved?
- How do other employees feel about the situation and the company in general?
- What is the company doing right?
- What are three things you enjoyed most about working here?
- What are three things you wish were improved at the company?
- What do you wish you had known before or at the beginning of your employment?
- What advice do you have for the next person in your position?
- Please complete the sentence "I don't know why the company doesn't just _____."

Terminating employees (whether it is a voluntary or involuntary situation) is never easy or fun, but it can position the organization for future success if done right.

CHAPTER 20

How to Have Millennials Show Up to Work and Meetings on Time

• • •

HOW OFTEN ARE WORKERS LATE to work? Is the nine-to-five schedule obsolete? Are employers becoming more lenient with worker tardiness?

CareerBuilder recently explored this topic with a January 2017 nationwide survey of more than twenty-six hundred hiring and human-resource managers and more than thirty-four hundred workers across industries. Here are the findings...

- 29 percent of workers admitted they were late to work at least once a month (up from 25 percent last year).
- 64 percent of employers and employees believe that the concept of working nine to five is an antiquated practice, but 53 percent of employers expect employees to be on time every day.
- 41 percent of employers have fired someone for being late.
- 29 percent say they have no problem with the occasional late arrival as long as it doesn't become a pattern (down from 33 percent last year).
- 69 percent of workers who arrive late stay later to make up for it (up from 62 percent last year).

- Top reasons for being late to work: traffic (49 percent), oversleeping (32 percent), bad weather (26 percent), too tired to get out of bed (25 percent), and procrastination (17 percent).

Even though these trends point to a greater employer lenience for tardiness, arriving to work or meetings on time remains a pertinent challenge that I hear frequently from my audiences of folks who manage Millennials.

Millennials have a 24/7, always-on approach to work, so coming in late—say, at 9:45 a.m.—isn't a big deal, since they've been sending work e-mails since they woke up at 7:00 a.m. and plan to work until 11:00 p.m. And other times, Millennials are simply unaware that their tardiness has an effect on those around them.

Whatever the case may be, the below should help managers.

6 STEPS TO GET MILLENNIALS TO SHOW UP TO WORK AND MEETINGS ON TIME

1. Believe the best. Leadership expert Andy Stanley says,

Occasionally, there are gaps between what we expect people to do and what they actually do. As leaders, we choose what to put in this gap. And what you as a leader choose to put in that gap will shape your culture. And what you put into that gap will also be what your staff puts in that gap. You will either assume the worst or believe the best. Developing a culture of trust is critical to the health of your organization. Trust fuels productivity. The message of trust is this...I think you are smart enough to know what to do, and you make a mistake, you will tell me, then fix it.

Stanley makes a compelling case to insert trust into the gap when you see your Millennial employee show up late. Choosing to insert your own assumption (for example: "all Millennials are lazy") could cause you to overreact or lash out and ultimately erode trust.

If the tardiness becomes a chronic issue, continue with the below steps.

2. Address quickly. Stanley says, "If you want to build a culture of trust, you must confront fairly and quickly and refuse to sit on it. Before I assume the worst, I should at least ask for the facts. The consequences of concealment are far greater than the consequences of confrontation."

Waiting so long that you react in anger toward the tardy employee is unacceptable and unprofessional. Or, waiting too long and beginning to document their every move, you run the risk of making the employee feel like he or she is being watched.

After a few offenses, approach the employee directly. Schedule a one-on-one, coffee run, or lunch where there is ample time for both the employee and the leader to discuss the issue. The person might not have a valid excuse or reason for the behavior, but he or she will appreciate you believing the best.

Don't let your fear of being a micromanager or bad manager get in the way of being the manager your employees need.

3. Diagnose the cause. While in conversation with the late arriver, take the posture of a coach trying to help the Millennial employee (like a doctor trying to diagnose the problem) and ask probing questions like...

- Are you late for some things, or everything?
- Is there a certain day or time when you're late?

- How do you feel when you are late?
- Does the amount of time you are late vary? (It's likely there is a psychological hurdle if the amount of time is always the same but a mechanical problem if it varies day to day.)
- What causes you to be late?
  - According to Diana DeLonzor, author of *Never Be Late Again: 7 Cures for the Punctually Challenged*, there are seven categories for late people:
    - The Deadliner: Subconsciously enjoy the thrill of the last minute rush. Rushing relieves boredom.
    - The Producers: Over-achievers who simply over-schedule their days and underestimate the amount of time their tasks will take.
    - The Absent Minded Professor: Prone to innocent flakiness or the condition of attention deficit hyperactivity disorder and get easily distracted on their way. They often lose track of time, misplace car keys, and forget appointments.
    - The Rebel: Actually enjoy the idea of knowing that other people are waiting for them.
    - The Rationalizer: Won't admit the problem and blame external factors.
    - The Indulger: Lacking in self-control.
    - The Evader: Struggle leaving the existing task until it's perfect or 100 percent completed.

These are not excuses. Knowing the tardiness tendencies is the first step in getting lateness under control.

Both parties have responsibilities: managers should take an active role in helping Millennials diagnose the cause, and Millennials must be open and willing to discover the causes or tendencies that cause them to be late.

ALTERNATE STEP: OFFER A FLEXIBLE SCHEDULE

Why fight biology, hardened habits, or extenuating circumstances (family obligations, medical issues, and so on) when a reengineered or custom schedule would allow the employee to be more productive and relieve you of some heartburn? Steps 1 to 3 may reveal that a flexible schedule would work best for the individual and team.

If you go this route, be prepared to explore other options for other employees, but you might be due for a nine-to-five shake-up anyway. (See chapter 14 for how to manage a Millennial remote team.)

4. Communicate the consequences. Don't assume that Millennials realize how their tardiness impacts others. Help them to see it clearly.

Quantify it: "When you're ten minutes late to a meeting with ten of your teammates, that is ten minutes times ten, which is a hundred minutes of unproductive time."

Help the Millennial to see the ramifications and consequences that his or her tardiness has on other people. For example: "Because you were fifteen minutes late, James had to fill in for you, and the client ended up having to wait." Or, "Not having you available online at 8:00 a.m. results in customer requests that sit for more than one hour."

Or consider putting it into a context Millennials might understand: "Imagine having an issue with your Netflix account, submitting a trouble ticket, and waiting an hour for someone to contact you. Would you tolerate that timeline?"

Also communicate some of the intangible consequences of being late: diminished trust, colleague resentment, and looking less responsible as a professional.

5. Discipline. Every employee, but especially the early-career Millennial, has a different learning curve when it comes to correcting tardiness. Some only need a subtle reminder, while others need disciplinary action.

Disciplinary action could include:

- Requiring that the employee make up the time.
- Docking his or her pay.
- Decreasing his or her bonus.

Enforcing steeper disciplinary action may be warranted if the behavior has negatively impacted the bottom line, the company culture, or a client relationship. (See chapter 19 for how to terminate a Millennial.)

6. Acknowledge improvement. If the Millennial employee's behavior improves, make it a priority to acknowledge it. (See chapter 21 for how to deliver recognition to Millennials.)

HOW TO HELP MILLENNIALS BE ON TIME

"Most people really hate being late and have tried many times to fix it," says DeLonzor. "Punctual people misunderstand. They think you're doing it as a control thing, or that you're selfish or inconsiderate. But it really is a much more complex problem than it seems."

Combine Millennials' inexperience and their different approaches to work with various psychological states, and you have a much more complex problem than someone just being fifteen minutes late. There are actually deeper psychological an behavioral problems at the core of tardiness.

Late arrivers tend to perceive time differently than their punctual peers. In *Never Be Late Again: 7 Cures for the Punctually Challenged*, DeLonzor writes:

> Part of my research included a test to measure the differences in how timely and late people perceive the passage of time. The test I devised is a simple one you can try yourself. Choose three or four pages in a book, mark the time, and start reading. Stop reading when you think ninety seconds have elapsed, then check your watch to see how accurate you were. I found that early birds, almost without fail, stopped reading before ninety seconds had passed, while lateniks put their books down well after the ninety-second mark.
>
> The researchers at Cleveland State University also included a time perception test in their study, this time using stop-watches. Interestingly, their results were similar to mine, with late people consistently underestimating the passage of time.

DeLonzor and Pauline Wallin, PhD, a psychologist in Camp Hill, Pennsylvania, have identified links between chronic lateness and certain personality characteristics, including anxiety, low self-control, distraction, ambivalence, and a tendency toward thrill seeking.

Ross McCammon, editor at *GQ* magazine, has this to say about being late:

> If you're late for a meeting, it's probably not because some unavoidable obstacle put itself in your way. It's because you didn't allow for the obstacle. You didn't spend time thinking about the obstacle. And if you didn't spend time thinking about the obstacle, you're not showing respect for the people you're doing business with. In other words, you are the obstacle. Because being on time is easy. Respecting time is the tricky part.

It's clear that tardiness is a messy mash-up of deep psychological problems, disrespect, misaligned priorities, and innocent, one-time traffic jams.

For managers of Millennials, getting them to be punctual is often more complicated. Not only are you battling psychological barriers but also Millennials' mobile-centric life, their wherever, whenever approach to work, and their inexperience with a structured work environment. Millennials made it to their university classes on time, but they also got to choose the times of their classes.

While the six steps above help you manage the Millennial who is punctually challenged, the below are tips you can encourage your Millennial employee to execute for themselves in order to become more punctual.

1. Time your routine. Write down your typical daily routine (eating break-fast, commuting to work, working out, etc.) and estimate how long you think it takes you to complete. Then spend a week documenting the actual time it takes to complete your various routines. Tools like ATracker Pro (www.wonderapps.se/ATracker) can help Millennials track how long certain tasks actually take throughout the day. Late people will likely be surprised how much longer their routines take than they think. This exercise is important to detach the unrealistic timelines from the brain.

2. Reverse engineer and add time. Reverse engineer the time needed to arrive punctually. Start with the time you need to be somewhere and track back how long it will take to get there or transition to the meeting. Be sure to factor in foreseeable delays (slow elevator, red lights, etc.). Once you've identified the approximate time needed to get there, add fifteen minutes. Timely people budget conservatively the time they need, while the chronically late budget exact times.

3. Embrace the wait. Often, people are tardy because they try to maximize their productivity by packing in as many activities as possible. So, arriving early to an appointment or meeting can feel uncomfortable or unproductive. To ensure that wait time is not unproductive, be prepared with a compelling activity like reading, listening to a podcast, catching up on e-mail or social media, calling a friend, or nothing—take in your surroundings and sit with your thoughts. Being early isn't a waste of time if you're prepared.

4. Prioritize sleep. Oversleeping is the second most common reason for arriving late to work. Sleep is critical for a productive and timely day. According to Shawn Stevenson, best-selling author of *Sleep Smarter: 21 Essential Strategies to Sleep Your Way to a Better Body, Better Health, and Bigger Success*, "High quality sleep fortifies your immune system, balances your hormones, boosts your metabolism, increases physical energy, and improves the function of your brain." To sleep better, Stevenson recommends that one get more sunlight during the day, avoid electronic screens before bed (or use a blue-light blocker), have a 4:00 p.m. caffeine curfew, get cool with a sixty-eight-degree-Fahrenheit room temperature, and use blackout curtains.

5. Establish an evening routine. Tomorrow starts with tonight. Establishing a consistent evening routine (heading to bed at the same time, dimming lights, meditation or prayer, etc.) alert the brain that it's time to wind down. Items you may include in your evening routine:

- Review your schedule and to-dos for the following day. Try to foresee any obstacles that might hinder you from being on time (weather, traffic, appointments are too far away, etc.).
- Lay out your clothes for the next day.
- Pack your work bag.
- Prepare your lunch or breakfast in advance.

The goal of the evening routine is to prepare your mind and body for sleep and to shrink the number of decisions to be made in the morning. Both will make the next day's prep more seamless, resulting in more margin to get to work on time.

OTHER HELPFUL TIME-MANAGEMENT TOOLS

Applebee's recently used gamification to help Millennials get to work on time. The restaurant chain created a program called BeeBlock, where employees would log into a smartphone and fulfill certain tasks (like showing up to work on time) to earn points and badges that could be redeemed for Xboxes, iPads, or other prizes. The effort led to a 20 percent reduction in staff turnover and larger average tickets.

If a custom game platform isn't in your budget, consider these tools to help Millennials get their tardiness on track.

Interruptive (www.interruptive.co)
Offers phone-call event reminders for Google Calendar. Users install the free Chrome extension, link it to their Google Calendar, and then set up phone-call interruptions for calendar events that require users to answer the phone as a way to remind and break users away from a task so they can be on time.

Toodledo (www.toodledo.com)
The $2.99 productivity tool offers task and appointment lists that seamlessly integrate with a user's e-mail and calendar. Toodledo lets users schedule reminders to arrive early via e-mail, text message, or even Twitter to help reduce the chances of being late to an event or meeting.

Leave Now (Apple App Store)
This free iOS app informs users exactly when to leave for an appointment. Users receive a reminder message on their device when it's time to leave. The app

automatically adjusts departure time and the reminder based on GPS tracking of traffic for various modes of transportation (walking, biking, driving, and public transportation). If you are running late, in a single tap, Leave Now sends an "on my way" text or e-mail on your behalf to let people know your estimated arrival time. (Bounce is a comparable app for Android.)

The reason the saying *80 percent of success in life is just showing up* is so famous is that so many people neglect to show up on time or at all. Help your Millennials get ahead and build trust by being on time.

CHAPTER 21

How to Use Recognition to Elevate Millennial Performance

• • •

ACCORDING TO BERSIN BY DELOITTE, a leading research-and-advisory firm, 87 percent of company recognition programs (a $46 billion market) are focused on tenure (years of service), yet tenure-based reward systems—a ten-year pin, a twenty-year gold watch, and so on—have little to no impact on organizational performance.

Josh Bersin, the founder and principal at Bersin by Deloitte, says,

> It turns out that many of these tenure-based rewards programs are really legacy programs from the turn of the century when labor unions forced management to give employees 'service awards' and hourly raises for tenure. Most large companies still have these programs today, yet only 58 percent of employees even know such programs exist. So for the most part they aren't creating much value.

Bersin by Deloitte has found that 83 percent of organizations suffer from a deficit in [employee] "recognition" and only 17 percent of employees believe their managers know how to recognize them well. And, according to an employee-engagement report by TINYPulse, 79 percent of all employees feel undervalued, due largely to a lack of recognition and appreciation.

Benefits of Recognition
Recognition programs done right can have powerful impacts on business performance.

Bersin by Deloitte found that companies that scored in the top 20 percent for building a "recognition-rich culture" actually had 31 percent lower voluntary turnover rates, and organizations with reward programs in place see a 14 percent improvement in employee engagement and productivity. According to Glassdoor.com, more than 80 percent of employees say they are motivated to work harder and stay at their jobs longer when they receive appreciation for their work.

It's clear that recognition has significant impact on employee engagement and retention and should be considered as part of any talent-management strategy.

Millennials and Recognition
According to Aon Hewitt and O. C. Tanner, one in four organizations finds its current recognition programs are ineffective for Millennial workers, and 38 percent of Millennials would like to see the recognition program at their current employer improved.

Rodney Mason, GVP of marketing with Blackhawk Engagement Solutions, an international incentives and engagement company, says, "Millennials are accustomed to attention and praise from their earliest days, and expect regular affirmation in the workplace. They are also prepared to switch jobs earlier and more frequently than previous generations, so employers need to take particular steps to maintain Millennial engagement."

Ultimately, the purpose of recognition is to reward effort and to encourage greater or continued effort. Elevated effort and performance occurs when employees feel inspired and incentivized to do more. Being recognized in a meaningful and consistent way strengthens Millennials' connection to their organizations and encourages them to become high-performing contributors.

PSYCHOLOGY OF RECOGNITION

Science confirms that employee recognition impacts workplace performance. When we feel loved or appreciated, our bodies create oxytocin, the well-known "love hormone." When oxytocin is present in employees, research shows they are more trustworthy and perform better at work.

Recognition also satisfies employees on a psychological level. After the human needs of survival (food, water, sleep) and safety (economic and physical security) are met, the next needs, according to Abraham Maslow's hierarchy of needs, are love/belonging (social, love, family, team) and esteem (importance, recognition, respect). Love/belonging and esteem are humans' most desirable most valuable psychological needs, and they can be met through recognition.

Recognizing Millennial employees boosts trust, engagement, retention, productivity, and satisfies at a psychological level.

WHAT DO MILLENNIALS WANT TO BE RECOGNIZED FOR?

According to 2015 employee research by Blackhawk Engagement Solutions, 85 percent of Millennials want to be rewarded for exceeding personal performance levels, followed by receiving a promotion and exceeding team performance levels.

Millennials are interested in meaningful recognition that helps them feel empowered. According to a 2016 Aon Hewitt and O. C. Tanner survey, the organization with effective programs for Millennials offer three key rewards vehicles: handwritten notes, experiential rewards (e.g., event tickets), and thank-yous from peers, managers, or next-level managers or section executives.

Is using compensation to recognize Millennials effective? Yes. Compensation is associated with the need for safety in Maslow's hierarchy, but it's not a primary concern that Millennials are looking for their employer to address. Millennials are likely to cover any compensation gap through their entrepreneurial spirit and resourcefulness as digital natives.

Beyond the threshold of what an individual needs to support his or her lifestyle, compensation is a weak motivator. Compensation fulfills Millennials' basic needs, but intrinsic motivations can fulfill deeper needs.

Is using promotion to recognize Millennials effective? Yes. Promotion, part of career advancement, satisfies the pinnacle human need of self-actualization (challenge, opportunity, learning, creativity) in Maslow's hierarchy.

It's important to note that recognition must supplement (and not replace) workplace accountability, feedback, and goal setting.

How to Recognize Millennials

Millennials have different values, expectations, and motivations from those of previous generations; thus, a new approach to workplace recognition must be considered. Here are seven tips on how best to recognize your Millennial employees:

1. Recognize specific behaviors or results. Be specific about what the Millennial employee did to receive the recognition and why that behavior/

result is important. For example, "Ashley, you continually make your colleagues and clients feel valued with your positivity, friendliness, and enthusiasm, so we would like to [insert reward], because that type of positivity is what clients appreciate."

2. Recognize company values. Adding the necessary context around recognition not only enhances feelings of belonging and esteem in Millennial employees, but it also reinforces company culture. What gets celebrated defines culture. The more you recognize specific behaviors that reinforce the culture, the better. Tie the recognition to the company's strategy so that the values and company culture can be reinforced with every recognition.

3. Recognize in every direction. Recognition received from peers can be more meaningful for Millennials because their peers have a better understanding of the work that they are doing. Organizations that leverage modern tools, like Achievers (www.achievers.com), to make their recognition programs more social and peer-to-peer will win over Millennials.

Recognition from leaders is also important for Millennials because it serves as an important indicator of the impact and direction of their work. Just make sure that any top-down recognition is personal and specific.

4. Recognize visibly and widely. Use the company blog, podcast, or team meetings to recognize Millennials. Tell the story behind the recognition and leverage the opportunity to reinforce expected behaviors and results. Make the people who are doing great things visible for everyone else to see and emulate.

5. Recognize in real time. Millennials' upbringing in an on-demand world has given them an appetite and expectation for real-time recognition. Integrate processes that enable peers and managers to recognize teammates in real time.

The recognition process needs to be effortless to ensure and encourage employees to participate frequently and in real time.

For example, we've mentioned Tango Card, a Slack integration that allows employees to send e-gift cards to teammates directly in Slack. Fond Rewards (www.fond.co/products/rewards) also provides a way for managers and peers to easily and regularly recognize one another.

While recognizing behaviors or results in real time isn't always possible, strive to recognize as soon as possible.

Warning: be careful not to overrecognize. Dishing out too many rewards can dilute the impact for the high achievers and embarrass the low achievers who know they didn't earn them.

6. Recognize with personalization. People don't quit companies; they quit people. Recognition that is personalized strengthens the bond between a manager and Millennial. Recognize Millennials with incentives that are relevant to their personal lives.

Millennials respond best when rewards are personal to them. Eliminate one-size-fits-all rewards and consider having Millennials choose their own rewards. Blueboard (www.blueboard.com) helps companies reward employees with unique experiences ranging from $150 kayaking outings to a $1,500 "James Bond" day that includes skydiving, an exotic car rental, and mixology lessons to $25,000 guided trips to Everest Base Camp. Blueboard also plans to offer a personalized concierge service that would allow employees to design their own day or night out.

Personalized recognition sends the message: "We recognize your good work. We value you. We're going places together."

7. Recognize, then coach. Success leaves clues. Help Millennials to understand the actions, steps, hard work, and so on that it took to receive the recognition. Then help them to identify ways they can maintain the effort so that they can continue to progress. Millennials expect ongoing learning opportunities and put a premium on professional development. Leverage the time you take to recognize a Millennial employee as an opportunity to coach and support his or her professional development.

THIRTEEN MILLENNIAL-RECOGNITION IDEAS

Here are a few ideas to get your Millennial-recognition gears turning:

- Grant special access to a leader.
- Offer a first look at some new tech.
- Award ownership in selecting their next project.
- Sponsor a ticket to a conference of their choice (you never know where inspiration will come from).
- Handwrite letters or notes to managers, peers, or parents without telling the Millennial employee.
- Grant a chance to appear on the company blog, podcast, or YouTube/media channel.
- Give an exclusive parking spot for a week.
- Offer tickets to an exclusive event.
- Make a donation to their charity of choice.
- Feature their story on the homepage of the company website or blog.
- Extend rewards or coupons to the Millennial's family.
- Allow the employee to rent a fantasy car for a week.
- Grant flexibility in how, when, or where they work.

A critical component for any twenty-first-century, high-performing workplace is recognition. Fill the air of your organization with gratitude and appreciation and be rewarded with Millennial loyalty and high performance.

CHAPTER 22

How to Help Millennials Overcome Failure and Handle Rejection

• • •

FAILURE IS A POPULAR SUBJECT these days. In fact, NPR recently analyzed popular speeches going back to 1774, and it identified "embrace failure" as the sixth-most popular theme. Failure even outranked themes like "be kind" and "dream big." What's most interesting is that of the thirty-eight speeches with the theme of "embrace failure," thirty-five of them were delivered after the year 2000.

Failure hasn't always been a popular theme.

The GI Generation, those born between 1900 and 1927, encouraged the emerging generations to minimize risk, follow the rules, and avoid failure. The Silent Generation (1928–1945) took this advice to heart and lived their lives that way. As Baby Boomers (1946–1964) came of age, they famously rebelled and embraced risk taking.

Taking cues from Baby Boomers, Generation X (1965–1980) adopted a risk-taking mind-set. Generation X was the driving force behind the tech boom of the 1990s in Silicon Valley. The new idea of failing fast and frequently gained traction there first before spreading to other industries and becoming the mainstream mantra of today.

According to a Babson College survey, 41 percent of twenty-five-to-thirty-four-year-old Millennials cited "fear of failure" as their biggest roadblock to starting a business, up from 24 percent in 2001. It would seem that Millennials are searching for safer paths toward success.

Millennials are interested in anticipating obstacles rather than stumbling through them. They will leverage today's abundant information, tools, and resources to minimize risk.

Millennials have a complicated relationship with risk. They've grown up in a connected world where failure is more public and permanent. One wrong move, and the Internet can immortalize one's failure. In addition, success is prioritized over failure on social media. Millennials don't see the missteps of their friends on social media, which gives the false illusion that they are the only ones experiencing failure.

Millennials also perceive risk differently from previous generations. Some would claim that climbing the corporate ladder is safe, while Millennials would call it risky. Some would claim that quitting a six-figure job to start a green-smoothie business is risky, but Millennials would call that safe because a business owner takes control.

Many Millennials grew up overprotected by hovering helicopter parents who would deflect anything that looked like failure. Now Millennials are entering the workplace, where some are experiencing failure for the very first time—and it's up to managers to help them thrive through it.

WHY IS FAILURE IMPORTANT?

Benjamin Franklin said it best: "The things that hurt, instruct." Failure is a teacher. Trial and error (emphasis on the error) is what forges stronger character.

Failure-free individuals grow into emotionally fragile professionals who are susceptible to anxiety and lack the grit to succeed.

The director of player development for the Pittsburgh Pirates, Kyle Stark, says,

> Failure separates those who think they want success from those who are determined to win. Failure narrows the playing field. The thin-skinned rarely win due to brittle egos and apprehensive attitudes. Thick skin comes from falling and failing. The falls produce wounds that heal and reveal a connection between resilience and a peculiar resolve which accepts failure as a temporary condition. They accept both good and bad so not to forfeit the blessing of learning from both.

> The thick-skinned prepare to win by increasingly expanding their willingness to endure pain in affirming the degree of true desire. They allow every challenge to serve as an opportunity to change for the better. They continue to learn that bitterness is poison and quickly purge its deadly influence on both their endurance and desire. They see a prize in every problem.

Millennials' altitude in their career and your organization is determined by their attitude toward failure.

How to Help Millennials Overcome Failure

Ultimately, people have two choices when it to comes to reacting to failure: to fail backward or fail forward. Leaders are in a unique position to help Millennials choose to fail forward and to view failure as deferred success.

Display empathy. Authority is given, but influence is earned. The quickest way to earn influence with Millennials is to listen. Listen and display empathy by stating something like, "I see that you're really disappointed. I know you really wanted to do better on this project." Or share your own struggles and stories of failure.

Believe in them. An authentic belief in the Millennial employee's abilities will prompt him or her to take more risks and bolder actions. Highlight the strengths, skills, and attributes that made you hire the person. Cultivate the belief that self-image is not dictated by external events. Millennials must understand that their self-worth is not based on their performance.

Encourage ownership. People are tempted to blame others for their failures. Don't tolerate Millennials pointing fingers and taking a victim mentality. Help them understand that they rob themselves of the learning and growth that's inside failure when they don't own their failures.

Emphasize the journey. Help them to view failure as a tollbooth instead of a roadblock. With a tollbooth, a price must be paid to move forward. Prepare the Millennial for the journey; don't prepare the journey for the Millennial.

Facilitate failure. Create environments where failing is easy and encouraged. Remove any fear or consequences of failure and communicate that failure isn't fatal or final.

Contextualize failure. Offer context around the failure. Help Millennials to see the failure as temporary. Putting it into perspective will help them see failure as a momentary event, not a symptom of a lifelong epidemic.

Challenge them. Challenging Millennials with tough assignments provides opportunities for failure and communicates that you believe in their ability to rise to the challenge. Resilience is a skill that must be intentionally developed and practiced.

Stress strengths. Failure can be minimized when people are operating in areas of their strengths. Help Millennials to be wary of laboring too long in areas of weakness. Spending too much time overcompensating for weaknesses increases the likelihood of continued failure.

Coach versus intervening. Resist the urge to intervene to assist a struggling Millennial. Allow the Millennial to marinate in the failure, but coach him or her to come up with a creative solution. Intervening only robs the Millennial of the opportunities to learn problem solving, develop resilience, and cultivate confidence to take on new challenges.

Affirm effort. Affirm the variables that the Millennial can control, such as effort, empathy, or strategy. Good effort, whether or not the employee failed, should be rewarded or recognized (see chapter 21 for more on recognition best practices for Millennials). Failing to try or put forth effort is unacceptable failure.

Move on. Have Millennials pause to unpack failures, but help them to understand that the past cannot be altered. Spending too long thinking about missteps can lessen self-confidence, stall progress, and divert focus. Coach Millennials to quickly forget the negative emotions of the setback and encourage them to press forward resiliently.

How Millennials Can Handle Rejection

Much like developing resilience in the face of failure, handling rejection is also like a muscle that must be developed and exercised. Not experiencing rejection and the "everyone gets a trophy" mentality has resulted in many Millennials (unknowingly) avoiding short-term pain for the guarantee of ten times the long-term pain.

Tim Ferriss, *New York Times* best-selling author of *The 4-Hour Workweek*, was rejected twenty-seven times by publishers before his book was picked up. Ferris believes that he persevered in the face of rejection because of "informed confidence." In other words, he had evidence that the content in the book worked. He had been speaking to audiences about it for years and had received overwhelmingly positive responses.

The best way to develop informed confidence is to test your plans, products, or ideas. Encourage Millennials to subject their ideas to the messy reality of everyday life (via a survey, blog, focus group, etc.) to see what feedback or response they receive. Help them to use any rejection as an opportunity to learn how to adapt the plan, product, or idea.

OTHER WAYS TO DEAL WITH REJECTION

- **Seek minor rejection.** Encourage Millennials to visit the local state fair or flea market and try to buy goods for half off the listed price. Or next time at Starbucks, have them ask for a 10 percent discount. In both situations, they are likely to receive immediate but minor rejection and will live to tell about it.
- **Limit extremes**. It's easy for Millennials who experience rejection for the first time in the workplace to allow their imaginations to get the best of them. They'll project extreme situations that are highly unlikely but intensify the rejection. Coach them through the likely ramifications and help them to become less emotionally overreactive when faced with rejection.

- **Depersonalize it.** Realize that most rejection is not personal. People can reject others simply because they are hungry, tired, distracted, or having a bad day.

How Millennials Can Mitigate Their Fear

The natural human reaction to failure and rejection is fear. If fear is limiting your Millennial team, this "fear setting" exercise can help to release Millennials from paralysis.

- On an 8 x 11 piece of paper, draw two vertical lines to divide it into three columns.
- At the top of the paper, write down one thing that you are anxious about, feel risky about, or are putting off.
- In the left-hand column, write down a bullet list of everything that could go wrong in a worst-case scenario. Be specific.
- In the middle column, write down a bullet list of what you can do to minimize the likelihood of the worst-case items happening. Be specific.
- In the right-hand column, write down what you can do to get back to where you are if the worst-case scenario happens.

When you put your fear, problem, or risk under a magnifying glass, you tend to realize that the worst-case outcome is very unlikely and/or very manageable. This simple exercise helps to put fear into perspective and can help Millennials overcome fear and face failure successfully.

Section 3
Develop Millennials

• • •

CHAPTER 23

How to Instill Work Ethic into Millennials

• • •

EMPLOYERS PURSUE IT, LEADERS EXUDE it, fulfillment is derived from it, customers expect it, success depends on it, and career progression is the result of it... what is it?

A strong work ethic.

Eric Chester, the author of *Reviving Work Ethic: A Leader's Guide to Ending Entitlement and Restoring Pride in the Emerging Workforce*, describes those with a work ethic as "positive, enthusiastic people who show up for work on time, who are dressed and prepared properly, who go out of their way to add value and do more than what's required of them, who are honest, who will play by the rules, and who will give cheerful, friendly service regardless of the situation."

Workers who view the work they do—fun or not fun, menial or noble—as a critical part of the bigger picture, execute it with excellence, and derive higher levels of satisfaction from it unlock more opportunities and become more promotable than those content with the minimum effort required.

With those types of benefits, why wouldn't someone want to cultivate a strong work ethic?

Work ethic is a value based on hard work and diligence. It's the principle that hard work is intrinsically virtuous or worthy of reward. However, work ethic is not something we are born with. It's a learned behavior. Work ethic is one of an individual's personal values, but much like a company's corporate values, it must be taught and modeled daily.

As I've noted, previous generations have defined success at work by time and tenure, but Millennials measure it by impact. Millennials ask themselves, "What's the biggest impact I can make with the limited time that I have?" This mind-set is often interpreted by managers as "lazy" because it clashes with previous generations' view of what hard work is and should be.

We must be careful when comparing a new generation of workers with previous generations when the way in which we work has changed so significantly over time.

Here are a few actions that can help instill a strong work ethic into Millennials...

- Clearly communicate the expected work ethic. Too many managers simply assume that Millennials ought to know it already. Stop assuming and tell them.
- Demonstrate the right work ethic daily. However, if you're not innovative and working smart or don't have a healthy work-life balance, Millennials may be deterred from following your example.
- Create channels for work ethic to be used. Ensure that Millennials are equipped and have access to innovative tools where they can put their unique skill sets to work.
- Connect work-ethic values to the big picture. The job of a leader is to paint a picture of the preferred future. Help Millennials connect their actions to the bigger picture.

Because of the shifting landscape of work and Millennials' varied approaches to work, one of the greatest challenges when you aim to instill work ethic into Millennials is defining a baseline for it. The best way to overcome this is...to let the customer define the work ethic. In other words, the behaviors that Millennial employees need to demonstrate should be defined by the needs of the organization's customers or clients.

If customers need...

- Reliability—then employees must be available or deliver products/services when or where customers need them.
- Quality—then employees must do everything in their power to produce high-quality products or service.
- Honesty—then employees must display integrity in their actions and in every interaction.
- Professionalism—then employees must dress, act, and prepare like professionals.
- Positivity—then employees must commit to serving the customer with positivity, friendliness, and enthusiasm.
- Delight—then employees must find ways to go the extra mile.
- Promptness—then employees must be timely in their responses, attendance, and deliverables.
- Expertise—then employees must demonstrate authority or a willingness to learn.
- Respect—then employees must be poised, diplomatic, and display grace. under pressure.
- Determination—then employees must embrace challenges and focus on solving the customer's problem.

It's the responsibility of the leader to understand what the customer or client needs and to clearly and consistently communicate the work ethic needed to satisfy those needs to their Millennial employees. Once the customer-defined work ethic has been established, give space to Millennial employees to see how they take ownership and execute their newly formed values.

As your customers evolve, so will the work ethic needed to create the best results for customers.

4 Critical Messages about Work Ethic to Share with Millennials

Here are four work-ethic messages to share with the Millennial generation who approaches work fundamentally differently than any other generation before them.

1. Own your work ethic. What makes work ethic so powerful is that you are 100 percent in control of it. You get to set the bar and get to decide how much hustle, focus, and diligence you inject into your work...and no one can take it away from you. A poor work ethic is a reflection on the individual only—no one else.

2. Consider your employer your number-one customer. A strong work ethic should be defined by the actions that create the best results for customers. How would your work ethic change if you were to consider your employer (or your manager or teammates) as your number-one customer?

Consider your work ethic as the product you are delivering. Will the customer be happy with the purchase? Will it be a repeat buyer? Will it recommend your services? Will it upgrade their purchase (aka give you a promotion)?

3. Tech should supplement (not replace) work ethic. Has work changed in the twenty-first century? You bet it has.

Thanks to technology and the Internet, the tools, rules, and pace of work have forever changed. But the effort, zeal, focus, and respect we inject into work should never change. Anything worth doing is worth doing well.

Leveraging technology to work smarter by automating and streamlining often takes hard work on the front end but allows for more time on the back end. Leveraging the saved time to pursue new endeavors or solve long-standing and complex problems for your organization or customers demonstrates a strong work ethic.

4. Patience, patience, patience. Work ethic is a muscle that takes time to grow and strengthen. It's a personal value that takes time to cement in one's soul. Don't try to microwave it. Instead, marinate in it daily, because it's a reflection of your character and integrity and, ultimately, your personal brand. Commit to developing a strong work ethic that will withstand the long, demanding, and high-flux career ahead of you.

Be satisfied but never content with the work ethic you offer to the world.

CHAPTER 24

How to Help Millennials Overcome Their Top Eight Weaknesses

• • •

HERE'S HOW MILLENNIALS TURN THEIR greatest workplace weaknesses into the strengths necessary to be effective next-generation leaders.

As a Millennial speaker who helps organizations better lead, engage, and communicate with Millennials, my audiences share with me the good, bad, and ugly about their Millennial workforces. Below are the top eight shortcomings that I've heard over the years and how you can help Millennials overcome each one so that they can become influential future leaders.

1. Poor work ethic. Millennials report working an average of 38.8 hours per week, much less than Generation X (47.8) or Boomers (47.1).

"Lazy" Millennials are redefining a strong work ethic. Thanks to technology and the Internet, the tools, rules, and pace of work have changed forever. Both managers and Millennials have to rethink what productive work can and should be in the digital age. Millennials are interested in leaning into technology to work smarter and to find work-life harmony.

Work has changed in the twenty-first century, but the effort, zeal, focus, and respect we inject into it should never change. Millennials who view their employer as their top client and consider their work ethic the product they deliver will build a reputation of excellence. Anything worth doing is worth doing well.

2. Devaluing face-to-face communication. Millennial women use texting three times more often than calling.

Millennials' high reliance on technology has resulted in a deterioration of other interpersonal skills. While Millennials have good reason not to answer your phone call, there is still tremendous value in face-to-face communication, and if leveraged appropriately, it can forge deeper connections.

With so many varied communication preferences in today's workplaces, Millennials can stand out by changing the channel and engaging in face-to-face communications. (See chapter 25 to discover how Millennials can best communicate face-to-face. And see chapter 8 for one tip to eliminate miscommunication across generations.)

3. Career impatience. Seventy-one percent of Millennials likely to leave a company within two years believe their leadership skills are not being fully developed.

Even though work is shifting to more project-based work with shorter turnarounds and timelines, managers continue to wrestle with the unrealistic career-advancement expectations of Millennials. Growing up in fast times and coming of age in an on-demand culture, Millennials have little patience for stagnation, especially when it comes to their careers.

Millennials who gain early clarity surrounding their career progression inside their organizations will be able to adjust their expectations and explore cross-collaboration opportunities to gain more experience and to put their anxious ambition to good use.

4. Frequent job-hopping. Sixty-six percent of Millennials expect to leave their organizations by the end of 2020.

Job-hopping isn't the resume red flag that it once was. Job-hopping into the same industry and position over and over again is the new red flag. Job-hopping into new industries or positions can simply reflect Millennials' desire to gain transferable skills in order to thrive in today's high-flux marketplace.

Millennials who set clear goals and objectives with specific timelines during the first few weeks of a new job are better equipped to justify and execute a job hop. While judgments on this are still subjective, Mary Ellen Slayter, a career expert at Monster.com, says to avoid stints of less than one year. Before hopping, notice how green the grass is under your feet before looking over the fence.

5. Dependency on feedback. Millennials want feedback 50 percent more often than other employees.

It's not surprising that Millennials want frequent feedback, considering they grew up gaming—which immersed them in continual feedback loops. Now that technology has enabled vast and fast connection, real-time feedback will become more of a workplace norm.

Millennials who take feedback into their own hands and exercise self-reflection on their past performance will develop a self-evaluation muscle that can be flexed in real time, creating greater self-awareness and productivity. Leveraging collaborative technologies like Slack, Waggl, 15Five or TINYPulse can satisfy Millennials' desires for real-time feedback. (See chapter 10 for a simple strategy to deliver feedback to Millennials.)

6. Fixation on flexibility. Eighty-eight percent of Millennials wish they could have greater opportunity to start and finish work at the times they choose.

Mobile technology has shifted work from a place to a space. Millennials have a boundaryless view when it comes to when, where, and how work can be done. Yet, it's important to be mindful of the timing expectations or requirements of colleagues and/or customers.

Millennials who gain clarity on the outcomes they are responsible for and achieve them routinely have the necessary credibility to earn greater flexibility. They should prove that those outcomes won't dip with increased flexibility by continuing to deliver efficient communication and satisfactory performance.

7. Lack of experience. Twenty-five percent of Millennials have taken an unpaid job to gain experience.

Millennials are often overlooked due to lack of experience. But what value does experience hold in a culture of perpetual beta? The school of thought that experience is needed to produce high-quality work is permanently out in today's digital age. In a world that moves fast, fresh perspectives and skills have new value. The new world of work will reward those experienced in being inexperienced.

Millennials who want to squash the lack-of-experience shortcoming must demonstrate honest gratitude for the people and processes that preceded them while applying conviction and a strong work ethic behind their ideas. (See chapter 26 for tips on how Millennials can successfully pitch their ideas.)

8. Acting entitled. Sixty-five percent of American adults think of Millennials as "entitled."

There probably isn't another word more synonymous for Millennials than *entitled*. Whether or not you believe Millennials are entitled, most American adults believe they are, and perception is reality. Millennials should do what they can to combat the label.

Millennials who demand or expect things too fast instead of being patient and respectful only expose their naiveness as young professionals. They should give effort, help, and support without expecting anything in return. They shouldn't demand anything but earn everything.

Looking for a proven and effective way to develop your Millennial workforce? Check out 21Mill.com, the first ever microlearning platform designed specifically to develop Millennials. (Full disclosure: I am a proud partner of 21Mill.)

CHAPTER 25

How to Improve the Communication Skills of Millennials

• • •

ACCORDING TO A RECENT GALLUP survey, "[Millennials] are more likely to communicate using newer technologies." Surprised?

Of course you're not.

For many Millennials, offline—especially face-to-face—communication seems archaic and outdated, since mass communication via a text or tweet can happen in a few thumb flicks.

The way people communicate varies by generation. The complexity of varying communication preferences based on age has caused real tension in today's workplace.

It's alarming how many clients share with me how often Millennials miss opportunities for promotion or closing sales due to their lack of face-to-face communication skills.

A blended communication skill set of high tech and high touch would serve any generation well today. However, the biggest communication gap seems to be in Millennials communicating face-to-face with previous generations that value such an interaction. Millennials who want to maximize their influence must become double threats and connect with others effectively online as well as genuinely offline.

Whether it's a meeting, presentation, or group discussion, every face-to-face communication is a ripe opportunity to make an impression and solidify a connection.

Share these five face-to-face communication rules with your Millennial team to elevate their influence.

1. Be prepared. Face-to-face communication deserves forethought. You'll waste your time and others' if you schedule a meeting and don't know the direction or purpose of the communication. Before the face-to-face communication, gather your thoughts and establish the purpose and desired outcome.

2. Be present. Face-to-face communication deserves full attention. Much like when driving a car, if you allow your mobile device to distract you, the likelihood of veering off course increases dramatically. Stay focused on the conversation at hand. Preparedness and intentional note-taking will help you stay present. Defuse the urge to multitask by getting caught up on e-mail, texts, and social media prior to the face-to-face communication. Do not check your phone unless you are expecting an urgent message—and communicate the urgent need up front, before conversing.

3. Be attentive. Face-to-face communication deserves full participation. Great conversation is like a tennis match. One person serves up his or her thoughts, and the other reciprocates—back and forth, back and forth. To successfully hit the ball over the net, you must pay close attention to the communicator's words, body language, and tone of voice. Resist the urge to hijack the conversation with personal stories or anecdotes. Instead, add to the dialogue with strong eye contact, clarifying questions, head nods, and a smile.

4. Be concise. Face-to-face communication deserves brevity. Building rapport with small talk can be helpful, but limit it to less than a few minutes. Put a time limit on the conversations so you both can stay on point. Preparation will enable confident and clear communication, and those whom you communicate with will appreciate your focus and clarity.

5. Be respectful. Face-to-face communication deserves appreciation. Ralph Waldo Emerson once said, "In my walks, every man I meet is my superior in some way, and in that I learn from him." Great advice. No matter whom you come face-to-face with, know that they can teach you something. Respect their perspective, appreciate their experience, and learn from it.

Face-to-face communication remains a critical skill set, and if used correctly, it can make anyone (especially Millennials) rise above the rest.

CHAPTER 26

How to Help Millennials Successfully Pitch Ideas to Management

• • •

IT'S NO SECRET THAT MILLENNIALS are eager to have an impact in the workplace with their ideas and innovations. In fact, 62 percent of Millennials would describe themselves as innovative. Additionally, 66 percent of Millennials say innovation is a key ingredient in making an organization an employer of choice, and 78 percent believe that innovation is essential for business growth.

With a knack and appreciation for innovation, Millennials are quick to pitch their ideas. Unfortunately, too often, those ideas are met with dismissive phrases such as, "Don't rock the boat," or, "This is always how we've done it," or, "Wait your turn."

Phil McKinney, retired CTO of Hewlett-Packard and current president and CEO of CableLabs, would call these kneejerk shutdowns "corporate or innovation antibodies." In his book *Beyond the Obvious: Killer Questions that Spark Game-Changing Innovation*, McKinney describes innovation antibodies as the "antagonist of the innovator."

As someone who got pitched a lot in the CTO role, McKinney has identified the primary barriers that keep Millennials from being heard and innovating within their organizations.

I recently sat down with McKinney to ask his advice on how Millennials can successfully pitch their ideas by overcoming the four innovation antibodies that plague today's organizations. Use these insights to empower your Millennial employees to innovate effectively.

Here are my questions and his answers:

HOW CAN MILLENNIALS OVERCOME THE FIRST INNOVATION ANTIBODY, "THE EGO RESPONSE?"

Typical ego responses are, "Oh, I already thought of that a long time ago," or "I have something better." An ego antibody is a person who has an ego response upon hearing your idea. Their immediate reaction is to shut you down because they don't want to look bad for not having the idea themselves.

The best way to get an ego antibody to support your idea is to write out three or four ideas on a piece of paper to review with them. Then wrinkle up the paper, lay it flat, put coffee cup rings all around it, and scratch on it.

Why is this important? You don't want the person you are pitching to think the idea is final. You want to clearly send the visual signal that these are just some ideas. Ask them for advice and council by asking, "What do you think?", "Am I missing something?", "What can you contribute?" Incorporate their comments into the final pitch so that it makes them a supporter for the overall idea.

How can Millennials overcome the second innovation antibody, "the fatigued response?"

Typical fatigued responses are, "You'll never get approval," "We tried that before," or "It won't fit our operation." A fatigued antibody has given up after years of hitting walls with their own ideas and innovations.

The best way to overcome a fatigued response is to engage with them and understand what it is they tried before. Rather than treating them as the antibody, treat them as an advisor and coach. Ask them what hurdles they ran into so you can learn how you would modify the approach when you encounter similar challenges.

How can Millennials overcome the third innovation antibody, "the no-risk response?"

The no-risk response typically are the people who have one of two titles, the Chief Financial Officer or the General Council. Their jobs are to manage risks so you'll likely hear them reject ideas by saying, "Not enough return on investment," or "We can't afford it."

To address these concerns design your idea by asking for a little bit of money, then prove it out, then ask for a little bit more money, then prove it again.

This allows everybody, including the senior management team and lawyers, to see progress being made before more money is allocated to the idea or project. Even inside an organization where they don't have a funding model in place, I would include this in the idea proposal because that will address the risk profile for some of the antibodies.

You can also point the management team or lawyers to other companies that have done similar kinds of innovation to see how they did it and how to deal with any legal concerns. In some cases the CEO, assuming you have a CEO who is supporting the innovation effort, just has to step in and make the call.

How can Millennials overcome the fourth innovation antibody, "the comfort response?"

The comfort response are people who are comfortable with the way things are. Typical responses will be, "We've always done it this way," or "Our customer likes it this way," or "Don't rock the boat." Organizations that don't pick up the pace and are stuck in this comfort mode won't be around much longer. They will get eaten alive by the other companies who are innovating.

The way to get around the comfort antibody is to find someone in a leadership position that is not of this comfort antibody. You need to find someone in a senior role who is pushing forward, changing the organization, and get them to act as a mentor. You will need that air cover sponsorship for getting around the other comfort antibodies.

Do you recommend leaders become more open to Millennial ideas?

My advice to leaders is to create a mechanism, a culture, and an environment that encourages the entire team to experiment. Find ways to make people comfortable so that they can try new things and fail; and it's not going to hurt their career.

Leaders have to remove friction from processes, open up doors, and stand back. You will be amazed when you unleash the full creative power of your team, the kind of impact they can have on your organization.

Innovative Millennials need to be aware of the four innovation antibodies; but also to keep in mind their own needs. If they are constantly being shut down by antibodies and their attempts to circumvent are continuously thwarted, then they are likely to move to an organization that will support your ideas.

CHAPTER 27

How to Create and Structure a Millennial Development Program

• • •

MILLENNIALS ARE POURING INTO THE workplace at the speed at which they'll be 75 percent of the global workforce by 2025. At that rate, understanding Millennials inside and outside of your organization becomes mission critical.

With a Millennial workforce of 43 percent, Bacardi, the largest privately owned set of spirits companies in the world, which owns such brands as Grey Goose, Bombay Sapphire, Martini, and Dewar's, is all in on Millennials. Developing Millennials as future leaders is crucial if Bacardi wants to successfully hand the business to its seventh generation of family members. Secondly, understanding the Millennials as Bacardi customers is crucial for the vitality of their business.

In light of this relevant need, Bacardi recently appointed Nim De Swardt as their global Millennials manager. It's her responsibility to "develop Millennial champions within their careers [at Bacardi] while leveraging them as a 'live think tank' of target consumers." De Swardt has created the Bacardi Rising Stars program, where emerging Millennial leaders will be equipped with the knowledge, expertise, and experiences to prepare them to be future leaders.

Here are five aspects of an unbeatable plan to mine the talent and insights of the Millennials in your organization as illustrated by Bacardi.

1. Be development rich. Seventy-one percent of Millennials who are likely to leave an organization in two years are dissatisfied with how their leadership is being developed. The number drops to 54 percent among Millennials planning to stay beyond 2020.

The Bacardi Rising Stars will initially be nominated by their managers. Once identified, they will be given live business projects to work on. Bacardi Rising Stars will also receive unparalleled exposure to executive leaders. The qualities that the program intends to build upon include high Emotional Intelligence (EQ), adaptability to change, being hyperconnected (self-starters), curiosity, commitment to a career at Bacardi, inspiration to others, strong communication skills, natural drive to succeed, and being a strong brand ambassador.

2. Go Millennial to Millennial. Fifty-five percent of Millennials say they're least likely to get along with someone from another generation.

Millennials get Millennials. It's important (at least at first) to create an environment where Millennials can connect with other Millennials. When trying to recruit Millennials, use Millennials.

As the global Millennials manager, De Swardt is the quintessential Millennial who has traveled the world and repeatedly job hopped while oozing with optimism and enthusiasm and is eager to make her mark on the world. De Swardt is well positioned to ingrain a "youthful spirit" into the organization and to connect and lead the emerging Millennials at Bacardi, because she is one.

3. Take a global focus. Fifty percent of Millennials want opportunities for international assignments.

Online access, a passion for travel, and immigration have made Millennials the most global generation to date. They have more in common with their international peers than those within previous generations. Millennials only notice diversity when it's absent. As a global brand, it's imperative that Bacardi reflect its global customer base in its "think tank" of Millennials. The Bacardi Rising Stars program will place a priority on creating a global community and a global mind-set.

4. Ensure executive buy-in. Fifty percent of Millennials believe their organizations could do more to develop future leaders.

The future leaders of Bacardi are encouraged by the vision, bold decision-making, and active participation of their CEO, who is the primary catalyst and supporter for the Rising Stars. Even though the Rising Stars program has many HR elements, the program will not be a traditional talent-development program but instead a business-led initiative where De Swardt will work directly with the CEO of Bacardi, Mike Dolan.

Through the Rising Stars program, Dolan is committed to driving change within the brand's corporate structures, remaining a relevant brand and employer in today's fast times and casting a vision for the future of work.

5. Infuse intrapreneurship. Seventy-nine percent would consider quitting their regular jobs and working for themselves in the future.

These are ripe times to be an entrepreneur, and Millennials are well equipped to dive into ownership. This presents a new challenge for organizations to recruit and retain Millennial talent.

Dolan provided De Swardt a "blank slate" to create the Rising Stars program. As a self-proclaimed intrapreneur (someone who acts like an entrepreneur within a larger organization), De Swardt intends to inject a new mind-set for the company by harnessing her inner "misfit, rebel, and instigator."

Like any great fearless entrepreneur, her goal is to "disrupt...in the most positive way possible."

CHAPTER 28

How to Gamify Career Paths to Retain and Engage Millennials

• • •

IF YOU'VE EVER TRACKED YOUR frequent-flyer miles, credit-card points, hotel rewards, or fantasy football scores, you've been engaged through gamification— the use of game-design techniques and mechanics in nongame contexts to solve problems and engage users.

It's no secret that Millennials are hitting the "restart" button on their careers at shorter intervals than ever before. In this chapter, you will learn seven ways gamification can help retain and engage Millennials.

Before turning twenty-one, the average American has spent two to three thousand hours reading books—but more than three times that playing video games. That makes the average Millennial very close to being a gaming expert, according to Malcolm Gladwell's ten-thousand-hour rule highlighted in *Outliers: The Story of Success.*

When humans achieve new levels in games, the brain releases dopamine, which prompts excitement, encourages exploration and trying new things, and helps combat the stagnation that can follow failure. The reward-motivated behavior induced by dopamine is the key to increased employee engagement, overcoming challenges, and increased innovation through exploration.

Organizations that learn to hack the Millennial brain by triggering innate reward systems with game mechanics can benefit from increased Millennial engagement and retention at work.

HOW BIG IS THE WORLD OF GAMING?

- Four out of five US households own a device to play video games.
- 97 percent of US youth plays computer or video games.
- 57 percent of Millennials play video games at least three times a week.
- 52 percent of gamers are women.
- 61 percent of CEOs, CFOs, and other senior executives say they take daily game breaks at work. More than half say they play "to feel more productive."
- The most subscribed-to YouTube channel with over fifty million subscribers is that of PewDiePie, a Swedish gamer who posts video-game reviews, run-throughs, and live streams.
- Twitch, the live video-game broadcasting service visited by a hundred million unique viewers a month, was purchased by Amazon for $970 million in 2014.
- Viewers of *ELeague*, an e-sports (professional video gaming) competition show, have watched 13.3 million hours of content across Twitch and the TBS channel.

WHY IS IT IMPORTANT TO CONSIDER GAMIFICATION IN THE WORKPLACE?

Today at work, there is a disengagement epidemic of epic proportions. Among Millennials, 71 percent are disengaged at work...the most of any generation.

According to the article "The High Price of a Grumpy Work Force" in the June 2016 issue of *Inc.* magazine, here are the benefits and costs of an engaged workforce:

- Engaged teams grow profits three times faster than disengaged ones.
- An unengaged employee costs an organization approximately $3,400 for every $10,000 in annual salary.
- Highly engaged employees are 87 percent less likely to leave a company.

Infusing the engaging elements of games into various aspects of work can reengage Millennial employees and ensure they remain contributors at your company—and one of the best ways to engage and retain Millennials is by clearly defining a career path for them.

How to Define Millennials' Career Paths Using Game Elements

1. Offer options. Games offer options of what to play, whom to play with, and when. Games offer customization of user profiles or avatars (game characters) with unique abilities, traits, and appearances. Gamers also thrive on the freedom to choose a specific mission or storyline.

Similarly, Millennials are interested in customizing their career tracks and the specific work they do. Millennials approach a career not like a ladder but like a cargo climbing net, which allows them to climb up (step into leadership roles), back (create more work-life balance), or side to side (collaborating across departments or trying new roles).

For example, Deloitte has a Mass Career Customization program that allows employees to customize their work preferences. The program transforms the corporate ladder into a "corporate lattice," allowing employees to move in many directions (not just upward or downward) and can repeat infinitely at any scale.

2. Provide hints. Games serve up hints when players are stuck to ensure they continue to play and stay engaged. The hints are calculated based on the direction of the player or the length of time it takes to overcome an obstacle.

Provide hints on what career paths Millennials might be best suited for based on their individual passions and strengths.

For example, Asana, a task-management and productivity company, offers employees access to executive and life-coaching services that provide employees with hints on how to pursue their passions, balance work and life, or take their careers to the next level.

3. Give control. With controllers in hand, gamers control their avatars' movement, decisions, and the ultimate outcome of the game.

Much the same way, Millennials are interested in having control of their careers. They desire ownership of their positions, tasks, and the outcomes.

For example, Valve (ironically, a four-billion-dollar video-game company) offers modular work, where employees get to select the projects they work on the same way they would if they were freelancers.

4. Deliver development. Gamers learn and cultivate skills through action and failing. In fact, according to Jane McGonigal's book *Reality Is Broken: Why Games Make Us Better and How They Can Change the World*, on average, gamers fail 80 percent of the time, and yet they still find the gaming experience enjoyable. Development is forged in the failing.

Gamers also have the option to enter tutorials where they can hone their skills or to practice a level over and over to master it.

Millennials want a clear picture of what is expected of them and what skills are required to level up and accomplish more at work. Communicate expectations clearly and provide environments where they can advance themselves throughout their career path.

For example, Zappos offers a system that allows employees to get certified and receive a pay bump with each new skill set acquired.

5. Promote collaboration. We build trust quickly with those whom we play games with. We trust they will play within the rules and that they will stick with the game. Growing up playing massive, online multiplayer games, Millennials came to understand that nothing significant can be achieved alone. The bigger the team, the more epic the win.

Millennials seek collaboration. They learn better and quicker in teams. Collaborating allows for career development and exposure to other career paths that might be a good fit for someone.

For example, Treehouse, a company that teaches people how to build websites and apps, has an internal collaboration and project-management tool called "flow," where employees can propose projects and then recruit people for them.

6. Communicate consequence. Gamers willingly struggle from level to level and puzzle to puzzle for the ultimate goal of saving the world. Gaming is engaging because the result is often bigger than ourselves, and we surprise ourselves with what we are actually capable of.

Millennials desire epic wins. Their definition of success is meaningful work. In games and in reality, they want to change the world. Communicate the consequence: "If you do this, you'll achieve that." If Millennials know the "why" of their work or your organization, they are more likely to stay on track, advancing along their career path.

For example, at Warby Parker, an eyeglass retailer, for every pair of glasses purchased, a pair is distributed to someone in need. There is a clear consequence for every pair sold, and the employees' work is bigger than themselves. So far, they've distributed over a million pairs of glasses to people in need—epic win!

7. Highlight progress. Games offer progress bars and leaderboards that inform where players have started, how far they've come, how they stack up, and how far they have left to go.

Clear visibility into the progress being made and the progress still needed in one's career is an extremely engaging and informative tool for Millennials.

For example, LinkedIn shows a "profile strength" progress bar that encourages users to achieve "All-Star" status by filling out their profiles 100 percent. The progress bar provides hints on what users can do to continue to enhance and strengthen their profiles. It's a subtle tool but immensely impactful.

Sensors, technology, big data, hyperconnectivity, and the surge of a generation of gamers into the workplace makes it easier than ever before to make use of and benefit from gamification at work.

Leverage the engaging and transformative traits of games to help define your organization's career paths, and you won't find disengaged Millennial employees, which could spell...

GAME OVER

CHAPTER 29

How to Structure and Deliver Training That Transforms Millennials

• • •

ACCORDING TO BERSIN BY DELOITTE, a leading research-and-advisory-services firm, talent development is the second-biggest challenge facing HR executives at organizations today. Bersin estimates that companies spend more than $130 billion per year on employee development, with leadership development taking up the single largest area of spending.

According to the article "The Secrets of Successful, Fast-Growing Businesses Today—and Plans for Tomorrow," in the September 2016 issue of *Inc.* magazine, 61 percent of the 2016 Inc. 500 CEOs and founders prefer to develop employees by providing outside training. However, only 28 percent have a formal leadership development program.

Unfortunately, the Inc. 500 are not alone when it comes to organizations not delivering employee training.

MODERN COMPANY TRAINING CHALLENGES

- **Lack of time.** One percent of a typical workweek is all that employees have to focus on training and development.

- **Evolving technology.** Technological change has led to a skills half-life of 2.5 years, and only 29 percent of learning functions claimed to be using "new learning technologies" to meeting their learning and development goals. Seventy-seven percent of workers say they do at least some of their learning on a smartphone or tablet.
- **Self-empowerment.** Workers spend five times more time learning on their own each week than from their employers, and three of four people invest their own money (an average of $339 each) in career-related learning.
- **Inadequate engagement.** On average, workers give their employers' learning and development opportunities a "Net Promoter" score of –31, and 92 percent of managers believe they would be more likely to use new managerial skills if the training was more engaging.
- **Absent follow-up:** 33 percent of managers say they hardly ever receive follow-up sessions to reinforce their training.
- **New generation of learners:** Only 38 percent of learning and development (L&D) professionals think they're ready to meet the needs of tomorrow's learners, and 62 percent of middle managers say that managers at their companies need more professional-development training.

While effective training and development is an issue for all employees, the issue is magnified among the Millennial workforce.

Of Millennials who are likely to leave an organization in two years, 71 percent are dissatisfied with how their leadership skills are being developed, yet 69 percent of Millennials aspire to be leaders in the next five years. And 60 percent of Millennials want training to develop their leadership skills.

Company perks, recruiting, customer service, and marketing are evolving to reach Millennials, so why is company training so far behind?

With ten thousand Baby Boomers retiring every day and a devastating lack of professional development for the generation who will replace the retiring leaders, it's no surprise that 89 percent of executives rate the need to strengthen, reengineer, and improve organizational leadership as an important priority.

THE SOLUTION FOR TRAINING MILLENNIALS

Because they grew up with ubiquitous connectivity and evolving mobile technology, Millennials think and act differently. They approach problems fundamentally differently; thus, they require an evolved learning approach.

Executed right, microlearning can satisfy the learning expectations and preferences of Millennials. Microlearning provides training in small learning units and short-term learning activities delivered in a convenient and accessible manner. Content is distributed in "microscopic" learning bursts that are typically two to fifteen minutes in length.

A powerful example of microlearning is that offered at 21Mill.com. 21Mill is an online microlearning platform built to help Millennials succeed in the workplace. 21Mill's training consists of twenty-one ten-to-fifteen-minute micro modules centered around Millennial-specific training topics such as "Developing a Strong Work Ethic," "Overcoming Entitlement," "Putting Down the Device," and more.

21Mill leverages microlearning to deliver on-demand, rich media content via desktop or a mobile device. 21Mill takes it one step further by offering a blended approach (online and offline) to training where learners execute their learning through real-world assignments, all the while tracking their accomplishments and receiving support from 21Mill professionals.

(21Mill.com is ideal for organizations with a growing number of Millennial employees who seek learning solutions that are catered to their learning style so that they can perform better at work. Request your free demo at www.21Mill. com. Full disclosure: I am a partner of 21Mill.com.)

6 ELEMENTS FOR DELIVERING TRAINING THAT TRANSFORMS MILLENNIALS

Millennials respond favorably to microlearning solutions like 21Mill because microlearning is:

1. Brief and beautiful. There is more competing for the time and attention of the emerging workforce than ever before. The media that Millennials consume is bite-sized; thus, the training they are most likely to consume has to be brief and succinct. Millennials also have a high expectation for technology to be simple, intuitive, and beautifully designed. Millennial training has to be beautiful. If the training content doesn't aesthetically mirror what Millennials normally consume, they will be less likely to engage and retain the information.

Microlearning doesn't require a long attention span, so there is less cognitive load on learners and information is easier to absorb, retain, and recall. Microlearning matches human brain-processing capabilities (especially those of Millennials), which makes it a fit for today's fast-paced and hyperconnected workplace.

2. Agile and accessible. Twenty-first-century employees are untethered. These are remote workers, bringing their own devices or applications to the job and finding new ways to execute work and structure their day. Training must be digitally native and mobile to be effective for the next generation of learners. It has to be agile and accessible to fit into the active lives of Millennial employees.

Microlearning delivers training in short intervals, so learners can easily insert it in their day-to-day lives. How and when Millennials learn is more important than what they learn, because the "what" won't matter if they never have the time to engage with it or if accessing the training is overcomplicated.

3. Instant and intelligent. Receiving a notification from Google Maps that traffic is heavy before you start your commute is informative and helpful. Information is being delivered instantly and intelligently these days, so why can't training take a similar form? You could receive an intelligent notification about powerful public-speaking tips instantly on your phone while walking to a meeting where you'll be presenting to the team.

Millennials turn to their smartphones to find just-in-time answers to unexpected problems. Information and learning is being accessed much differently today than in years past. Deploying intelligent learning via quick how-to articles, videos, or interactive infographics where learners can pull down the content for instant application makes microlearning ideal for Millennial training.

4. Collaborative and communal. A majority of workplace learning happens via on-the-job interactions with teammates, managers, and in-house subject-matter experts. Creating communities where Millennials can learn from experts, managers, and their peers and also contribute their own experience or expertise is impactful and empowering.

When microlearning offers collaborative technology and a communal environment, it helps to build relationships, diminish silos, shrink geographies, enhance personal influence, and promote sharing.

5. Relevant and relatable. The accelerated change happening at work and in business means that everyone needs to commit to continuous learning. This also means that training has to be hyperrelevant to the specific and evolving challenges Millennials face at work. If the content isn't relevant and relatable for the learner, retention and recall of the information will suffer.

The microscopic nature of microlearning content allows for quick creation of content and fast consumption by the learner. Creating training that addresses a relevant need and provides a solution or applications that are relatable for the learner is key for engagement.

6. Blendable and bindable. For the digitally dependent Millennial generation, it's imperative that their training merge digital with real-world activities. Offline, in-person, or classroom training remains impactful and transformational in today's digital age. A blended approach to training binds one's learning.

Microlearning platforms like 21Mill that prompt, encourage, and reward Millennial learners for real-world interaction and application is extremely effective for binding the learning.

To prompt development, sustain engagement, achieve transformation, and improve retention among your Millennial workforce, use microlearning.

CHAPTER 30

How to Cure (or Curb) Millennials' Career Impatience and Job-Hopping

• • •

A CONSISTENT COMPLAINT AGAINST MILLENNIALS is about their unrealistic time-lines for being promoted. They want a pay bump in a few months, a promotion a few months later, and the title of CEO by the end of year one. Growing up in fast times and coming of age in an on-demand culture, Millennials have little patience for stagnation, especially when it comes to their careers.

According to the US Bureau of Labor Statistics, as of April 2016, Millennials have held an average of 7.2 jobs from age eighteen through twenty-eight. A 2016 Gallup report revealed that 21 percent of Millennials say they've changed jobs within the past year, which was more than three times the number for non-Millennials. This Millennial turnover is costing the US economy $30.5 billion annually.

As work cycles continue to spin faster and project timelines become short-er, Millennial employees will move up or move on with greater frequency than previous generations.

Managers need to get more comfortable with the accelerated career-ad-vancement expectations of Millennials and arm themselves with a few strate-gies to satisfy Millennials' desire for career progression and stop job-hopping.

How Many Millennials Want to Move On or Up?

- Only 50 percent of Millennials strongly agree that they plan to be working at their current companies one year from now.
- Only 16 percent of Millennials see themselves with their current employers a decade from now.
- 71 percent of Millennials likely to leave a company within two years believe their leadership skills are not being fully developed.
- 93 percent of Millennials are eager to learn about new job opportunities, which means only 7 percent are fully satisfied in their current roles.

Unlike previous generations, Millennials are not attached to their employers and are eager for new opportunities and experiences.

How Millennials Approach Career

Millennials grew up in households where their parents preached and exemplified company loyalty. Millennials then had front-row seats to see companies not reciprocate their parents' loyalty. This burned the lasting impression in the minds of Millennials that company loyalty and job security are illusions.

Thus, Millennials approach their careers like entrepreneurs, with a desire for ownership and development at every turn. Today's high-tech and hyperconnected world has encouraged and enabled Millennials to sustain ownership and development of their careers.

Previous generations viewed career success as tenure, titles, and tangibles (cars, a house, a boat, and so on). Millennials view career success as having an impact.

Previous generations viewed career like a ladder, where each rung is a step closer to career success. Millennials view career like a military cargo-climbing net, where each rung (up, down, or side to side) represents an opportunity to have an impact while building the transferable skills needed to sustain a long, multi-industry, retirement-free career.

Having a resume littered with various positions and/or job hops is no longer the career hindrance it once was. In fact, according to a Robert Half survey, 57 percent of Millennials who were asked, "Is job hopping losing its stigma?" responded yes.

The type of job hopper that employers are wary of is one who moves around in the same industry, taking the same position or job level over and over again. However, if your job changes reflect career advancement or a brand-new field, more and more hiring managers are likely to be receptive to hearing about the diverse skill set gained from those experiences.

Job-hopping into new industries or new positions can simply reflect a desire to gain transferable skills in order to thrive in today's high-flux marketplace. For Millennials, internal or external job-hopping offers opportunities to gain diverse perspectives, new experiences, and skills needed to thrive in the turbulent twenty-first-century workplace.

4 FACTORS CAUSING MILLENNIAL CAREER IMPATIENCE

The top two reasons that Millennials leave for new jobs are to obtain more money and benefits and more career opportunities. This is likely true of every generation, but Millennials want to acquire these things faster than previous generations. Here are a few factors that contribute to Millennials' career impatience:

1. A crowded workplace. Fifty percent of male and 48 percent of female Millennials say they are "being overlooked for potential leadership positions." Often, Millennials are blocked from advancing in an organization as Baby Boomers delay retirement. Many Millennials experience impatience because no advancement opportunities exist or because the time they will likely have to wait to advance is longer than that of previous generations.

2. Exposure and access to opportunity. I recently stated in a workshop, "If Millennials aren't happy or engaged at work, they can jump on LinkedIn and find a new job by lunchtime." Immediately following that statement, a Millennial in the crowd blurted out, "Why wait 'till lunch?"

The abruptness of the response surprised me, but the sentiment behind it indicates Millennials' ownership attitude and impatience about career moves. In an age of endless options and on-demand information, a new opportunity is a finger swipe away. The power has shifted to the job seeker.

Connectivity has increased exposure and access to more opportunities. Millennials are connected to more sources of information (people, social networks, Glassdoor.com, and so on) where new opportunities can be explored and exploited.

3. Alternate work options. Roughly 70 percent of Millennials see themselves as working independently at some point in their lives rather than being employed within a traditional organizational structure. Economist Paul Zane Pilzer projects that 50 percent of the workforce will be participating in independent work by the year 2020.

Not only are organizations competing with their competitors to attract and retain Millennial talent, but they are also competing with the entrepreneurial desire of Millennials themselves. It's never been easier to start a business.

Millennials will consider entrepreneurship to supplement a stagnant career or as an alternate career entirely.

The rise of remote working also provides alternate channels for work. Millennials have waited longer to marry, buy houses, and have kids, which has given them more flexibility to explore new locations and ways of working.

4. Development stagnation. Only 28 percent of Millennials in 2015 felt that their current organizations were making "full use" of the skills they currently have to offer. No one wants to experience stagnation in their development, but this is the first generation that doesn't have to "bite the bullet" or "just be thankful they have a job." They are enabled and equipped to find an organization or position that will develop them.

Underemployment breeds discontent. In chapter 36, we explore how you can move your Millennial employees from underemployed to hyperutilized. This will help reinvigorate Millennials as they reignite their development, exploring new opportunities and accomplishing challenge tasks.

5. Promotion disparity. For as far back as any of us can remember, time and tenure have been the grounds for promotion. The view was that someone must be in a position for a certain amount of time to gain the skills and knowledge necessary to move into a new position.

However, 68 percent of hiring managers believe that Millennials have skills that previous generations don't. So for a generation entering the workplace with unprecedented skills and knowledge, where does that put them on the promotion timeline?

A look at UK Millennials showed that 83 percent actively disagree that people should expect to spend a minimum number of years in a job before they can be promoted. And only 8 percent of Millennials believe people should stay in a position for a minimum number of years before they can be promoted, regardless of performance.

Growing up when the world's answers have been curated into a search engine and with endless how-to video tutorials has forced Millennials to reject the notion that a precise amount of time is needed to master a skill or to learn everything there is to learn in a position.

As highlighted in chapter 38, success, training, and learning are happening faster. And, by default, Millennials are leveraging a rookie mind-set (more about this in chapter 40) and their digital resourcefulness to expedite learning and development.

The reason many Millennials job hop is because organizations ask them to sacrifice their learning and development to align with the organizations' planning needs (aka promotion timelines). For a generation who wants ownership of career, this causes its members to become impatient and move on.

When rigid timelines surround career progression, Millennials get impatient. Putting boundaries on a boundaryless generation doesn't bode well for Millennial retention and engagement.

Millennials believe that promotion should be based on merit more than time or tenure. In other words, if they are qualified, they should be able to move up, or they'll move on.

Below are a few ideas on how to satisfy Millennials' desire to be promoted or change positions.

6 WAYS TO CURE (OR CURB) MILLENNIALS' CAREER IMPATIENCE AND JOB-HOPPING

To fully satisfy the diverse needs and desires of your Millennial team, consider using a combination of these approaches:

1. Mine the motivation. Millennials are accustomed to external motivators. Perks, trophies, and praise were used to motivate Millennials as they grew up. Because of this, many Millennials lack the internal motivation to overcome career impatience. If you want to deepen the determination and motivation of your Millennial employees, it's up to your leaders to cultivate it.

The responsibility rests on leaders to cast a compelling vision and help Millennials discover their personal (intrinsic) motivation in achieving the vision and progressing within the organization. Help them to identify the necessary grit that won't let them quit.

Millennials who gain early clarity on their internal motivations and career progression goals will be able to adjust their expectations and be better equipped to explore cross-collaboration opportunities to gain more experience and to put their anxious ambition to good use.

2. Commit to coaching. Coaching is the leadership style that resonates most with Millennials. Millennials were raised in organized activities where they were consistently surrounded by coaches. They view coaching as their path to greatness. The best coaches train, guide, and advance while taking deep interest in those they coach.

Effective coaching builds trust, instills loyalty, and helps Millennials become valuable faster. Coaching allows a leader to reflect the progress and impact a

Millennial is having at the organization and to recommend the right opportunities where Millennials can continue their growth and development.

Coaching allows leaders to anticipate when a Millennial is struggling, frustrated, bored, or underemployed before he or she decides to leave the company. Leaders should reemphasize, however, that there is no quick recipe for job satisfaction. It's a slow, uncomfortable, and complicated process.

3. Connect with contribution. Parents encouraged Millennials to have a say at an early age. Access to the Internet also gave Millennials a platform for contribution and to have a voice. They now carry this desire to contribute into the workplace. Leaders who create opportunities for Millennials (no matter their tenure) to contribute and cocreate will be rewarded with Millennial loyalty and longevity.

Too often, organizations underestimate the ability and desire Millennials have to contribute. Underestimation leads to resentment, and underemployment leads to impatience. Create environments that encourage and channels that enable contribution.

4. Motivate with movement. To satisfy Millennials' desire to gain transferable skills, get them moving throughout the organization. Millennials don't view career paths as linear, like a ladder, but rather multidimensional, like a military cargo-climbing net. They might be interested in moving left and then back down before moving up.

Be transparent and proactive in your communications about the available opportunities throughout the organization. Networking or social events, job shadows, and online job directories are good examples of ways to help Millennials explore movement throughout the organization.

Taco Bell's corporate office has a strategy in which it loans employees to other companies. If an employee notices a project at another company that he or she is interested in, the employee can request to be loaned out on a temporary basis to work on it. This is a nontraditional approach for a generation that approaches career and learning nontraditionally.

5. Develop for departure. Offer the training, coaching, and mentoring necessary for Millennials to develop themselves out of their current roles or the organization. Why develop someone out of the organization? Because the alternative of *not* developing workers and having them stay and underperform is much worse.

Liz Wiseman, author of *Rookie Smarts: Why Learning Beats Knowing in the New Game of Work*, believes that a rookie mentality—approaching work or a job/task for the first time or from a new perspective—is the key to faster learning, better performance, and persisting through failure. (We explore this concept in more depth in chapter 40.) Departing Millennials can make room for new "rookies" ready to perform better and can bring the rookie mentality to their new role or company, further advancing themselves or that organization.

If Millennials depart your company, they might not know how good they had it, because they have nothing to compare it to this early in their career. When they experience the lack of development at another organization, they can boomerang back to your company. These become your best company ambassadors. Leverage them wisely.

CHAPTER 31

How to Eliminate Entitlement in a Millennial Workforce

• • •

MOST AMERICAN ADULTS—71 PERCENT—THINK OF Millennials as "selfish," and 65 percent think Millennials are "entitled."

WHAT IS ENTITLEMENT?

Entitlement is the feeling or belief that you deserve to be given something (such as special privileges). Entitlement can show up in students, customers, parents, employers, managers, and employees.

Dr. John Townsend, psychologist, leadership expert, and best-selling author of *The Entitlement Cure: Finding Success in Doing Hard Things the Right Way*, defines entitlement in two ways...

- An attitude that I am not responsible for my impact on you. (Examples: I can be late to meetings, a clock watcher, or not be a team player.)
- An attitude that I deserve special treatment. (Examples: I don't need to work my way up, I don't need to start at the bottom, and I don't need to play by the rules.)

Entitlement can be a heavy anchor for any generation's journey toward success. It can make the most seasoned professional blind to his or her weaknesses, complacent, or resentful.

MILLENNIAL EXPLANATION OF ENTITLEMENT

Entitlement is perhaps the top word associated with the Millennial generation. Some of the Millennial behaviors labeled as entitled are...

- Expecting to land a job upon graduating from college.
- Demanding a certain salary or promotion.
- Assuming specific flexible hours at work.

Unaddressed entitlement in your Millennial workers can result in unethical behaviors, higher turnover, underperformance, lower job satisfaction, and/or loss of leadership influence, as Millennials might view their managers as unreasonable, hardheaded, or irrelevant.

But before we can address the entitlement issue, we must understand the external factors that have created Millennial entitlement (or at least the perception thereof).

Parenting. I grew up playing competitive ice hockey in Colorado. One year, we were fortunate enough to win the state championship, at which point I expected to receive a trophy...a big one. But every other year when we fell short of the championship, my fellow Millennial teammates and I never expected a trophy. Instead, the "everyone gets a trophy" advocates were...our parents.

To a high degree, entitlement is a learned behavior. Millennials never thought of themselves as entitled, but their parents believed they were entitled to everything—thus the emergence of "helicopter parents." It may have been a noble parenting style, but it had unexpected ramifications that infused different behaviors and expectations into an entire generation.

Fast Times. We live in fast times, changing times. In fact, famed futurist and author Ray Kurzweil believes that we will experience not a hundred years of progress in the twenty-first century but twenty thousand—thanks to technology.

Today's high-tech times have created a new, connected era in which opportunities are abundant and accelerated success is the new reality.

Did you know that during the nineteenth century, it took the oil tycoon John D. Rockefeller forty-six years to make a billion dollars? Starting in the 1980s, it took Michael Dell fourteen years to achieve billionaire status. It took Bill Gates twelve years. In the 1990s, Yahoo's founders, Jerry Yang and David Filo, earned a billion dollars in four years. The founder of eBay, Pierre Omidyar, did it in three. And in the late 2000s, Groupon's Andrew Mason made a billion dollars in two years.

We live in a much different world than we did even ten years ago, which is why there are much different employees emerging in today's workplace.

Millennials have new expectations of what's possible and are less tolerant of what once was because of today's fast times. This results in behaviors that are perceived as "entitled," because Millennials...

- are less tolerant of not moving fast.
- are better educated on today's "new world."
- live in a world where success can be achieved faster.
- have mastered tools (technology, apps, software, etc.) that have leveled the playing field.

- have been empowered by the Internet and mobile devices to create something for themselves.
- have an abundant and boundless mind-set that provides them with endless optimism, confidence, and passion.

These behaviors might make Millennials entitled...or it might make them the next generation of workers.

Culture. The on-demand, instant-gratification culture that Millennials grew up in and the Great Recession, when they came of age, produced new levels of anxiousness over their careers. This situation now interferes with their ability to prioritize any other perspective but their own.

Science confirms that when we are anxious or stressed, our minds prioritize our own perspectives and needs. Today's culture encourages individuals to prioritize self over others.

Knowledge and skill shift. Sixty-eight percent of hiring managers say that Millennials have skills that prior generations do not. For the first time in history, the emerging generations have knowledge and skills that previous generations do not.

Some Millennials' entitlement stems from their view that they are more knowledgeable in select areas, giving greater weight to their viewpoints or actions there. Millennials may overstep traditional workplace or hierarchy boundaries to share their unique perspective or expertise to help their teams be more innovative and efficient.

Ownership. The connected world has empowered Millennials to take ownership. Glassdoor and LinkedIn allow ownership of one's career. YouTube allows ownership of one's content. Instagram and Snapchat allow ownership of one's personal brand. Netflix allows ownership of one's content consumption.

The Internet has offered Millennials personalization and customization at every turn of their lives, and now they expect the same control at work and in their careers.

Millennials are skeptical of "paying their dues" due to the mistrust between employer and employee that they've witnessed firsthand in their parents' situations. Thus, Millennials approach their career like free agents, taking ownership and looking for new opportunities or creating their own through entrepreneurship.

The rejection of the traditional career path and workplace norms is perceived by many as "entitlement," but perhaps a better descriptor is "ownership." Millennials are not interested in spending hours commuting to work, working for years in the mere hope of promotion, and sitting at a desk from nine to five for the only reason that "this is how it's always been." That's the opposite of ownership.

Millennials are interested in ownership, freedom, legacy, and impact during their careers, not just at the end. This is a noble quest that any generation can get behind.

Human nature. Entitlement is a human condition that is not exclusive to Millennials. Humans are selfish by nature. We have to work hard and intentionally to overcome or suppress our selfish behaviors.

Maturity is the ability to see and act on the behalf of others, while immaturity is not seeing things from someone else's point of view. In many cases, it's natural for Millennials to exude entitlement because they are immature in their grasp of workplace dynamics.

In addition, the human brain continues to develop until a person is around twenty-five. Buying a house, getting married, and having kids helps to accelerate maturity and an others-first mentality, but Millennials are waiting longer than previous generations did to enter those life stages.

The above factors are not excuses for but rather explanations of Millennial entitlement.

Now that we have a better understanding of Millennial entitlement, let's look at ways to overcome Millennial entitlement at work.

How to Eliminate Entitlement in a Millennial Workforce

If entitlement is a disease, Townsend says that the antidote is "the habit of doing what is best rather than doing what is comfortable to achieve a worthwhile outcome." Those who wait for life to come to them are entitled and ultimately are not successful.

It can be daunting for leaders to confront an entitled individual or an organization filled with entitlement. But overcoming entitlement can be done. It's a process. Here are some strategies to help.

Smash silos. Working in silos (or in the absence of a team) can produce the feeling that success happens independently and thus cultivate an attitude of entitlement in the individual. Finding ways to get people collaborating, brainstorming, working, and playing together helps erode entitlement.

Own failure. Company cultures and leaders that own failure are positioned well to stamp out entitlement. After a failure, nonentitled leaders and employees will ask themselves, "What did I do to contribute to this?" and, "What could I have done differently?" Pride is an early indicator of entitlement. Leaders must model the behavior of pointing fingers at themselves more than at others.

Seek agreement. Russell B. Lemle, PhD, an associate clinical professor in the Department of Psychiatry at the University of California San Francisco, writes, "Entitlements are unilateral. We award them to ourselves. By contrast, agreements are jointly consented, arrived at together. Researchers have confirmed that [relationships] flourish when both parties feel they have a voice in decisions."

Seek agreements that are good for the individual and for the organization.

Lemle recommends four actions to find more agreement in relationships...

- Learn to tolerate frustration. The normal reaction when we don't get our way is discomfort. Sitting with that feeling, rather than immediately acting to end it, enables us to connect with [the other person].
- Make a request instead of demanding compliance. Ask once; if you get no for an answer, modify the request.
- Remember that what we want is a personal preference—not a right. Inquire about [the other person's] wishes and put them on par with your own.
- Be flexible and strive for compromises that are amenable to both parties.

Lemle explains, "Wanting our way is not the same as being entitled to our way. Though we may feel a strong imperative how something should go, we must ensure that [the other person] has equal input. If we impose our position, we deny the legitimacy of [the other person's] experience and encroach upon his/her autonomy."

Reinforce responsibility. We spend so much time writing and editing an organization's mission statement because we know the power those words have to guide the organization. Words have a profound power to impact organizational change and ultimately change employee attitudes.

Employee entitlement can be eliminated using words. Townsend recommends eliminating employee entitlement by getting employees to shift their attitudes from "I deserve" to "I'm responsible." An attitude or culture of "I deserve" is severely disempowering because it relies on external forces that are out of an individual's control. "I'm responsible" is extremely empowering because it gives control or ownership—something Millennials are familiar with and longing for—to the individual.

Here are a few examples of attitude shifts:

- "I deserve a great job. I'll wait for someone to hand me a job."
  - Change to: "I'm responsible for securing a great job. I'll do what it takes to find and secure a great job. I'm responsible for networking, acquiring in-demand skills, or interviewing well. I'm responsible for helping my employer become a better workplace."
- "I deserve a promotion. I'm going to wait until someone gives me the promotion I deserve."
  - Change to: "I'm responsible for my work ethic and the quality of my work. I'm responsible for executing my job responsibilities with excellence every day. I'm responsible for informing management of my career aspirations. I'm responsible for building the skills necessary for promotion."
- "I deserve to work whenever and wherever I want. I'm going to find an employer that will give that to me."
  - Change to: "I'm responsible for meeting the needs of my customer or employer. I'm responsible for helping my manager understand how I can bring more value with a flexible schedule. I'm responsible to maintain high performance no matter when or where I work."

In each of the above "I deserve" scenarios, the individual is robbed of choice and control because of an entitled attitude. In every "I'm responsible" scenario, the individual is empowered with choices and control.

Doing our best doesn't entitle us to anything. Instead, it elevates our chances of being rewarded for our work and acquiring what we desire.

It's important to note that there are healthy forms of deserving. For example, we deserve fair compensation for the work that is required of us. It's when deserving and our desires for more, better, faster overtake us that we slip into an "I deserve" attitude and mind-set that is dangerous. This is something every generation is guilty of and remains susceptible to.

Be responsible. Choose to persevere with patience. The selfish "I deserve" attitude will only weakens resolve.

Model servant leadership. To stamp out entitlement in ourselves and in emerging generations, leaders must practice servant leadership.

According to Robert K. Greenleaf, author of *The Servant as Leader*, servant leadership is the philosophy and set of practices that enriches the lives of individuals, builds better organizations, and ultimately creates a more just and caring world. "The servant-leader is servant first. It begins with the natural feeling that one wants to serve, to serve first," says Greenleaf.

A servant leader prioritizes the needs of others first. A servant leader always asks the question, "Why don't I?" instead of, "Why don't they?" As famed author Simon Sinek puts it, "Leaders eat last."

It's up to leaders to expect more, to raise the lid of Millennials' potential by modeling servant leadership so that Millennials are equipped to model it for Generation Z.

4 ENTITLEMENT-ENDING PHRASES TO COMMUNICATE TO MILLENNIALS

- Don't demand a voice, earn a voice. Before making demands, make an effort. Give your effort, help, and support without expecting anything in return.
- Be content but never satisfied. Be humble, yet confident. Be grateful, yet hungry.
- Prioritize marinating over microwaving. The most rewarding and strongest careers, skills, and expertise are built slowly and steadily. Persevere with patience.
- Do your best and forget the rest.

Section 4
Engage Millennials

• • •

CHAPTER 32

How To Use Employee Experience To Increase Millennial Engagement And Job Satisfaction

• • •

ACCORDING TO DELOITTE'S 2017 GLOBAL Human Capital Trends report,

> A productive, positive employee experience has emerged as the new contract between employer and employee. Just as marketing and product teams have moved beyond customer satisfaction to look at total customer experience, so is HR refocusing its efforts on building programs, strategies, and teams that understand and continuously improve the entire employee experience.

Before exploring the idea of "employee experience" and its impact on the Millennial workforce, let's first review the impact and importance of experiences.

THE IMPACT OF EXPERIENCES

Experiences (terrible, average, or great) are at the core of our lives as consumers. We know the difference between an extraordinary experience (the hotel that remembers your room preferences, meal choices, and specific needs) and a terrible experience (the waiter forgets your drink order, brings out the dishes at separate times, and goes missing when you're ready for the check).

Experiences matter. They impact our satisfaction, loyalty, relationships, happiness, buying decisions, and they shape us as human beings.

Research shows that humans derive more meaning and joy from experiences than objects, so when faced with the decision to buy a new thing for the family or go on vacation, they prefer to go on vacation and create an experience.

Though experiences may be momentary, they stay with us in the form of memories. Similarly, the experiences we have at work have the capacity to positively or negatively shape the connections we have with our managers, coworkers, and the company as a whole.

So, if experiences are so critical and we put so much value on a good experience, why are great experiences missing from inside of our organizations?

WHAT IS EMPLOYEE EXPERIENCE?

Jacob Morgan, author of *The Employee Experience Advantage: How to Win the War for Talent by Giving Employees the Workspaces They Want, the Tools They Need, and a Culture They Can Celebrate*, explains that organizational priorities are shifting to focus more and more on "people and bringing humanity and experiences into our organizations."

Morgan believes that organizations have evolved from utility (basic components of work), to productivity (getting the most out of people), to engagement (making employees happy and engaged), to employee experience. "If employee engagement is the short-term adrenaline shot, then employee experience is the long-term redesign of the organization," says Morgan.

Morgan defines attention to employee experience as "designing an organization where people want to show up by focusing on the cultural, technological, and physical environments." Said another way, employee experience is the approach to delivering excellent experiences to employees inside of an organization throughout the life cycle of employees. It's the impact an organization's processes, policies, and programs have on its people.

The core of the shift to employee experience is creating organizations where people want, not need, to show up to work. Organizations can no longer assume that employees need to be present or have to show up. They must instill a desire to be there.

Employee experience has recently emerged as a top priority in organizations as a way to foster innovation, recruit and retain top talent, improve customer and employee satisfaction, and increase overall company performance.

Deloitte's 2017 Global Human Capital Trends report sums up why employee experience is emerging as a top priority:

In a digital world with increasing transparency and the growing influence of Millennials, employees expect a productive, engaging, enjoyable work experience. Rather than focus narrowly on employee engagement and culture, organizations are developing an integrated focus on the entire employee experience, bringing together all the workplace, HR, and management practices that impact people on the job. A new marketplace of pulse feedback tools, wellness and fitness apps, and integrated employee self-service tools is helping HR departments understand and improve this experience. Through new approaches such as design thinking and employee journey maps, HR departments are now focusing on understanding and improving this complete experience and using tools such as employee "Net Promoter" scores to measure employee satisfaction.

THE RISE OF EMPLOYEE EXPERIENCE

A major contributor of the rise and relevance of employee experience is the growing representation of Millennials in the workplace. The presence and expectations of Millennials have required organizations to fundamentally redefine their structure and purpose.

Previous generations learned to keep silent about the change they wanted, but Millennials are vocalizing the change they want. Change and the shift to employee experience will accelerate when Millennials account for 50 percent of the global workforce by 2020. More experience-seeking Millennials in the workplace means that a shift to experience-centric organizations is needed to attract, retain, and engage the Millennial worker.

To contend in tomorrow's talent war, organizations must rethink and reengineer how to deliver a signature experience for its greatest asset... people.

THE IMPORTANCE OF EXPERIENCES

According to Cornell University psychology professor Dr. Thomas Gilovich and colleagues Dr. Amit Kumar (University of Chicago) and Dr. Matthew Killingsworth (University of California), "Experiential purchases (money spent on *doing*) tend to provide more enduring happiness than material purchases (money spent on *having*). Waiting for experiences tends to be more pleasurable and exciting than waiting to receive a material good."

When people spend money on experiences, their satisfaction increases over time. When people spend money on material purchases, their satisfaction decreases over time. Also, people's experiential purchases are more closely associated with their identities, connections, and social behavior.

In addition, Dr. Gilovich says, "We feel more compelled to talk about our experiences and we get more out of doing so. Talking about experiences, furthermore, tends to be more socially rewarding as well."

It seems that employees view work as a material purchase, because, according to research done by Glassdoor, there is a clear relationship between years of experience and happiness at work. Older workers tend to be less satisfied. Each additional year of experience leads to a decrease in overall employee satisfaction.

The goal of employee experience is to shift Millennials' relationship with work from considering it like a material purchase, where satisfaction decreases over time, to an experiential purchase, where the anticipation of going to work is exciting and job satisfaction increases over time.

For Millennials who grew up in a world of abundance, their basic needs have been met, so they naturally look to fulfilling their higher needs. According to Maslow's hierarchy of needs, these would be love/belonging (social, love, family, team) and esteem (importance, recognition, respect). These are all benefits that can be delivered via carefully executed employee experiences. (There's more on Maslow's hierarchy and Millennials' psychology of recognition in chapter 21.)

Benefits and salary are expectations for Millennials. Millennials aren't interested in simply filling a job. Instead, they want meaning, strong company culture, and extraordinary experiences at work.

Millennials don't look to corporations for job security. Instead, they recognize that their networks and skills will provide any security and stability they seek. This new shift redirects the responsibility of the organization to delivering a place where folks want to show up instead of where they have to.

Almost all recruiters—90 percent—say that the current job market is candidate driven, which is up from 54 percent in 2011. In today's global and candidate/employee market, focusing on the employee or candidate experience can be a competitive advantage—especially for garnering Millennials, who put a premium on experiences and have elevated expectations of how products, services, and employment are delivered to them. For example, 77 percent of Millennials say some of their best memories are from an event or live experience they attended or participated in.

Morgan urges organizations, "We have to focus on designing employee experiences, which is the long-term organizational design that leads to engaged employees. This is the only long-term solution. Organizations have been stuck focusing on the cause instead of the effect. The cause is employee experience; the effect is an engaged workforce."

Research reveals that organizations that focus on employee experience far outperform organizations that don't. They develop and retain high performers, and become beacons for new top talent. And strong employee experiences drive strong customer experiences.

Enhancing the employee experience is critical for companies wanting to remain competitive in today's global economy. Creating engaging employee experiences is a key differentiator and will become increasingly more important for engaging and winning the war on talent.

How to Implement Employee Experience

Millennials are the most disengaged at work of any generation: 71 percent. To offset this Millennial engagement epidemic, organizations must design employee experiences. Morgan looks at employee experience as "the intersection of employee expectations, needs, and wants and the organization design of those expectations, needs, and wants."

Nearly 80 percent of executives rated employee experience very important (42 percent) or important (38 percent), but only 22 percent reported that their companies were excellent at building a differentiated employee experience. And 59 percent reported they were not ready or only somewhat ready to address the employee-experience challenge.

Because employee experience is very human-centric, organizations will (and should) take very different approaches to it. Here are three items to consider when designing the employee experience:

- **Know your people.** The best experiences are catered to the individual. The better you know the Millennials in your organization, the better the experience you can deliver. Designing a rich employee experience isn't just *for* Millennials; it must be done *with* them. Because experience is subjective, it's crucial to connect with those to whom the experience will be delivered. Leaders must be committed to connecting with Millennials. Consider creating Millennial-employee personas and use them to develop journey maps.
  - Companies such as Cisco, IBM, GE, and Airbnb have used hackathons to collect employee ideas about how to enhance the employee experience. Emerging technology and trends in people analytics can also assist organizations in predicting employees' expectations, needs, and wants. IBM has saved over $130 million by using people analytics to predict which employees are at risk of leaving the company and notify managers to prevent it.
- **Deliver holistically.** Employee experience must be end-to-end service that spans the entire life cycle of Millennial employees—hiring, day-one orientation, onboarding, training, promotion, offboarding, and so on. The employee experience must also cover the workspace, technology, leadership, diversity, organizational structure, career mobility, employment brand, HR services, and company perks. Also consider all

segments of the workforce—part time, freelance, etc. Changing "job descriptions" to "job experiences" is a subtle change but can get the candidate and employer beginning to think in the right direction.

- Nike, Telstra, and Commonwealth Bank of Australia have developed mobile apps, new user experiences, and new service-delivery solutions to improve their employee experience holistically across onboarding, recruitment, and self-service applications. In addition, companies such as Apple, Google, and Facebook have designed their workplace facilities holistically to incorporate exercise, collaboration, health and well-being, food, and nature to enhance the employee experience.

- **Revisit routinely.** The employee experiences that are developed and delivered must be routinely revisited for necessary course corrections or adjustments. Create open feedback systems and pulse surveys (simple, fast, and frequent surveys that provide quick insights into the health of a company, designed to be done weekly or every few weeks) to measure impact instead of annual or biannual engagement surveys.

- TINYPulse and Culture Amp are strong workplace tools for delivering pulse surveys. Using an employee "Net Promoter" score that reflects the value of the employee experience can be helpful for tracking and measuring purposes.

EXAMPLES OF COMPANIES EMBRACING EMPLOYEE EXPERIENCE

- Airbnb has an appointed "chief employee experience officer" whose job it is to serve employees in a number of different ways. A few include building a healthy and satisfying food program, providing employees with the latest technology, recruiting the best and brightest talent, and ensuring that their buildings are spaces for an optimal work environment. Airbnb's employee-experience team touches every facet of Airbnb and aims to drive the company's health and happiness. Other companies that have chief employee experience officers are Cisco and Pandora.

- Adobe recently combined its customer-experience organization with its human-resources and facilities organizations to create the new "Customer and Employee Experience" organization. The focus of the new organization is the people who are essential to Adobe's business—their customers and employees—and the understanding that people want the same fundamental things: to be treated with respect for their needs and their time, to find the information they need quickly, and to feel invested in a long-term relationship, whether it's with the employer or the brand. Adobe is committed to injecting employee experience into the thinking of every one of their employees, regardless of role.

- Ford Motor Company launched a global listening tour to better understand what is effective and ineffective in its employee experience. Based on the findings, the Ford HR team will deliver high-impact, innovative workforce solutions and experiences that improve workers' lives. Ford's group vice-president of human resources and corporate services says, "Our mission is to make employees' lives better by changing the way we think about work, feel about work, and the way we do our work differently."

Prithvi Shergill summarizes the power of employee experience very well in *The Economic Times* article "Employee Experience in the Time of Uncertainty":

An enhanced employee experience impacts key individual and collective drivers of business growth—passion, proficiency, productivity and performance. How exactly? By putting employees first, they are now more emotionally invested in the mission and are committed to the same beliefs as that of the organization which multiplies capability, contribution and commitment. A passionate workforce is willing to go the extra mile to seed, nurture, and harvest ideas to add value. By building individual proficiencies and providing opportunities for employees to fulfill their potential organizations are able to ensure the relationship with their workforce goes beyond the contract. Greater productivity and performance enables employees to enhance the 'value zone' in every interaction with clients and stakeholders they interact with leading to higher levels of customer satisfaction.

Many of the ideas and strategies in the coming chapters (and throughout the entire book) can contribute to enhancing the overall employee experience for your Millennial workforce. Execute them well and watch Millennial engagement, job satisfaction, and productivity increase.

CHAPTER 33

How to Engage Millennials in Meetings

• • •

MILLENNIALS CONTINUE TO GET RAZZED for having their heads buried in their phones. For managers of Millennials, this behavior is most frustrating in the midst of a meeting. The finger flicks and swipes can make the most seasoned manager's blood boil.

If the small Yondr pouches that lock smartphones shut with a wireless signal while in the "no-phone zone" aren't an option for your meeting, then what's a person to do?

This challenge extends beyond the business environment. I recently spoke to a roomful of highly esteemed doctors from around the country, where many asked me about how to get their Millennial residents to turn off their phones while in the classroom.

My answer to the doctors is the same for business leaders wondering, "How do I get Millennials to ignore their phones while in a meeting?" That answer is: you're asking the wrong question. The better question is, "How do I create more engaging communications?"

You can't control the attention of Millennials. Even if you get them to power down their devices, that doesn't mean you'll win their attention. Instead, you'll earn Millennial resentment and the label of an irrelevant and outdated leader. The only thing you can control is the message and its delivery. The secret to engaging Millennials in meetings is crafting captivating content.

As a professional speaker, every time I step onstage, I am competing with the audience's hundreds of pending e-mails, endless status updates, continuous news stories, and a new high score in Fruit Ninja...all in the palms of their hands. My content has to be more gripping than the next post of their favorite Instagram follow. My delivery has to be more dynamic than a sports highlight.

There's more competing for our attention than ever before. It takes intentional communication to cut through the noise. It's a battle, and it starts in the preparation and extends through the delivery. Having an audience turn off its phones is the lazy way out.

Attention can no longer be expected. It must be earned. Whether in the conference room or classroom, take responsibility for the attention of your Millennial audience. Prepare meticulously and deliver with passion and brevity. Here are a few other ideas to consider when engaging mobile-dependent Millennials...

- **Tell a story.** Stories remain timeless as a way to captivate any audience.
- **Ask questions.** What's 12 minus 5? I'll bet you just answered that question in your head before continuing to read. Questions are inherently engaging.
- **Use images.** Humans think in images. Take a cue from Instagram's success with Millennials and supplement your message with appealing images.
- **Be shocking.** The unexpected and surprising will attract the attention of the most mobile addicted.

- **Simplify.** Simplify the message to its bare essentials and simplify the logistics by cutting the time of all future meetings in half.
- **Cocreate.** Prior to the meeting, ask attendees to help create or shape the content.
- **Draw in digitally.** Pull engagement through mobile devices. I use Poll Everywhere (www.polleverywhere.com) to engage my audiences with live polls.

If, for some odd reason, phones must be shut off, then you must present a clear and compelling case for *why* they cannot be used.

Today's Millennial worker and the ever-evolving times demand for transformed communications. Today's tech should be your motivator to be a better communicator.

CHAPTER 34

How to Attract Millennials with the Right Company Perks

• • •

NAP PODS, FREE LUNCHES, AND unlimited vacation days aren't enough to capture the attention and loyalty of Millennials. Transform your company perks and attract Millennials with these six tips.

Most Millennials—66 percent—expect to leave their organizations by 2020. Companies are at risk of losing a large percentage of their next-generation talent if they fail to adjust how they retain Millennials. That's why cultivating workplace culture and incentives that keep employees happy and productive is critical.

One solution to consider for overcoming the Millennial-retention issue is the right set of company perks. Company perks pack the potential to attract new and retain existing Millennial talent.

In fact, 64 percent of Millennials care about company perks and benefits (compared to 54 percent of Generation X and 51 percent of Baby Boomers). And "perks and benefits" are the number-two thing behind "culture and values" that Millennials want to know about a company.

According to employee gift-box company Perkbox, 69 percent of eighteen-to-twenty-four-year-old Millennial employees in the United Kingdom say that company perks are crucial to their job satisfaction, compared to about half of Baby Boomer employees.

"Millennials see [company perks] as something employers should do as standard, whereas older employees see it as a bonus," says Saurav Chopra, co-founder of Perkbox.

Take company-perk cues from Inc.'s 2016 50 Best Workplaces...

- 46 percent have on-site fitness facilities.
- 74 percent offer on-site meals.
- 86 percent match employee 401(k) contributions (typically 3 or 4 percent of income).
- 28 percent have on-site health-care clinics.
- 64 percent offer paternity leave.
- 74 percent give time off for volunteering.
- 84 percent let employees telecommute.
- 24 percent offer unlimited vacation.

6 Tips for Using Company Perks to Attract (and Keep) Millennials

1. Blend work and life with perks. Ninety-nine percent of Millennials agree that "more and more, I'm trying to find balance in my life."

Basecamp, a web-application company based in Chicago, pays for employees' hobbies and for their staff to have fresh fruits and veggies at home. Johnson & Johnson provides a concierge service to run errands and even stand in line for concert tickets.

More than ever before, work and life are blending. Thanks to mobile communications, we bring more work home with us and bring more of our personal lives to work.

Many of today's company perks reflect Millennials' desire to experience more of life at work. It's not as much about having access to ping-pong tables as it is having elements that reflect their life outside of work.

To attract and retain Millennials, blend work and life by integrating the "life" aspects of your employees or community into the workplace.

2. Make perks an experience. Over 70 percent of directors and managers say that their employees value experiences over things, or at least a combination of the two.

New Belgium Brewing Company employees receive a one-week trip to Belgium after five years there. Yahoo provides employees with corporate outings like concerts and backyard barbecues. Freeborn & Peters, a full-service law firm headquartered in Chicago, has an annual "luggage party" where four employees are randomly chosen for an all-expense paid trip to Las Vegas.

Since 77 percent of Millennials say that some of their best memories are from an event or live experience they attended or participated in, companies have a unique opportunity to win Millennial affinity by delivering an unforgettable experience.

Creating company perks that Millennials can't help but tell everyone about will work wonders for your attraction and retention efforts.

3. Make perks appeal to Millennials. Eighty percent of Millennials say they would like to work for a company that offers student-loan repayment assistance.

CommonBond of New York City and PricewaterhouseCoopers contribute $1,200 a year to help employees repay student loans. IBM, GE, and Accenture help nursing mothers (most being Millennials) by providing the necessary materials and funds to ship breast milk home when they're traveling for work. Premier Staffing of San Francisco expects employees to devote twenty days a year to community service.

Rather than other low-tech perks in their workplaces, 80 percent of Millennial workers prefer tech-forward perks like augmented/virtual reality. Whether it's innovative tech perks, student-loan repayment, help with being a new parent, or the resources to develop as a professional, addressing the specific interests and desires of Millennials with company perks can result in company loyalty.

Don't know what appeals to your Millennial workers? Ask them.

4. Emphasis company culture with perks. The number-one thing that Millennials want to know about a company is its "culture and values."

Be purposeful with your perks. Patty McCord, former chief talent officer at Netflix, says that some benefits favored by tech companies, such as in-office hammocks and personal chefs, are "a race to the ridiculous." She notes, "Perks are designed to make people happier at work, but you're not accomplishing anything just by giving people more stuff." Aligning company perks with company culture and values can be much more useful.

Here are a few good examples of companies offering perks that align with their company culture and mission.

- Zynga, an online and mobile game company, has an on-site video arcade.
- Mattel, Inc., a toy-manufacturing company, offers employees up to six-teen paid hours off to participate in their kids' school events.
- Airbnb, a community-driven hospitality company, provides employees with $2,000 a year to spend on properties on the home-sharing site anywhere in the world.
- Burton, a snowboarding outfitter, provides employees the day off to hit the slopes if two feet of snow falls in twenty-four hours.
- Pandora, a music-streaming company, offers free in-office concerts to its employees.
- REI, a retail and outdoor-recreation services company, offers an em-ployee-challenge grant where employees get $300 in products for an outdoor activity as long as it's a challenge—like backpacking in the High Sierras, running a marathon in Thailand, etc.

5. Highlight the inherent perks. Seventy-one percent of Millennials likely to leave a company in the next two years are unhappy with how their leadership skills are being developed.

If retaining and engaging Millennials is your objective, make it a consistent and high priority to highlight the development perks that are inherent in the work. Extract the learning and developmental benefits that are built into the day-to-day tasks and responsibilities.

A few examples could be...

- Opportunities to meet, collaborate, and learn from forward-thinking and brilliant people.
- Building products and services that add value to others and that you can be proud of.
- Failing in a supportive environment with an understanding and uplifting team.

6. Leverage the greatest perk. The greatest perk is hearing that your company values you. Tell your people early and demonstrate it often.

CHAPTER 35

How to Avoid the Top Two Reasons Millennials Leave Companies

• • •

ONLY 16 PERCENT OF MILLENNIALS see themselves with their current employers a decade from now.

One of the greatest talent challenges currently facing employers is engaging the Millennial generation, who recently became the largest share of the US labor market. The absence of Millennial loyalty and engagement represents a serious threat to the longevity of any business.

In Deloitte's recent 2016 Millennial Survey, it collected the views of nearly 7,700 Millennials representing twenty-nine countries around the globe. All participants were born after 1982, have obtained a college or university degree, are employed full time, and predominantly work in large (one hundred-plus employees), private-sector organizations.

The survey focused on Millennials' values and ambitions, drivers of job satisfaction, and their increasing representation on senior management teams. The below is a summary of the results of the survey.

WHY ARE MILLENNIALS LEAVING ORGANIZATIONS?
The lack of leadership development and flexibility.

The primary factor contributing to the decline of Millennial loyalty is the Millennial belief that businesses are not doing enough to bridge the gap to ensure that a new generation of business leaders is created. Millennials feel underutilized and believe they're not being developed as leaders.

- 63 percent of Millennials believe their leadership skills are not being fully developed, and yet the number-one most important driver in Millennials' evaluation of job opportunities is the ability to progress and take on leadership roles.
- Only 24 percent of Millennials are "very satisfied" with the learning opportunities and professional-development programs at work.

The secondary factor contributing to Millennials leaving organizations is the lack of workplace flexibility.

- 88 percent of Millennials wish they could have greater opportunity to start and finish work at the times they choose.
- 75 percent of Millennials would like to start to work from home or other locations where they feel more productive, or do so more frequently. Only 43 percent currently do so.

HOW TO KEEP MILLENNIALS FROM LEAVING AN ORGANIZATION
According to Deloitte's 2016 Millennial Global Survey, there are three key actions to ensure that an organization can retain Millennials.

1. Identify, understand, and align with Millennials' values.

Millennials intending to stay with their organizations for at least five years are far more likely than others to report that it has a positive culture and focuses on the needs of the individual. Millennials believe that the most important values a business should follow for long-term success are putting employees first and having a solid foundation of trust and integrity.

Millennials choose employers whose values reflect their own; 56 percent of them have "ruled out ever working for a particular organization because of its values or standard of conduct."

Millennials choose employers who demonstrate a strong sense of company purpose beyond financial success—87 percent of believe that "the success of a business should be measured in terms of more than just its financial performance."

2. Satisfy the demands Millennials have of employers.

Beyond pay and financial benefits (which drive Millennials' choice of organization more than anything else), the most important drivers of employer choice for Millennials are: work-life balance, opportunities to progress/be leaders, flexibility (i.e., remote working and flexible hours), sense of meaning from work, and professional-development training programs.

Millennials report high levels of employee satisfaction when the following features exist: open and free-flowing communication, a culture of mutual support and tolerance, a strong sense of purpose beyond financial success, active encouragement of ideas among all employees, strong commitment to equality and inclusiveness, and support and understanding of the ambitions of younger employees.

3. SUPPORT MILLENNIALS' AMBITIONS AND PROFESSIONAL DEVELOPMENT.

Millennials would like to increase the time devoted to leadership-skills development from 2.7 to 4.5 hours a week—an increase of two-thirds. Millennials demonstrate more loyalty when there is an emphasis on leadership development.

For the 68 percent of Millennials likely to stay over five years with a company, they say that they have support/training widely available to progress in leadership roles. Make training and development support widely available.

Millennials intending to stay with their organization for more than five years are twice as likely to have a mentor (68 percent) than not (32 percent). Encouraging mentorship promotes loyalty.

(Looking for a proven and effective way to offer leadership development for your Millennial workforce? Check out www.21Mill.com, the first ever microlearning platform designed specifically to develop Millennials. Full disclosure: I am a proud partner of 21Mill.)

HOW ONE COMPANY IS WORKING TO RETAIN MILLENNIALS

On July 26, 2016, Susan Peters, GE's senior vice-president, human resources, sent an e-mail to more than three hundred thousand GE employees around the world informing them that the long-standing practice of annual reviews was over.

GE ran a pilot with thirty thousand employees in which managers gave constant feedback about employees' work though an app called Performance Development at GE (PD@GE). Employees were also able to use the app to receive real-time feedback at any time.

GE is not alone in ending the annual-review process. LinkedIn, Adobe, Cisco, and many others have adopted alternative ways to review their employees.

GE's PD@GE is one of many new initiatives that are positioning the company well to attract and develop Millennial talent.

1. Delivering real-time feedback. The death of annual reviews has created the birth of real-time feedback. Millennials want 50 percent more feedback than other employees.

2. Empowering managers to be coaches. GE managers are still expected to meet with their employees but will now act more like coaches, guiding their employees toward the established goals. For a generation that grew up on teams being coached at every turn of their lives, Millennials will welcome this new approach.

3. Offering work flexibility. A permissive approach to paid time off was rolled out recently where GE employees can coordinate with their manager to take the time they need to relax and recharge outside of work. Peters mentioned, "You need greater flexibility to create a schedule that works with your life"—88 percent of Millennials wish they could have greater opportunity to start and finish work at the times they choose.

4. Enhancing parental-leave benefits. GE allows ten weeks of parental leave and has a "GE Babies" program that offers moms and dads personalized advice from registered maternity nurses. It is piloting a new program called "Moms on the Move" that enables traveling US moms who are nursing to ship their milk back home for their babies. These are all enticing benefits for Millennials, who make up a majority of new moms in the workplace.

5. Making development a high priority. GE has cultivated a culture of learning by launching "several new digital learning platforms," expanding the "number of global learning centers," enhancing its leadership courses across two hundred locations worldwide, and continuing to invest "$1 billion on employee learning and development every year." As we've seen, 71 percent of Millennials likely to leave a company in the next two years are unhappy with how their leadership skills are being developed.

CHAPTER 36

How to Move Millennials from Underemployed to Hyperutilized

• • •

MOST MANAGERS WHO SEE AN empty chair at a Millennial's desk or a Millennial sinking a lot of time into social media while on the job would chalk his or her behavior up to laziness or lack of focus. However, in my experience working with hundreds of organizations on this topic, I have discovered that often, the behavior occurs because the Millennial is underemployed.

Underemployment is similar to when schoolteachers consider a student a disruption in the classroom because he or she finishes the day's work or test before anyone else and starts talking to peers out of boredom.

Millennials leverage technology and collaborative tools like social media to streamline and systemize their work. They can work smart. As long as managers are still managing the input (time) of their Millennial employees rather than the output (results), they may underestimate just how much their Millennial employees can contribute. Do not confuse working smart with laziness.

4 WAYS TO MOVE MILLENNIALS FROM UNDEREMPLOYED TO HYPERUTILIZED

Provide examples of satisfactory work. A clear and relevant example of excellent work is fundamental in aiding employees to achieve hyperutilization.

Sixty-one percent of Millennials say they need "specific directions from their boss" to do their best work.

Leaders must cast vision—a vision of the "why" behind the work and a vision for the quality of the work. People tend to meet the expectations of those who lead them. Raise your Millennial expectations, and you will raise the lid on the potential of your Millennial employees.

Make additional projects available. It's probably an understatement to say that today's organizational leaders have too much on their plates. Yet, today's underemployed Millennial employees would pounce on the scraps from that plate. In fact, one in four Millennials are "asking for a chance" to show their leadership skills. Whether they vocalize it or not, they want to prove that they have what it takes.

Make it a priority to check in with your Millennial employees on a daily or weekly basis to ensure they have enough to work on. Then communicate the other projects that are available should they want to elevate their impact on the organization.

Create a transparent and cross-collaborative work culture. Seventy-four percent of Millennials prefer to collaborate in small groups, and 38 percent of Millennials feel that outdated collaboration processes hinder their companies' innovation. A transparent culture creates trust and enables Millennial employees to align their unique passions and strengths with company priorities and initiatives.

Transparency creates the necessary visibility and accessibility an employee needs for action. The more empowered a Millennial employee feels to collaborate across teams, the greater the potential for innovation and stronger team outputs.

Support personal and professional development. Fifty percent of Millennials believe their organizations could do more to develop future leaders. When

Millennials' appetite for development isn't satisfied, they will feed the need outside the organization. This is why Millennials are notorious for having "side hustle" or passion projects outside of their full-time jobs.

Leaders should encourage development, and where possible, help Millennials identify areas where they can apply their "side hustles" to their jobs. For example, if a Millennial enjoys blogging, perhaps he or she could launch a company blog or become a contributor for an existing one.

Stop making excuses for your Millennials' disengagement at work. Do not settle for an underemployed Millennial workforce. Instead, raise the bar and see how it responds.

CHAPTER 37

How to Use Flexible Work to Engage Millennials

• • •

IN CHAPTER 14, WE HIGHLIGHTED how you can best manage remote Millennial workers. In this chapter, we will highlight Millennials' desire for remote/flexible working and the benefits of offering it to them.

FlexJobs, the leading online service for professionals seeking flexible jobs, recently surveyed three thousand people and uncovered how critical flexible work is for employers to attract, engage, and retain Millennials.

Flexible work is typically defined by the flexibility in the amount of hours worked, the scheduling of hours worked, the place of work, and in how work gets completed. Flexibility in how work gets completed—rethinking legacy processes and procedures or using new tech and tools—isn't directly covered in the FlexJobs survey but is an increasingly attractive component of work for Millennials.

According to the FlexJobs survey, here are Millennials' top five most important factors when evaluating a prospective job:

1. Work-life balance (84 percent)
2. Work flexibility (82 percent)

3. Salary (80 percent)
4. Work schedule (65 percent)
5. Benefits (48 percent)

Three of the top five most important factors Millennials use to evaluate a potential job center on flexible work. Most Millennials—75 percent—who are interested in work flexibility have college or graduate degrees, and 20 percent are already at a managerial level or higher.

The FlexJobs survey also found that Millennials show a stronger preference—over that of other generations—for working at places besides the office such as coffee shops, coworking spaces, and so on.

Why do Millennials want flexible work options? One reason is that 40 percent of Millennials identify themselves as "working parents" and are interested in work-life balance.

Another reason is that 70 percent of Millennials say the desire to travel is the primary reason to work. Last, no Millennials (or any other generation surveyed) "cited the office during traditional hours as their location of choice for optimum productivity."

How do employers benefit from offering Millennials flexible work options?

- **Bottom-line savings.** Thirty-five percent said they would trade a 10 or 20 percent cut in pay for more flexibility.
- **Boosted focus.** Twenty-seven percent are willing to forfeit vacation time.
- **Higher input.** Twenty-two percent would be willing to work more hours.

- **Heightened loyalty.** Eighty-two percent say they would be more loyal to their employers if they had flexible work options.
- **Reduced turnover.** Thirty-four percent of Millennials have left a job because it did not have work flexibility.
- **Increased productivity.** Sixty percent said they would be more productive at home versus an office.

Leverage the clear benefits of flexible work or run the risk of losing Millennial talent to a competitor who does offer it.

How to Engage Millennials with a Revised View of Hard Work

• • •

ONE OF THE MOST PROMINENT strikes against the Millennial generation is their "poor work ethic."

We covered in chapter 23 how to help Millennials develop a strong work ethic. In this chapter, I'd like to challenge the assumption that most Millennials lack work ethic. How can we compare a new generation of workers with previous generations when work has changed so significantly?

As mentioned in chapter 31 and according to Shane Snow's book, *Smartcuts: How Hackers, Innovators, and Icons Accelerate Success,*

> It took the oil tycoon John D. Rockefeller 46 years to make a billion dollars...The 1980s computer baron Michael Dell achieved billionaire status in 14 years; Bill Gates in 12. In the 1990s, Jerry Yang and David Filo of Yahoo each earned ten figures in just four years...Pierre Omidyar, founder of eBay, three years to [make a billion dollars]. And in the late 2000s, Groupon's Andrew Mason did it in two.

It's clear that success has accelerated and work has changed drastically since the nineteenth century when Rockefeller built his oil empire. More recently, the creator of Snapchat, Evan Spiegel, turned down $3 billion in 2013, less than two years since launching. He was twenty-three years old.

A recent GE commercial humorously highlighted the new era of work that is being ushered in by a new generation. In it, a Millennial's parent tries to pass down an old manufacturing hammer to his recently hired son, only to find out that he will be writing the code for the manufacturing machines to share information with each other instead of swinging a hammer. Befuddled and convinced that the son lacks work ethic, the father tries to shame the Millennial by asking, "You can't pick it [the hammer] up, can you?" The Millennial responds, "I don't need it."

Work has changed. Thanks to technology and the Internet, the tools, rules, and pace of work will never be the same again.

Today's entrepreneurs are launching successful businesses with only a single Instagram account. Building a business still takes intense dedication and relentless hustle, but there has never been more opportunity to work smarter—doing more with less—than in today's hyperconnected world.

Too many people have a dated view of work and equate laziness with what is actually working smart. A recent Carvana ad amusingly epitomizes how Millennials are leveraging technology to work and live smarter. The Millennial in the ad describes laziness as the "mother of invention" and states, "Where there is a will, there is always a way to make it easier. What you call lazy, I call brilliant."

Amber Fehrenbacher, chief marketing officer of SuretyBonds, says it this way: "With answers to any possible question in the palm of their hand, in most situations, Millennials tend to take the fastest route. That's not laziness. That's problem-solving."

Mobile and collaborative technologies have enabled work to be streamlined, automated, and outsourced. If more can get done in less time today, then why are we still defining work ethic by time input and tenure? Today's work ethic should be defined by outputs and problem-solving ability.

A very different "work ethic" is needed for swinging a hammer than for machine coding. After all, it's entirely likely that the Millennial in the GE ad will create more output writing code for countless machines in one hour than his grandfather or father would have swinging a single hammer for an entire week. No disrespect is meant here—that's just the new reality of work.

Leaders who understand and run their organizations with today's new reality of work in mind will engage and resonate with Millennials.

"[Millennials] can code and develop apps and algorithms that will change the world. It is time to get over their shortcomings, and get down to twenty-first-century business," says the CEO of Peak Sales Recruiting Inc., Eliot Burdett.

Accomplishing more work in less time and then leveraging the additional time to solve complex problems, spend time with family, or pursue a side venture is the new calling card of a hard worker of the twenty-first century.

The "poor work ethic" label should now be reserved for those who refuse to retool and relearn for the current century of work.

How to Design Workspaces
That Engage Millennials

• • •

THE ENVELOPE OF TODAY'S WORKSPACES is being pushed further and further. Facebook recently moved into its new forty-three-thousand-square-foot "garden-roofed fantasyland" office. Apple has built a new Cupertino campus that resembles a giant alien spacecraft. And plans for a new Mountain View headquarters at Google have proposed miles of supertransparent glass and an interior workspace that can be reshaped by cranes and robots according to the company's needs.

If Steve Jobs taught us anything, it's that design matters. The better the design, the better the experience and the higher the engagement. The same applies to today's workspaces.

When deciding if they wanted to work at a company, 78 percent of Millennials were strongly influenced by how innovative it was. It's no wonder so many of today's tech giants are investing heavily into new, innovative workspaces. Besides creating functional workspace, the office's design is being used as a recruiting and employee-engagement tool.

What does the design of your workspace communicate to potential new hires and existing employees? Providing workspaces that entice collaboration and offer unique experiences are a must. At work, 79 percent of Millennials would rather be mobile than static.

It's become more and more challenging to engage the next generation of employees at work. Work-life integration has replaced work-life balance. Nowadays, we take home more work, and we want more life at work. More employees (especially Millennials) are looking for companies that offer rich and immersive experiences at work. And that starts with the physical workspace.

Here are four workspace elements that will engage the Millennial worker.

1. Collaboration. According to the 2014 Qualtrics Millennials in Tech Survey, 74 percent of Millennials ranked a collaborative work environment as the first or second most important characteristic they look for in the workplace. The quickest way to boost collaboration is to observe where your team naturally gravitates. Once you pinpoint the high-traffic areas, encourage collaboration by offering food or drinks nearby, placing stools or high tables there, or streaming Wi-Fi to the area.

2. Flexibility. Millennials are more productive and ultimately have a better impression of their employers when they have workplace flexibility. In fact, 90 percent of managers believe that workers are more productive when given the flexibility to choose when and how they work. Cater your workspace to meet a wide range of needs and interest by offering solo workstations, mobile workstations (e.g., desks with wheels), small team rooms, large conference rooms, lounge areas, and relaxed community areas.

3. Value infusion. Company values that are visible on a daily basis will help to engage the Millennial generation, who is massively motivated by meaningful work. Bring your company values to life by naming meeting rooms after each value, writing them on the walls, printing them on business cards, looping them on digital displays, or creating images or badges that employees can share on social media.

4. Well-being. Millennials value a healthy lifestyle and are interested in blending that lifestyle with work. Natural light enhances energy and results in more productivity; find ways to leverage natural light in your workspace. The right colors can brighten moods. Color psychologists have found that green promotes calm, blue is stimulating, and yellow spurs creativity. Other perks that can promote a healthy workspace: ergonomic chairs, meditation spaces, nap rooms, dogs at work, and standing desks.

For more examples and inspiration on how you can create an innovative workspace, search for "modern workplace" or a related search term on Pinterest.

Barry Salzburg, former global CEO of Deloitte Touch Tohmatsu Limited, recently said, "To attract and retain talent, business needs to show Millennials it is innovative and in tune with their world-view." Leverage an innovative and forward-thinking workspace as your catalyst for Millennial engagement.

CHAPTER 40

How to Increase Millennial Engagement and Productivity

• • •

WHEN IS NOT KNOWING MORE valuable than knowing? When does experience become a deterrent? What value does experience hold in a culture of perpetual beta? Is stubborn experience the enemy of innovation?

As work cycles spin faster and faster, professionals are continuously faced with never-before-seen challenges and uncharted territory. As the pace of work accelerates, our capacity for learning must keep up. The shifting landscape of work is forcing us to approach work, no matter our ages, as if we were rookies.

People often find themselves operating at their best when they are rookies—new to an undertaking, doing something for the first time. Liz Wiseman, president of The Wiseman Group and author of *Rookie Smarts: Why Learning Beats Knowing in the New Game of Work*, believes that a rookie mind-set will be an imperative skill set for any future professional.

After studying four hundred workplace scenarios, comparing how rookies and veterans each tackled work assignments, Wiseman arrived at some compelling and countercultural insights about learning. She analyzed the data by performance level, looking for the key differentiators between how rookies and veterans approached their work and the situations under which they excelled.

Wiseman defines a rookie as someone who has never done a type of work and a veteran as someone who has previous experience with it, each regardless of age.

According to Wiseman, here are twelve reasons that rookies trump veterans in the new world of work:

1. Rookies listen more and learn faster.
2. Rookies bite off smaller pieces of work.
3. Rookies are four times more likely than veterans to ask for help.
4. Rookies seek out expertise 40 percent more often than veterans.
5. Rookies inject a spirit of fun into everything they do at work.
6. Rookies have significantly higher levels of self-awareness than veterans.
7. Rookies are 12 percent more likely than veterans to persist in the face of failure.
8. Rookies are twice as likely as veterans to believe that they have something to learn.
9. Rookies tend to deliver more timely solutions despite having a steeper learning curve.
10. Rookies work cautiously and minimize risk by frequently checking in with stakeholders.
11. Rookies are more attuned to politics, although veterans possess greater political savvy.
12. Rookies are 40 percent more likely than veterans to work harder and put in longer hours in response to pressure or scrutiny (while veterans are 30 percent more likely to feel debilitating or significant pressure not to fail).

While these findings are not age dependent, it's safe to assume that many of today's Millennials operate like rookies. A rookie mentality is natural for Millennials due to their limited experience as working professionals and because of the high-flux world they grew up in that demanded adaptability. Today's information and knowledge is widely accessible and no longer concentrated among a select few.

For all the veterans with valuable experience, Wiseman encourages you to "renew your mind and skills and combine your hard-won wisdom and experience with the naive brilliance and vitality of a rookie." It's critical that veteran leaders treat Millennials as "full" and ready to contribute with their rookie smarts.

A rookie mind-set is the key to faster learning, increased self-awareness, and persisting through failure. Leaders who nurture the built-in rookie mind-set of Millennials will not only unlock these benefits but will also gain their engagement at work.

The school of thought that experience is needed to lead and innovate is permanently out in today's digital age. The new world of work will reward those experienced in being inexperienced.

CHAPTER 41

How to Engage Millennials in Company Succession Planning

• • •

THE TERM "BRAIN DRAIN" WAS first used to describe the movement of scientists and technologists to America from postwar Europe. Because today the chances of US talent emigrating to other countries is low, brain drain is now more commonly used in reference to Baby Boomers retiring without transferring their knowledge or expertise to successors. In other words, brain drain is the result of not having a succession plan.

In 2011, the first Baby Boomers turned sixty-five years old. Over the next nineteen years, ten thousand Baby Boomers will turn sixty-five each day. In 2029, all Baby Boomers will be sixty-five years old and over. Of employers at Fortune 1000 companies, 62 percent believe that future retirements will result in skilled-labor shortages over the next five years.

Companies will be facing the reality of brain drain in the coming years (if not already) with increased intensity. Having a succession plan, a process for identifying and developing new leaders who can replace previous leaders, is essential.

THE SEVERITY OF BUSINESS BRAIN DRAIN

Knowledge-intensive industries such as education, health and medical, finance, federal government, distribution, and any employment structures that are heavily weighted toward scientists, engineers, and other experts are in jeopardy of being impacted most severely by brain drain.

Here are some startling numbers behind the impending brain drain...

- Baby Boomers account for approximately 29 percent of all jobs, and 56 percent hold leadership positions.
- Baby Boomers own four million companies, which make up 66 percent of all businesses with employees.
- An estimated $10 trillion worth of businesses will change ownership in the next twenty years.
- Seventy-five top HR and IT executives at midsize-to-large US-based companies answer these questions this way:
  - Is the threat of losing business-critical expertise more or less an issue than it was five years ago?
    - More (78 percent) / About the same (22 percent) / Less (0 percent)
  - How frequently do you lose a top manager or other expert without a successor?
    - Never (16 percent) / Sometimes (60 percent) / Frequently (24 percent)

Organizations big and small are in danger of bleeding critical know-how at unprecedented rates. Yet, despite this urgent concern, few employers are actually doing anything to reduce the impact that brain drain will have on their organizations.

- 68 percent of employers have not analyzed the demographics of their workforces.
- 77 percent of employers have not analyzed the retirement rates of current employees.
- Only 19 to 37 percent of employers have taken action to prevent Baby Boomer brain drain.

The vacancies left behind by Baby Boomers will be too large for Generation X to fill. Thus, the bulk of the Baby Boomer replacement will be by Millennials. For this reason, recruiting and retaining Millennials is likely to become even more competitive moving forward.

5 STEPS TO TURN BRAIN DRAIN TO BRAIN GAIN

A plan for knowledge transfer enables a company to secure valuable knowledge and properly equip the next generation of leaders.

1. Analyze your workforce. Gather data about your current employees' ages, tenures, salaries, and job types to assess the risk of brain drain. Gain a clear understanding of the retirement picture over the next three to six years. Identify the areas of the business that are most vulnerable to brain drain.

2. Reexamine retention efforts. If slowing Baby Boomer departures is necessary, reexamine retention policies and benefits that might improve seasoned-worker retention. Benefits could include compressed work schedules, flextime, remote working, phased retirement, and/or sabbaticals.

For example, the retail pharmacy and health-care company CVS Health provides a "Snowbird" program that encourages older pharmacists and employees in cold climates to spend the winter working in stores in warmer locations. This is a solution that works well for the business because it retains seasoned workers while meeting the demand for extra help in serving customers who also winter in the warmer locations.

3. Prepare and engage potential retirees. Approach potential retirees and ask for their active involvement in capturing their knowledge. Emphasize their continued value to the organization with the appropriate context, tone, and candor. Be sensitive to the fact that they might be hesitant at the idea of divulging all of their hard-won knowledge. Consider providing incentives for them to share it with Millennials.

If a supportive company environment has been established, the most seasoned leaders and workers will be willing to help prepare the next generation and will take pride in the legacy they can leave behind.

Active involvement is critical from retirees, because they possess tacit knowledge that is difficult to replace. Tacit knowledge (as opposed to formal, codified, or explicit knowledge) is the kind of knowledge that is difficult to transfer to another person by means of writing it down or verbalizing it. An example of tacit knowledge is how to speak a language. You probably don't remember formally learning to speak your native language; nor did you formally teach it to your children. It is the kind of knowledge or skill that is acquired by just being around others.

Seasoned workers often have tacit knowledge that they are not even aware that they possess and don't see how valuable it can be to others. Transferring tacit knowledge works best in an established relationship (like parent to child), which is why a healthy relationship between Baby Boomer and Millennial is crucial for knowledge transfer and plugging the brain drain.

Last, 94 percent of employers report that having a succession plan positively impacts their employees' engagement levels. And, according to TransAmerica Center for Retirement Studies, 68 percent of Baby Boomers envision a phased retirement plan. Potential retirees will be grateful and more engaged when a succession plan has been established.

4. Identify emerging leaders. It's important to establish a Millennial depth chart for the critical positions that are likely to become vacant. At 38 percent, Millennials make up a majority of the 2017 workforce. By 2020, they will be 50 percent, and by 2025, the workplace will composed of 75 percent Millennials and Generation Z.

It won't be difficult to identify a Millennial eager to lead, since 91 percent of Millennials aspire to be leaders. The challenge comes in finding the Millennials who will stick around after the knowledge transfer is complete, since 66 percent of Millennials expect to leave their companies by 2020.

Consider reading more chapters in the "Engage" section of this book for strategies to retain Millennial employees. It's important to document and archive as much of the knowledge-transfer content as possible in case Millennials who receive the knowledge decide to exit the company.

Over 90 percent of Millennials say that working at a company with a clear succession plan would "improve" their level of engagement. Why is that? A succession plan provides Millennials with a sense of career advancement and opportunities to learn and grow, and it demonstrates that there is a defined career path—something Millennials crave.

Note that 65 percent of Baby Boomers say that Millennials have sought them out for guidance, and 58 percent of Millennials turn to Baby Boomers, rather than Generation X, for professional advice. Leverage Millennials' natural gravitation toward more seasoned workers and their knack for collaboration to ensure an effective knowledge transfer.

Here are a few other ideas on how to engage Millennials in the knowledge-transfer process:

- Emphasize the opportunity for mentoring. Seventy-five percent of Millennials want mentors.

- Stay connected with Millennials to keep them well informed through-out the knowledge-transfer process.
- Tie knowledge-transfer opportunities to the larger company mission. Millennials want to make an impact and to be part of the growth.

By actively facilitating the transfer of knowledge and skills from Baby Boomers to Millennials, companies can mitigate the effects of brain drain and prepare Millennials for important leadership roles.

5. Initiate knowledge transfer. Consider these knowledge-transferring approaches to future-proof your organization against the potential greatest brain drain the world has ever seen.

- **Courses.** Have senior leaders teach courses (inside classrooms, webcasts, or webinars) where they can showcase their knowledge and expertise.
- **Reciprocal mentoring.** What veteran employees know and what novice employees know are often complementary. In reciprocal mentoring, Baby Boomers have a chance to mentor and learn things that might aid them in an encore career, and Millennials are likely to remain at a company when they are in a position to grow and contribute.
- **Infographics.** Veteran employees can distill their expertise into info-graphics that can be easily consumed by emerging leaders. Have them team up with the design team or create these infographics themselves.
- **Video recordings.** Task a Millennial team to capture a professional video of experienced workers sharing their knowledge and expertise. Not only will Millennials be excited to contribute to an innovative project, but they will have a front-row seat to soak up the wisdom. Then create a YouTube-like resource where the videos are accessible company wide and easily searchable.

- **Coaching.** Partner emerging leaders with senior leaders in a more formal coaching structure. Keep the exchanges candid and conversational.
- **Shadowing.** Give emerging leaders front-row seats to various leadership processes and procedures, meetings, site visits, or operations abroad.
- **Screencasts.** Task experienced workers with screencasting (digital recording of a computer screen with audio narration) how they effectively source leads, prioritize e-mails or to-do lists, use internal platforms, or navigate the company intranet.
- **Involve senior leaders.** Have senior leaders participate in the new-hire onboarding process, training, or cross-department training programs.
- **Intergenerational teaming.** Routinely pair emerging leaders with seasoned leaders, and/or arrange the workspace in a way that encourages emerging leaders to collaborate and interact with other generations.
- **Podcast.** Task a Millennial team to launch, produce, and host an internal company podcast where experienced employees can be interviewed to draw out their tacit knowledge.
- **Culture of learning.** Create a company culture that puts a premium on learning, where employees are empowered and encouraged to practice in-the-moment learning. Create an environment of learn-it-alls instead of know-it-alls.
- **Leader vlogs.** Encourage senior leaders to use their smartphones or laptop cameras to capture their workplace productivity tips, perspectives on the industry, career advice, and the vision of the company. Share the videos via an internal vlog (video blog).
- **Leader onboarding.** Onboarding shouldn't be reserved just for new hires. Bank of America has an onboarding program to help new executives adapt to the corporate culture and learn from senior executives.

Strive to capture all knowledge transfer via video, audio, or written word so that the details can be compiled on a company wiki, SharePoint, blog, or other venue where it can be readily available to current and future employees and where it can be continually updated.

Examples of knowledge worth transferring...

- Top salespeople share the stories of their biggest wins.
- Senior programmers screencast their daily workflow.
- An HR manager teaches a course covering how he or she tackled a challenge that is sure to repeat itself.
- An experienced technician records a video about how to safely and swiftly repair customer equipment.
- A senior leader discusses his or her passion for the industry and respect for the company history on a podcast.

Don't be caught flat-footed as workplace demographics shift. The shift represents opportunity to gain a competitive advantage and prepare your next-generation leaders.

HOW ONE COMPANY IS COMBATING BRAIN DRAIN

The below is an excerpt from the *Bloomberg Businessweek* article "As Boomers Retire, Companies Prepare Millennials for Leadership Roles," by Jeff Green.

BAE, a multinational defense and aerospace company, similarly has been preparing for the retirement cliff for several years, says Andrew Muras, the company's advanced learning manager. BAE adapted a NASA program developed a decade ago when the U.S. space agency started to lose expertise from the lunar landings as senior engineers retired. Realizing it would need that knowledge for missions to Mars, the agency asked engineers who'd worked on the Apollo mission to share what they knew in meetings with new engineers.

[One NASA spokesperson said, "If we want to go to the moon again, we'll be starting from scratch because all that knowledge has disappeared."]

When BAE learns that an employee with deep institutional knowledge plans to retire, whether in a few months or a couple of years, a knowledge-transfer group of about a half-dozen people of varying ages working in the same area is formed. The teams meet regularly over months to talk and exchange advice. Younger workers elicit tips, and in some cases older ones gradually hand off tasks to junior employees. The program began as a pilot in 2013; during the past two years, BAE has expanded it across the company. It eventually wants to hold as many as 60 sessions a year.

BAE has quantified the payoff of its knowledge-transfer efforts by looking at variables such as direct and indirect costs and productivity. 'We're saving on average between $120,000 to $180,000' per project, Muras says. Devoting more time preparing Millennials for leadership roles may also encourage them to stay with the company.

The bottom line: Companies that don't plan for generational management shifts risk falling behind and losing out to their competitors.

CHAPTER 42

How to Get Millennials Teaming and Collaborating Across Generations

• • •

THERE IS NO DOUBT THAT teaming and collaborating are mission critical for any company. In fact, around 75 percent of employers rate teamwork and collaboration as "very important," and 97 percent of employees and executives surveyed believe that lack of alignment within a team directly impacts the outcome of a task or project.

What workplace teaming and collaboration is supposed to look like is different across generations. When building connections across generations, appeasing everyone is not feasible. However, neglecting to build generational cohesion can leave the team exposed and organization vulnerable. Communication and collaboration challenges will always exist across generations; it's a tension to manage instead of a problem to solve.

WAYS TO GET MILLENNIALS TEAMING AND COLLABORATING ACROSS GENERATIONS

1. Showcase knowledge. Make it clear that every employee has something to teach and something to learn. Create informal or formal settings where employees can share their expertise in a specific area. The content doesn't have to be business or industry related...think TED-like presentations. Perhaps even consider creating a TEDx event for your organization and have employees submit their ideas for topics. The collective sharing of expertise and passions will not only alert Millennials of the wealth of knowledge that surrounds them but will provide helpful context for how or when to approach the individual for help or collaboration on a project.

2. Generational training. Training on who the generations are, motivators for each one, and how to work together is helpful for greasing the wheels of generational collaboration. Generational training creates awareness and appreciation, builds empathy, and helps a multigenerational workforce find common ground in their similarities and differences. This knowledge can be especially helpful as more and more Millennials have begun to lead Generation X and Baby Boomers.

3. Affinity groups. Launch a young-professional affinity group (a group formed around a shared interest or common goal), where all generations are welcome to learn and grow together. Creating opportunities for employees to have regular cross-generational contact is important to diminish misconceptions in the minds of employees.

4. Reverse mentoring. Reverse mentoring is a learning relationship where the mentor is younger than the mentee. Creating two-way conversations where both parties are learning and can see the value the other brings to the workplace can lead to effective teaming and collaboration. (See more about reverse mentoring in chapter 9.)

5. Team-building activities and events. A generationally diverse workforce requires intentional team building. According to a 2015 poll by The Go Game, 79 percent of Millennials found that "team" or "culture" building activities in their organizations significantly helped retain talent; 88 percent of Millennials and 76 percent of Baby Boomers said team building was worth the time and effort.

Team building done right can be a strong Millennial retention tool, but forced and antiquated styles of team building can be a Millennial repellent.

Effective team-building activities for Millennials should be...

- **Collaborative.** Avoid activities that encourage independent involvement or single out a team member. Instead, focus on activities that require team effort.
- **Meaningful.** Resist team building for the sake of team building. Ensure that each activity or event has a worthwhile purpose with outcomes that make a difference.
- **Dynamic.** Millennials will disconnect if the activity is poorly organized, overly complicated, or begins to drag.
- **Innovative.** Mobile or virtual games can inspire creativity and prompt Millennials to collaborate with teammates.
  - Gelling: Akeakami Quest is a team-building application that puts teams on a virtual deserted island where they must exercise effective communication techniques and work as a team to succeed. The game is specifically designed for Agile and Scrum teams, but the game can improve any team's overall performance. (You can find the game in Apple's App Store.)
  - The Go Game (www.thegogame.com) couples mobile technology and skilled game producers to offer innovative and fun team-building activities. Examples of a few of the games include building bicycles for charity, creating a continuous musical lip-dub video, producing a short film, and a treasure hunt to collect toys or supplies for charity.

Effective team-building activities and events cultivate stronger connections that equip teams to communicate better, make decisions faster, and ideate bigger.

6. Flatten hierarchy. Ever since the dawn of the Internet, power and ownership have shifted toward individual consumers and employees. The information age has created more democratization in the business world. For leaders to optimize their diverse, multigenerational teams, they need to increase collaboration and ownership.

Adaptability and agility are highly valuable team traits to possess in a high-flux world. Creating a corporate structure that lets ideas be exchanged more effortlessly and seamlessly throughout the organization is not only attractive to Millennials but a necessity for any organization to remain relevant.

To get the most out of cognitive diversity, each generation (no matter one's rank or role in the organization) should lead. A flatter hierarchy builds trust across generations and creates transparency that enables each generation to understand the value of their colleagues' contributions.

7. Enhance technology. A relevant struggle when it comes to cross-generational collaboration is enhancing technology to optimize Millennials and meet their innovative expectations without overwhelming or alienating other generations who are used to the existing processes.

This very tension represents a ripe opportunity for generational teaming and collaboration. Millennials can coach (aka reverse mentor) previous generations about the benefits of the new process and the best practices for integrating it into one's daily workflow.

Don't shy away from technology. It's gotten easier since you've been ignoring it.

THE BOTTOM LINE

With more generational diversity in the workplace than ever before, getting Millennials to team and collaborate across generations is a challenging and historic endeavor.

For generations to work well together, organizations must foster environments that encourage collaboration, support teamwork, and promote generational understanding so that the unique strengths of every generation can be mined for the greater good of the entire team.

CHAPTER 43

How to Engage and Retain Millennials Using Work-Life Harmony

• • •

IN THE PAST, WORK WAS a location. Today, work has shifted from a place to a space. The tech shift from fixed communications to mobile communications has redefined how and where we work.

In the past, all working professionals would get into their cars and make their morning commutes to work. They would arrive at a building, and upon entering it, they would begin work. At 5:00 p.m., they would exit the building and drive home, and once they were at home, they weren't tempted to work anymore because they didn't have the capacity to do so.

Today, 42 percent of employees feel obligated to check in with work while on vacation, according to Randstad's Employee Engagement Study. The study also found that Millennials were the generation "most inclined to remain 'on' during off hours."

For Millennials, the never-offline and always-available workplace is all they know. To them, turning off work at 5:00 p.m. is an antiquated practice. Due to their always-on approach to life, Millennials see no problem with blending work and life. Checking e-mail before they get out of bed in the morning, then shopping online while at work, exchanging texts with their managers after 8:00 p.m., and then catching up on e-mail on Sunday afternoon is native to them.

Every generation seeks a healthy work-life balance, but it's Millennials who most demand it from their employers. In today's employee market, creating work-life balance for Millennials is a compelling competitive advantage.

WHY WORK-LIFE BALANCE MATTERS TO MILLENNIALS

1. It defines success. Millennials don't view climbing the corporate ladder or owning tangible items (job title, house, salary, car, and the like) as success. According to the 2016 Millennial Survey by Deloitte, 16.8 percent of Millennials evaluate career opportunities by good work-life balance, followed by 13.4 percent who look for opportunities to progress and 11 percent who seek flexibility (i.e., remote working and flexible hours). For many Millennials, success is having control over how and when they work and accumulating various life experiences, both of which are enabled by a better work-life balance.

2. They're always on. Millennials are the first generation to enter the workforce with access to technology that enables them to seamlessly work remotely, which 75 percent of Millennials want more opportunities to do. Millennials are eager to capitalize on the new technological capabilities (that they are already familiar with) to create more flexibility and thus a better work-life balance.

3. They're moving up. According to EY's Global Generation Research, nearly one-third of Millennials say that managing their work, family, and personal responsibilities has become more difficult in the past five years. And 47 percent of Millennial managers around the globe reported an increase in their hours at a time when many are moving into management and starting families (compared to 38 percent for Gen X and 28 percent for Boomers).

4. They're dual income. According to a 2015 EY study, Millennials find it harder to achieve work-life balance because they are almost twice as likely to have a spouse or partner who works at least full time than Boomers (78 percent versus 47 percent).

The bottom line is that Millennials are entering a stage of life when they are marrying, buying homes, and having children at the same time that the demands of work are increasing, while they are equipped (and sometimes expected) to work 24/7. It's no wonder that Millennials value work-life balance higher than all other job characteristics such as job progression, use of technology, and a sense of meaning at work.

Millennials aren't alone, according to the 2016 LinkedIn Censuswide Study. Nearly half of American workers would forgo the corner-office job and a high salary to gain more flexibility in their schedules.

Yet, despite a growing desire for a better work-life balance, only 53 percent of workers say their employer values work-life balance, and only 43 percent say their employers offer programs and policies that allow for flexibility, according to a 2016 survey from the American Psychological Association.

THE BENEFITS OF A HEALTHY WORK-LIFE BALANCE

1. Enhances health. Achieving a fluid balance between work and life can improve physical, mental, and social health. Some studies have correlated taking time off from work with a reduction in health issues like coronary heart disease. Authors of *Willpower: Rediscovering the Greatest Human Strength*, John Tierney and Ron Baumeister, state that midday breaks can replenish an employee's willpower and improve judgment and decision-making in the afternoon. Removing oneself from work also allows for more time to invest in social relationships—with a spouse, kids, friends, family, and so on.

2. Increases productivity. Research shows that employees who take time off are more productive. Removing oneself from work, via a workout or nap for example, can recharge the brain to face the day's remaining challenges. In the *Harvard Business Review* article "The Productivity Paradox: How Sony Pictures Gets More Out of People by Demanding Less," Tony Schwartz wrote, "Human beings perform best and are most productive when they alternate between periods of intense focus and intermittent renewal."

3. Boosts creativity. In 1974, Art Fry invented the iconic Post-it Note during his "15 percent time," a company program at 3M that allowed employees to use a portion of their paid workday to pursue their own passion projects. This type of program has since been adopted by companies like Google and Hewlett-Packard, who see how creativity unburdened from day-to-day work can lead to massive breakthroughs.

4. Improves retention. Employees (especially Millennials) who are able to easily manage work and nonwork-related responsibilities because they have some measure of control over their work schedules are likely to experience higher job satisfaction. Employees who have the margin and control to deal with pressures and responsibilities at home are likely to be more present while at work, happier employees, and less inclined to leave the company.

HOW MILLENNIALS VIEW WORK-LIFE BALANCE
Balance doesn't mean working less, but it can mean something different to each Millennial employee.

- **Long-term.** Millennials aren't driven by the thought of working hard for the next forty years and then retiring. Rather, they are driven by the idea of building a life and career that can withstand the continuous reinventions and pivots that their long-term careers in the twenty-first century will require.

- **Integrated.** Millennials are more interested in leveraging today's tech to integrate work and life versus just balancing them. The term "work-life balance" implies that work is separate from life, but in reality, it's all life. Forcing people to put work and life into separate boxes that never overlap is unrealistic in today's always-on world.

- **Engaged.** Millennials view work-life balance as being fully engaged with the task, activity, or people they are currently involved with. Work-life balance isn't necessarily about physical time and place, but it is about the state of mind and mental margin that Millennials experience. (Some Millennials may need help from leaders to turn off the distractions to ensure they can be fully present in order to maximize a balance.)

- **Fluid.** Millennials want work-life balance to be fluid, free, and flexible to prioritize whatever (work or life) is most important that day. To them, work-life balance means not having rigid boundaries between work and life. A more fluid approach ensures less stress.

- **Personal.** Millennials want all aspects of their professional and personal lives to receive the same level of attention, priority, and progress. They want a healthy mix of achieving professional goals and time to pursue personal goals. A sense of freedom and flexibility to be fulfilled and supported in both their personal and professional endeavors is critical. An example might be traveling for work and then staying an extra day to explore the area (while remaining available to be reached for work-related items that come up)—or getting what needs to be done at work and then attending a child's school function later that day.

With so many varying definitions of work-life balance, it's safe to assume that what constitutes work-life balance is an individual preference. Each Millennial will define it differently, which should be expected since each person has different responsibilities, goals, aspirations, and family commitments. To Millennials, work-life balance is about what matters most to them as individuals and taking the steps to achieve it.

My 21Mill.com business partner and fellow Millennial, Steven Cohen, has a powerful analogy for how Millennials should view work-life balance:

> Stop thinking your life needs to be "balanced." Balance implies things need to be of equal relation in order to reach success. I believe your life from birth to death should be thought of as a symphony. A great symphony is played with many different types of instruments and each played at different levels of intensity at different times during the performance. Sometimes you need to play the drums really hard or a flute really soft. Your commitments, just like instruments in a symphony, need to be adjusted to whatever is most important at that point in time. The goal is not to have work-life balance. It is to have work-life harmony.

Dan Thurmon, author of *Off Balance on Purpose: Embrace Uncertainty and Create a Life You Love,* says, "The perpetual quest for balance ends up limiting growth, progress, and the quality of life." Thurman suggests that perfect balance is unachievable and, upon closer inspection, undesirable. We must be open to forcing ourselves off balance on purpose when we need to give an area of life more attention.

HOW TO CREATE MORE WORK-LIFE HARMONY FOR MILLENNIALS

How companies help Millennials achieve work-life harmony will differ depending on the company culture and business realities—customer-facing teams won't have the same flexibility that a team of developers might have. But nonetheless, work-life harmony should be a workplace element that is pursued and consistently reevaluated by any organization.

Consider a few of these strategies to unlock more work-life harmony for your Millennial employees:

- **Observe employees.** Where in your organization or throughout the day might Millennial employees experience frustration, heavy workloads, or stress? Increased mistakes, excessive absenteeism, physical exhaustion, or general unhappiness might be warning signs that employees are lacking work-life harmony.
- **Survey employees.** Because work-life harmony will look and mean something different to everyone, it's important to ask your Millennial employees what type of work-life harmony would be most useful, productive, and desirable for them.
- **Offer training.** Work-life harmony can be a fluffy and ambiguous topic, so offering training that offers specific strategies and tools to achieve harmony would be helpful to many employees, especially for Millennials who are young in their experience of juggling work and life priorities. (Training topics might include: how to set up a home workspace that limits distractions; health and wellness; prioritizing to-dos and task management; how to reduce stress; etc.)
- **Structure flextime.** Allowing Millennials to choose *when* they work is fundamental in their achievement of work-life harmony. Consider structuring flextime with weekly hour requirements that they can choose how to allocate (for example, PwC boasts compressed workweeks—longer hours per day for fewer days per week) or with a weekly hour range, or have requirements only for what work needs to be completed. (In chapter 37, we cover how employers benefit from offering Millennials flexible work options.)

- **Enable telecommuting.** Allowing Millennials to choose *where* they work is also fundamental in their achievement of work-life harmony. Offering telecommuting to workers provides additional freedom for them to care for personal items while still getting work done. (In chapter 14, we cover how to manage a remote Millennial team.)
- **Relabel flexibility.** Because mobile technology and ubiquitous connectivity have enabled today's work to be completed anywhere and anytime, flextime and telecommuting shouldn't be considered "perks" or things that must be earned over time. Millennials view flexibility as a standard work function, and employers that label it as a perk will seem outdated. (In chapter 34, we cover how company perks can engage Millennials.)
- **End working weekends.** JPMorgan Chase recently joined other Wall Street banks in telling its employees to take weekends off in order to improve their work-life harmony.
- **Remove exclusivity.** Millennials may not have as many family responsibilities (kids, grandkids, aging parents, a house, etc.), but they have similar desires to find harmony between work and life (travel, education, etc.). Don't make work-life harmony options exclusively for senior employees.
- **Encourage efficiency.** According to a UK study from the Mental Health Foundation, after working long hours, 27 percent of employees feel depressed, 34 percent feel anxious, and 58 percent feel irritable. Avoid pushing employees to work longer hours. Instead, enable and encourage Millennials to leverage their digital resourcefulness to work smarter and with greater efficiency. Focus on output (results), not just input (time spent).
- **Involve family.** Finding creative ways (family-friendly events or a "bring your pets to work" day) to involve Millennial employees' families (spouses, parents, kids, or pets) is a powerful way to integrate life with work.

- **Prioritize health.** A healthier workforce leads to reduced stress, boosted productivity, and fewer absences. Extended periods of working can force Millennials to sacrifice health and fitness. Offer health and wellness training, provide well-being classes (such as yoga), use standing desks, create nap rooms, start a company sports team (kickball, softball, etc.), conduct walking meetings, or offer discounts to a local gym.
- **Promote breaks.** For Millennials at work, Snapchat is the new smoke break. Build in time when workers are encouraged to take rejuvenation breaks from work. Taking breaks has been shown to increase productivity levels.
- **Nurture creativity.** Allowing Millennials the time and space to exercise creativity will provide a better sense of balance, keep them mentally fit, and will nurture the innovative thinking that is crucial for any organization operating in today's age of disruption. Creative outlets can include puzzles, video games, or off-the-wall side projects.
- **Permit volunteering.** Allowing Millennials time off to pursue volunteer or charitable work can keep them happy and in harmony.
- **Give parental leave.** One of the life stages that requires Millennials to focus on life over work is having a baby. Recently, a number of high-profile companies have announced their robust policies surrounding parental leave. Facebook and IKEA now offer new parents (mothers and fathers) four months of paid baby leave. Netflix recently began offering unlimited parental leave.
- **Support vacationing.** Encourage Millennials to take advantage of their vacation days or consider expanding the number of vacation days offered—or eliminate the accrued-vacation policy and offer unlimited vacation...you might be surprised how few vacation days Millennials will actually take.
- **Provide childcare.** Working Millennial parents will experience less stress and find more harmony if childcare is available on-site or if there is a discount at a nearby childcare center.

- **Lend help.** Providing Millennial employees with access to services to help them with personal errands or household responsibilities reduces stress and allows more leisure time away from work. On-site or nearby services might include: dry-cleaning, meals, auto repairs, gift wrapping, or a concierge service that coordinates other miscellaneous needs. Be sure to ask Millennials what services might be most helpful, since they might already be using apps like TaskRabbit or Goodservice for these needs.

Whatever work-life harmony strategies you decide to use, be sure to back them up with your example. Leaders must promote and exemplify the work-life harmony that they wish to see in their Millennial workforce.

The change starts with you.

Section 5
Work with Millennials

• • •

CHAPTER 44

How to Leverage Millennials
for Company Innovation

• • •

CHALLENGING THE STATUS QUO IS not only a fundamental mandate for all leaders, but it's critical for companies who want to remain relevant.

The goal of leadership should be to point people to a better future. Betterness precedes progress. Progress precedes change. Change precedes challenge.

Although it's difficult and often uncomfortable, challenging the status quo is where leadership begins.

In the book *The Leadership Challenge*, James Kouzes and Barry Posner teach that "Leaders must challenge the process precisely because any system will unconsciously conspire to maintain the status quo and prevent change."

An organization left unchanged will conspire against its own effectiveness and relevance. The people, habits, or structure of an organization can get in the way of the growth of the organization if the status quo remains unchallenged.

Who's best positioned to challenge the status quo? The next generation of leaders...the Millennials.

Leadership expert and author Andy Stanley shared in his May 2016 leadership podcast,

> Every idea and approach has a shelf life, and the next generation idea is more than likely not going to come from the current generation. A leader's IQ goes down the longer they remain in an organization. The person that has been in an organization the longest is least aware of the culture of the organization. It's often fresh eyes that bring the best ideas.

One generation's status quo is another generation's challenge to improve.

Stanley recommends that organizations create a "listening culture"—where an organization is open to the next generation challenging the status quo, where leaders can get behind the next generation rather than seeing it as a threat. It's important not to mistake a challenge to the status quo as a challenge to the existing leadership.

Stanley suggests making an organization's mission and vision permanent but the approach temporary. Leaders should remain open minded and open handed about the approach and create systems or procedures where ideas can easily bubble up. Ask team members to be raving fans publicly and honest critics privately. Behind the scenes, encourage young leaders to "make it better."

"If [young] leaders in an organization have permission to challenge the status quo, everybody wins," says Stanley. The Millennial leader feels heard. A possible good idea is gained. The organization remains relevant. And it creates environments that attract leaders, because leaders want to be listened to and they want to feel like they are influencing their own destiny.

Effective twenty-first-century organizations create listening cultures and empower Millennial leaders to be champions of challenge and change.

CHAPTER 45

How to Have Millennials Successfully Challenge the Status Quo

• • •

IF MILLENNIALS ARE GOING TO successfully challenge the status quo, they must keep certain rules in mind.

In chapter 44, we discussed that one generation's status quo is another generation's challenge to improve. And ultimately, Millennials can save your company from irrelevance if they are empowered to be champions of challenge and change.

Considering the fast times we're living in, the *way* of an organization shouldn't be set in stone like the *why* of an organization should be.

Leaders intuitively evaluate and critique everything around them, always looking for ways to improve. Many Millennials have a tendency to evaluate and critique before they even achieve a leadership position. Millennials have a natural knack for challenging the status quo.

While more and more organizations seem to want to hire Millennials who are independent, entrepreneurial minded, and champions of change, there can be plenty of growing pains as Millennials learn the appropriate posture, timing, and tact it takes to successfully challenge the status quo.

What Millennials need to know about challenging the status quo:

1. Challenge the status quo of your sphere of influence, not necessarily the entire organization.
2. Don't change for the sake of change. The proposed change should be linked to a picture of the preferred future.
3. Until the change is confirmed, be an honest critic internally but a raving fan externally.
4. Learn and appreciate the history of the organization. We are all standing on the shoulders of those who went before us.
5. Don't make every conversation about change or challenging the status quo, because you will likely tire those around you and lose influence.
6. Understand that there has to be some predictability and stability. Constant change isn't sustainable.
7. Appreciate that there is a right tone, timing, and language when challenging the status quo.
8. Realize that public loyalty creates private influence. Support a leader's decision or instruction publicly, and then approach the leader privately to verbalize how it could be better.
9. Never verbalize frustration with a process or instructions in front of other team members. It's unhealthy and disrespectful.

Communicate these nine rules early and often to your Millennial workforce so that they have the clarity and blueprint on how best to challenge the status quo at work.

How to Adjust to Millennials' Workplace Communication Expectations

• • •

IN THIS CHAPTER, WE'LL DISCUSS how today's fastest-growing social network will soon disrupt how you communicate at work.

In April 2009, Ashton Kutcher beat CNN to become the first person with one million followers on Twitter. All the media attention surrounding Kutcher's challenge served as a tipping point in helping Twitter move from a niche network to a mainstream communication tool.

Many believe that Snapchat, a video-messaging application valued at over $25 billion, is on the verge of the same tipping point as DJ Khaled, considered the first Snapchat celebrity superstar, racks up three million views in a single "Snapchat story."

Whether or not you believe the hype, it's hard to argue with the numbers. Snapchat is the fastest-growing social network, boasting a hundred million active users who post four hundred million snaps per day (Twitter users were posting fifty million tweets per day in 2010), which accounts for seven billion daily video views, outpacing many cable networks.

Why is this important to you?

Over 60 percent of American smartphone users between the ages of thirteen and thirty-four use Snapchat, and the social platform is growing 69 percent among Millennials ages twenty-five to thirty-four, according to ComScore. You should take interest because Snapchat is rapidly shaping the communication preferences of the generation that is expected to make up 50 percent of the global workforce by 2020.

How will Snapchat change Millennials' (and Generation Z's) communication preferences as they enter the workplace?

1. A surge in urgency. Snapchat content has a one-day lifespan—then it disappears. This has created an urgency that's uncommon in a world full of distraction. Imagine if your e-mails disappeared in twenty-four hours. It would create a new level of attention and urgency. Perhaps this explains why Generation Z teenagers respond the fastest to e-mail, with a thirteen-minute or less response time, followed by Millennials (ages twenty to thirty-five) with a sixteen-minute average response and older generations taking twenty-four to forty-seven minutes to respond.

2. A higher value on transparency and authenticity. Because Snapchat content is time bound, the content creator experiences less pressure to create the perfect image or video. Users are liberated to be their true selves, to communicate authentically and express themselves in the moment, knowing their content won't live online forever like a Tweet or Facebook post would. Ever since fake social-media personas became common, the Millennial and Z generations have been on a quest to find a channel where more transparent and authentic connection could occur. Snapchat seems to satisfy that desire.

3. Stronger storytelling. Pictures used to be for saving memories. With Snapchat, the emerging generation is using pictures to talk. Most social networks display the newest content first. However, Snapchat displays a user's content in chronological order. This provides a much more familiar feeling—it's how we tell stories. Users can be taken on a journey, all while having two-way interaction with the storyteller.

4. It's simple and succinct. Discover, a way to explore Snapchat stories from different editorial teams, only offers—at the time of this writing—nineteen channels. Snapchat has intentionally limited the selection, even removing brands like Yahoo who weren't adapting their content to the Snapchat audience, so that users can access content easily. The ten-second window to post content also forces users and brands to be concise. Keeping communication simple and succinct on Snapchat is, in the words of DJ Khaled, "major key."

5. Increased mobile video and multimedia. For the emerging generations, communicating with text or drawings overlaid onto images or videos via a mobile device is the new norm. In fact, Cisco predicts that nearly three-fourths of the world's mobile data traffic will be video by 2019. Expect to see more Snapchat-like video and multimedia communications to begin seeping into your organization as more Millennials and Generation Z pour into your workplace.

You will be impacted by Snapchat sooner than you think, because behaviors have a funny way of rippling up the generations these days. Remember when you heard someone vow never to be on Facebook, take a selfie, or text an emoji? Next thing you know, you see them posting a selfie on Facebook with the "face with tears of joy" emoji as the sole description.

The world is moving fast, and communication is moving faster. Stop dismissing and start connecting with the communication tools and trends that are sure to impact the future of business.

CHAPTER 47

How to Get Millennials to Answer Your Phone Call

• • •

THE SECRET TO GETTING A Millennial to answer your phone call is...you don't.

Texting has overtaken calling as the most popular mobile function across all generations, with Millennial women using SMS three times more often than calling, according to the mobile research agency RealityMine.

Phone calls have been second fiddle to texting since 2007, when Americans sent and received more text messages than phone calls, thanks largely to the launch of the iPhone and to Millennials. The iPhone was texting nirvana for Millennials because of its virtual keyboard, multitouch interface, predictive text technology, and—the saving grace of the entire Millennial generation—automatic spell check.

With texting being the universal go-to mobile function, why are so many managers still frustrated with Millennials not answering their phones? Let me help put one final nail in the Millennial phone-call coffin.

The real reason that Millennials won't answer your phone call is because it's unproductive. More specifically, a phone call is...

1. Distracting. Calls can sever focus, disrupt workflow, and draw people away from crucial projects.

- Texting allows users to respond at a convenient time between tasks.

2. Presumptuous. Calls presume that the person you are calling should drop everything and adhere to your agenda.

- Texting (like e-mail) is passive communication that doesn't presume a real-time interaction.

3. Superfluous. Calls give the perception of more airtime, so callers can neglect to gather the necessary information up front and talk until they land on the intended message.

- Texting forces you to put your thoughts into words, which can be edited or condensed, and allows you to communicate the essential information for maximum efficiency.

4. Ineffective. Missed calls result in phone tag, a supremely idiotic and unnecessary game in an age of bountiful communication alternatives.

- If a picture is worth a thousand words, is an emoji worth half that? Texting is effective and efficient. Ninety percent of all SMS text messages are read within three minutes.

5. Time-consuming. The time cost of a "quick five-minute call" can exceed twenty minutes, including the salutations, pleasantries, small talk, good-byes, and time it takes to refocus on the original task, which, some experts say, can take twenty-three minutes after a disruption.

- Texting limits unnecessary salutations and the exchange of irrelevant information, and the time cost can be as low as a few seconds.

After a recent keynote presentation I delivered on the topic of communicating to Millennials, I was approached by an audience member who was anxious to share his experience of communicating with them.

The gentleman was a manager of a team of Millennials, and he described his initial frustration with his team not answering his phone calls. Rather than demanding that the team cater to his communication preference, he decided to test texting. "Much more productive," he said.

The gentleman now texts his Millennial team every afternoon before his commute home. In the message, he provides the necessary correction or direction his team needs to be efficient and effective. "After my texts, it surprises me how often I find my team that evening back online, eagerly working," he proudly told me.

Is a phone call still valuable? Of course. A phone call can still be necessary, welcome, and, in some instances, productive. The tone or urgency that can be conveyed in a human voice remains powerful. But if you're interested in elevating the productivity of your Millennial workforce, consider a text. (See chapter 8 for a strategy to effectively communicate with Millennials and chapter 25 to learn how to help Millennials improve their face-to-face communication skills.)

How to Set a Company Dress Code Millennials Will Get Behind

• • •

TODAY, 50 PERCENT OF MANAGERS say employees dress less formally than they did five years ago. And 58 percent of employees say they would prefer to work at a company that has a business-casual, casual, or no dress code. "Dressing up for work continues to go out of style," says Brandi Britton, district president at Robert Half Los Angeles.

THE SHIFT FROM BUSINESS FORMAL TO BUSINESS CASUAL

Hewlett-Packard is credited with the idea of allowing more comfortable clothes for "casual Friday" in the 1950s. Then, in 1966, the Hawaiian garment industry helped further promote a relaxed dress code with the 1966 "Aloha Friday" campaign that encouraged Hawaiian businesses to let their employees wear Hawaiian shirts to the office once a week.

Then, in 1992, Levi's capitalized on the growing assumption that a relaxed dress code leads to happier and more productive employees. Levi's marketing team created "A Guide to Casual Businesswear," a pamphlet that showed professionals casually dressed in Levi's products, and sent it to twenty-five thousand HR departments around the country. It was a huge success. In 1992, only 66 percent of companies had either a full-time or part-time casual dress code, but by 1995, that number increased to 90 percent, and Levi's had record sales of $6.2 billion, up 10 percent from 1994. Levi's had successfully introduced the entire country to business casual.

Chances are, if you work in an office today, your attire is more casual than ever before.

REASONS FOR THE CONTINUED CASUALIZATION OF THE WORKPLACE

- **Competitive job market.** Since more than half of job seekers said a company's dress code is either very important or moderately important when it comes to accepting a job offer, companies are using flexible dress codes as a way to attract talent...especially Millennials.
- **Rise of remote working.** Working at a coffee shop, coworking space, or at home alleviates the need to dress formally.
- **Increased visibility and awareness.** Instagram, Snapchat, YouTube, and so on provide outsiders an inside look into the culture and dress codes of other companies around the world. This increased exposure has instilled new expectations—especially for the emerging generations—of what dress codes could and should be.
- **Impressions are changing.** More and more, the appearance of suits (even in client-facing roles) strikes people with fear of an audit than it does with the impression of professionalism. The consumer impressions of what a professional person looks like is also loosening. People are more open to tattoos, beards, piercings, and such, which is why Starbucks, PetSmart, and other retailers and employers have relaxed their dress codes in each of these categories.
- **Surge of Millennials.** The below describes why and how companies are relaxing their dress code for Millennials.

COMPANIES WITH UPDATED DRESS CODES

- **JPMorgan Chase & Co.** Once known for its strict attire and etiquette, this financial-services firm has expanded business casual "firmwide." CEO Jamie Dimon recently realized that the company's dress code was "significantly out of date."
- **MassMutual.** This insurance and financial company replaced its formal dress code with a simple guideline: "Dress appropriately." The company stated that the new dress code is designed, in part, to create a work environment that's more familiar and appealing to Millennials—a plus from both a recruiting and retention perspective.
- **Crowe Horwath LLP.** This accounting and advisory-services firm experimented with a daily extension of casual Fridays and then officially introduced a new "Dress for Your Day" policy. A video highlighting the policy states, "Personal reputation and brand is reflected in our dress and we trust our people to exercise good judgment in their choices based on the location and the nature of work they are performing each day." The firm plans to use the video as a recruitment tool for Millennials, also stating, "If you are looking for a workplace where you are...encouraged to bring your full self and style to work, we hope you pursue an opportunity with our firm."

To have professional industries such as banking, insurance, and accounting embrace less formal dress codes is confirmation of the strong momentum behind workplace informality.

A common reason that many of the above companies and others are relaxing their dress policies is to lure Millennials. The sheer size of the Millennial generation and its desire to work for companies that reflect its values have companies rethinking their dress policies.

WHY COMPANIES SHOULD RETHINK THEIR DRESS CODES

Some professionals are still split on the topic of dress code. Some question the seriousness, professionalism, and productivity of companies with flexible dress codes. Others question the culture, relevance, innovation, and management of companies with strict dress codes.

So, why consider updating yours?

"It's an employee's market. People wearing suits and more formal attire seem to return in tougher economic times," says Brandi Britton. She adds:

> More casual dress codes seem to be the trend when economic times are good and it's an employee-driven market. If there are more jobs than there are people, what are you as an employer doing to attract talent to your company? You do the things employees want: they want money and they want perks such as a more casual dress code. Right now, companies are having to be competitive for talent.

As the demand for Millennial talent grows and more Millennials step into decision-making roles, expect the trend toward more casual to grow.

Mark Zuckerberg is the business inspiration for 40 percent of Millennials, they say. With that much Millennial attention on the founder of Facebook, Zuckerberg's choices to wear a hoodie to meet investors and to wear the same gray T-shirt and jeans every day to be more productive have influenced the next generation of professionals' views of appropriate workplace dress.

In addition, by 2020, at least half of US households will be participating in the gig economy (independent work), and 70 percent of Millennials might reject traditional business to work independently. People dressing formally while working independently is unlikely.

Employers' dress policies are being held accountable by the desire and possibility of Millennials to work for themselves, where they can dress as they wish.

THE BEST DRESS CODE FOR MILLENNIALS AND YOUR MULTIGENERATIONAL TEAM

During a networking event before a recent presentation of mine, Lauren Williams, principal at the CPA firm Johnson Lambert LLP, expressed her company's desire to change its existing dress code:

> We wanted to set a tone that we are a professional services firm and we should dress the part. However, when we're at the office, we do not have many clients visiting (as we go to them more than they come to us) and our office had become more casual over the years as our partners relaxed enforcement of the business casual dress code.

I recommended that the company explore smart casual.

Smart casual can be considered a combination of casual, business casual, and business dress codes. Formal and casual clothing pieces can be mixed and matched to combine into a "smart" ensemble. It's considered neat, conventional, and professional yet relatively informal—the best of all the dress-code worlds.

The advantage is that smart casual is ambiguous, which caters to Millennials' desire for flexible dress and to other generations' desire to keep it professional. The disadvantage is that smart casual is ambiguous and might require more guidelines than other dress policies.

I followed up with Williams a few months later to see how the transition to smart casual went. She told me:

> Our goal for smart casual was to allow people to wear jeans any day of the week (previously we only wore jeans on Friday) or wear tailored shorts along with a nice shirt tucked in. Jeans shouldn't have holes and should be more fitted and put together. No tennis shoes or flip-flops. More tailored outfits regardless of the fabric involved.
>
> We previously allowed certain cargo shorts, flip-flops etc. that do not fit in with the new dress code. Enforcing the new code for those people was initially a challenge but given the lenient boundaries of the new code, most people adapted nicely.
>
> The benefits of the smart casual dress code are that we have a younger demographic of people in our office and through reading about trends, we learned that the easiest thing you can do for Millennials to make them happy is let them dress how they want. Given that we are a professional services firm, we applied some boundaries to that but overall employees are empowered to wear what works for them to get them through the work day and into the evening. Another benefit has been with recruiting. It is a selling point to potential new hires that we have smart casual dress in the office.
>
> We continue to dress business casual and business professional at client sites and for various professional events, but we have received very positive feedback from employees. Overall I think we found a nice balance between 'looking the part' and allowing people to dress comfortably and appropriately for the office.

Smart casual encourages Millennials to be unique and individualistic—a Millennial's dream.

4 KEYS WHEN REVISING THE COMPANY DRESS CODE

- **Overeducate.** Don't assume that Millennials (or any employees) know the difference between casual and business casual. It's up to employers to educate their employees and provide the necessary dress guidelines and examples. The top two most common dress-code violations managers see at work are employees dressing too casually (47 percent) and employees showing too much skin (32 percent).
- **Make it simple.** Complexity breeds confusion. Multiple dress code rules and scenarios can be as stifling as the formal dress code you are trying to avoid. Take cue from MassMutual's simple dress guideline, "Dress appropriately."
- **Geography matters.** Someone in San Francisco, California, might have a different interpretation of business casual than someone in Atlanta, Georgia. Factor in all locations and seasons when creating an updated dress policy.
- **Start at the top.** Often, the dress code is a reflection of the style of company leaders (especially for small and medium-size businesses). Ensure that each leader buys into and models the appropriate dress.

"This is always how we've dressed" is not an acceptable answer in today's twenty-first-century workplace. Revisit your company's dress code to ensure it is positioning you for next-generation growth and success.

CHAPTER 49

How to Get Millennials to Put Down the Device

• • •

HUMANS HAVE A PAST WITH resisting change.

Around 370 BCE, Socrates warned against writing because it would "create forgetfulness in the learners' souls, because they will not use their memories." People railed against the first newspapers, arguing that it socially isolated readers and would erode face-to-face communication. When radio and television arrived, many were fearful that they would distract children, diminish performance in school, and turn their brains to mush.

Today, we have an endless, on-demand combination of writing, radio, and television all rolled into smartphones. If anyone were going to be concerned about forgetfulness, social isolation, distraction, and mushy brains at some point, it would be today.

Creating healthy limits around mobile devices couldn't be more important as augmented reality and virtual reality—forecasted to generate $150 billion in revenue by 2020—become more mainstream. The next generation of employees will have to strike the right balance between interpersonal skills and participating in the most immersive virtual worlds humanity has ever seen.

But that's easier said than done. Technology is addicting, especially for Millennials, who grew up on it and have created a stronger dependence on it than other generations.

Science tells us that the dings of our devices release dopamine in our brains. Dopamine is a neurotransmitter that helps control the brain's reward and pleasure centers. Dopamine is the same chemical released when someone is smoking, drinking, or gambling. It's addictive because it's a pleasurable brain sensation.

Just like an alcoholic will turn to the bottle during stressful times, Millennials turned to mobile devices and social media during the stressful and confusing times of their adolescence. This created a sense of security and dependence on technology that many of them still carry with them as young professionals. Today, many Millennials abuse mobile and are addicted to social media. Too often, mobile has become a crutch, a mindless escape to consume instead of a tool for creation or to enable productivity.

Remember when companies offered their employees a "smoke break"? For Millennials, Snapchat is the new smoke break.

However, Millennials aren't the only guilty party. Every generation's digital behaviors are infringing on the opportunity to create genuine human connection. A recent report from the media information and analysis company Nielsen found that Generation X spent the most time using social media (six hours and fifty-eight minutes per week), followed by Millennials (six hours and nineteen minutes per week), and then Baby Boomers (four hours per week).

As the world goes mobile, it's critical not to vilify mobile but rather to find ways to manage it instead of it managing us. We must ensure that today's tech tools are not limiting our focus and connection with others.

Because, on the other hand, mobile will be the lens through which we interact with the future world. An artful, tricky balance between use and abuse must be struck.

Technology isn't bad, just like gambling isn't bad. It's an imbalance that is hazardous: too much gambling is dangerous, and too much technology is unhealthy.

Balance is best, and finding the right balance starts with leaders.

5 Actions Leaders Can Take to Help Millennials Put Down the Device

Model. Today's best leaders are double threats. They leverage technology for enhanced learning, productivity, and influence while maintaining strong offline communication skills in order to listen, collaborate, and inspire. A healthy balance of mobile-device use is critical in establishing the necessary credibility and capability to lead in a hyperconnected world.

To effectively influence Millennials' mobile-device usage, a leader must have his or own mobile usage under control and in good balance. Leaders have to appreciate (and use) the power of mobile, the pitfalls of too much or inopportune usage, and integrate it successfully.

Asking Millennials to "get off the phone" will only create resentment and position a leader as irrelevant or outdated. Speaking from a place of authority and credibility is crucial if Millennials are going to listen and/or take you seriously.

Track. Encourage Millennials to take an active role in monitoring how much time they spend on their devices. Ironically, there are apps to help individuals track their smartphone use. Encourage the use of the below tools so that Millennials can take back their productivity.

- Checky (www.checkyapp.com) tracks how many times users turn on their phones in a single day.
- BreakFree (www.breakfree-app.com) incorporates the usage-tracking features found in many similar apps, but it differs in that it breaks down the information into an easy-to-understand "addiction score."
- Offtime (www.offtime.co) helps users unplug by blocking distracting apps and/or games and filtering communications.
- Forest (www.forestapp.cc) is a gamified app where users are rewarded by the growth of a virtual tree for not touching their phones.
- Moment (www.inthemoment.io) tracks users' device usage and allows users to set daily limits; the app notifies if someone exceeds them.
- Flipd (www.flipdapp.co) allows users to lock their phones for a set period of time without the option of unlocking once the limit has been set.
- AppDetox (Android App Store) users can set their own parameters on an app-by-app basis so users can still access them at the appropriate times.
- Unplug (iOS App Store) users can monitor their daily device usage, explore the results, set daily limits, and earn rewards for cutting back.
- Freedom (www.freedom.to) is a cross-platform application that lets users set a list of distracting sites and block them either on a schedule or during sessions that users turn on at will.

These tools will help Millennials quantify the magnitude of their addiction or dependence on their devices. Gaining personal buy-in is important for Millennials to take the necessary steps in correcting their unproductive and unfocused behaviors.

Emphasize. Use the results of tracking as an opportunity to emphasize the purpose, perks, and power of disconnecting. Take time to emphasize messages like...

- Often, just the presence of a device in your hand or on a table can create an invisible barrier between you and another person.
- Social media can be misleading. Social-media activity has a filter, figuratively and literally—people only show what they want you to see. It doesn't communicate the whole picture and can spark feelings of depression if you're not careful.
- The constant distractions offered by a device limit innovation and ideas. Uninterrupted thoughts and conversations spur greater creativity.

Emphasize the purpose, perks, and power of disconnecting through your actions...

- Give employees a glimpse of what real connection feels and looks like.
- Make them see and feel what it's like to have undivided attention uninhibited by a device.
- Deliver unexpected experiences or thought-provoking questions that result in genuine curiosity.

Use chapter 25 to emphasize how Millennials can improve their communication skills.

Trial. Once mobile dependence is quantified and verified (and the power of disconnecting to connect is communicated) by someone, leaders can take steps to set up the necessary boundaries or guidelines. Consider trialing a specific mobile-free zone in the office, a no-mobile hour, or a mobile-free lunch. Model or encourage participation in the trials but never mandate it.

After the trial, ask employees what their results or outcomes were from participating in it. Adjust the trial accordingly or consider turning it into a permanent part of the workplace or company culture.

Balance. Mobile devices are a new staple in the fabric of life. Going back to a post-mobile workplace is impossible in a world where there are more active mobile devices than people. For Millennials, who will be using mobile for the rest of their lives as their wallets, maps, keys, cameras, and phones, etc., expecting them to ditch mobile isn't realistic or a productive long-term solution.

We are living through an era of mobilization, so it's important that you be an advocate of mobile and play your part in helping your workforce master the tool. If there are specific work-related tasks that Millennials can perform better or faster on a mobile device, then consider folding them into the process and/ or making them best practices for the team.

Balance is best and a must.

Finding balance has become increasingly difficult with the enhanced ability and urge to multitask with our devices.

HOW MULTITASKING IS THWARTING YOUR PRODUCTIVITY

What do leprechauns, the Loch Ness monster, and multitasking all have in common? They're all myths. Your colleague can't multitask; you can't multitask...no one can. Even the tech-savvy, multidevice-juggling Millennials can't. Yet, on a daily basis, we cling to the multitasking myth as we work across multiple devices and systems, trying to squeeze more productivity out of our day.

We are all guilty of trying to multitask. You'll probably even be tempted to try it a few times while reading this chapter. You may glance at an e-mail, send a text, add a task to your to-do list, or create a calendar reminder.

Today's work environments and culture are carnivals of distracting multitasking demands. And it's costly. Researchers estimate that we lose 28 percent of an average workday to multitasking ineffectiveness. And a Microsoft study found that it can take us up to fifteen minutes to refocus after an interruption. Imagine what the cumulative loss of focus and productivity is over a career or what loss it is to a business.

WHY WE "MULTITASK"

- **It's ancestral.** Multitasking was a necessity for survival. Our ancestors had to survey the foreground while assessing the threats in the background.
- **It's tempting.** Humans produce as many as fifty thousand thoughts a day. We are constantly tempted to change direction and pursue new thoughts and ideas.
- **It's addictive.** Media multitasking produces dopamine squirts in our brains.
- **It's necessary.** Many of us believe that we must multitask to get everything done. Workers change desktop windows and check e-mail or other programs nearly thirty-seven times an hour.

WHY MULTITASKING IS A MYTH

According to Gary Keller, author of the number-one *Wall Street Journal* and *New York Times* best-selling book *The One Thing: The Surprisingly Simple Truth*

Behind Extraordinary Results, the term "multitasking" first appeared in the 1960s to describe what computers did, not people. Computers were becoming so "fast" that a whole new word was needed to describe a computer's ability to quickly perform many tasks at once.

Originally, the term "multitasking" referred to multiple tasks alternately sharing one resource (the computer's CPU). However, the interpretation of "multitasking" has shifted to mean multiple tasks being done simultaneously by a resource (a person).

Today's computers give the illusion that everything happens at the same time, when in reality computers have to switch back and forth to process and can only process one piece of code at a time. Humans operate the same way: we can only process one piece of information at a time. Thus, multitasking, as we think of it, is a myth.

THE REALITY OF MULTITASKING

Can you listen to a podcast and drive at the same time? Sure. Humans can do two things at once. But we cannot focus effectively on two things at once. And oftentimes, we rely on muscle memory to help us perform one of our simultaneous tasks.

It's very likely that if you got lost while driving, you'd turn the podcast down or off so that you could fully focus on the more complex task of finding your way. Or, if the roads you were driving on became icy, your retention of the podcast content would drop significantly as your focus shifted to driving safely.

If you are instant messaging a peer during a conference call, texting while having a conversation, or e-mailing during a team meeting, you are actually switching between the tasks. Researchers refer to this as "task switching."

Interestingly, it's been proven that younger brains can switch between tasks with greater effectiveness than older brains. This explains why Millennials and Generation Z (the post-Millennial generation) give the illusion that they are elite multitaskers. In reality, their brains just allow them to switch between tasks with greater ease and less loss of focus.

You can still manage to extract the necessary and important information while you task switch, but don't think for a second that you are 100 percent present and delivering your best performance within each task. Our brains simply do not allow it.

WHAT TO DO WHEN FACED WITH MANY TASKS?

- Appreciate the limitations of your brain and your focus.
- Start small. Block off fifteen minutes to hyperfocus on one activity or task.
- Throughout the day, decide what matters most in the moment and give it your undivided attention.
- Quiet your world so you can conquer what matters. Build a work bunker—silence your phone, close e-mail and social media, turn Wi-Fi off, and so on.

We will never achieve 100 percent distraction-free work. Distractions aren't a problem that can be solved but rather a tension we must manage. Hopefully, with a renewed perspective on task switching, you can better manage this tension and avoid the devastating productivity costs—for it is said that those who chase two rabbits will not catch either one.

Fight on for your focus.

CHAPTER 50

How to Have Millennials Use Social Media More Strategically at Work

• • •

SOCIAL MEDIA IS A BROAD term for Internet-based tools used on laptops, tablets, and smartphones that allow for community-based input, interaction, content sharing, and collaboration. Social media received mass adoption from Millennials early on and now is in widespread use among all generations.

More and more social-media-inspired communication tools like Slack, Yammer, and Facebook at Work are gaining high adoption thanks to the surge of Millennials into the workplace and ubiquitous connectivity.

Four-time *New York Times* best-selling author and CEO of Vaynermedia, Gary Vaynerchuk, said,

> Every year the world becomes a little smaller, a little more social, a little more connected. Creating content that allows us to share our experiences, thoughts, and ideas in real time is becoming an intrinsic part of life in the 21st century, in fact, it's getting to the point that we're making a statement when we don't share or choose not to connect.

According to research firm PricewaterhouseCoopers, 78 percent of Millennials say that access to the technology they like makes them effective at work.

Some of the other benefits of social media at work include: streamlined communications; efficient collaboration; effective relationship building; brand building (personal and corporate); talent scouting; info gathering; and promoting products, services, events, and so on.

According to CareerBuilder, 28 percent of employers report that they've fired people for using the Internet for nonwork activity (such as using social media) during the workday, and 18 percent have dismissed employees because of something posted on social media.

Some of the risks of social media at work include: misinterpreted posts, a high level of distraction, oversharing of personal information, company misrepresentation, replacement of face-to-face communication, and sharing of sensitive or illicit content.

THE DOS OF SOCIAL MEDIA AT WORK

Here are some social-media dos and don'ts to emphasize with your social-savvy Millennial employees:

- **Be respectful.** Intent matters. Have the right intent and treat others as you want to be treated.
- **Know and follow your company's social-media guidelines.** Neglecting the guidelines can get you fired, sued, or both. Also consider the company's code of ethics.
- **Proofread before posting.** Correct poor grammar, unnecessary slang, or misspelled words.
- **Use a disclaimer** (if your name is closely associated with your employer). Make it clear when you are posting your personal opinions.
- **Check privacy settings.** Decide what accounts might need to be private or set up a separate business or personal account.

The Don'ts of Social Media at Work

- **Don't complain.** Don't complain about work over social media (no matter how private the account). Consider discussing your work challenges with friends or colleagues face-to-face.
- **Don't share confidential company info.** Keep information such as budget, future plans, rumors in the office, etc. confidential. Also, beware that sensitive info does not sneak into the backdrop of a photo.
- **Don't fight with customers on social.** Handle complaints and criticism calmly and respond with the type of positive, empathetic words that you would like to receive if you had an issue.
- **Don't post illicit content.** Don't post anything that could damage you professionally.
- **Don't spend more time** on social than is necessary for productive work.

7 Productive Ways Millennials Can Use Social Media at Work

Restricting social media at work is unrealistic in a world dominated by mobile social networks, and it can actually hinder Millennial productivity. Encourage Millennials to use social media strategically and effectively.

1. Get help. Use social media to get input on a project or product. Connect with an expert or thought leader who can weigh in on an issue. Or consider leveraging tools like Survey Monkey or Twitter Polls to get help, feedback, or answers to a question via social media.

2. Collaborate with colleagues. Collaboration technologies like Slack, Yammer, Facebook, or Google Drive are tools that Millennials are familiar with and can leverage to increase productivity, streamline messaging, share documents, and more.

3. Search for talent. Use social media (specifically LinkedIn) to find freelancers, experts, contractors, or job candidates.

4. Listen to customers. Use social media to actively listen to what potential or current customers are saying about your product, industry, or competitors.

5. Connect with customers. Communicate with customers in real time across multiple social networks about new promotions, exclusive offers, new store openings, or updated product features.

6. Promote events or products. Company announcements, events, or products can be promoted (externally or internally) via social media.

7. Receive real-time feedback. Receiving feedback from in-person small groups, at a trade show, or other public setting can be tedious, time-consuming, and costly. Social media offers a simpler and more real-time way to receive feedback and gauge customer interest while the product or service is still in progress.

3 Exercises for Millennials to Get Their Social Media Usage under Control

1. Self-audit your social media usage at work. Download the free tool RescueTime (www.rescuetime.com). It tracks how the user spends time online and provides tools to help him or her be more productive. (Chapter 14 also has a list of tools that could help audit social-media usage at work.)

Ask yourself the following questions:

- How often do you use social media daily?
- What are your productive habits on social media?
- What are your counterproductive habits on social media?
- What social networks interfere with your productivity?
- When and where do you need to limit or quit social media?
- What are two or three things you can do to be more productive in your social-media use at work?

2. Adopt a productivity technique. Research has confirmed that the human brain needs routine breaks to remain functioning at a high level. Select one of the techniques below and implement it for one day. At the end of the day, take five minutes to review your productivity. Repeat this process for the other three techniques and consider adopting one that improves your productivity. Only check social media during the allotted break time.

- **Pomodoro method.** Set a timer for twenty-five minutes, and when it goes off, take a short break for five minutes. After four of these sessions, take a longer break of thirty minutes.
- **Ninety-minute work blocks.** Work in ninety-minute intervals with twenty-minute breaks between work sessions.
- **52–17 method.** Work for fifty-two minutes and then break for seventeen minutes before getting back to work.
- **Two fifteen-minute breaks per day.** Block out two planned, fifteen-minute intermissions in your day—one in the midmorning and the other in the midafternoon. (Note: 3:00 p.m. is the least productive time of the day, so consider scheduling the break over that time.)

3. Replace social media with another rewarding activity.

In many ways, Facebook, Instagram, and Snapchat are the new smoke breaks at work. However, instead of consuming social media during your next work break, try one of these productivity-boosting activities:

- Take a walk
- Daydream
- Read
- Listen to a podcast
- Doodle
- Nap
- Chat with colleagues
- Meditate
- Plan a trip or vacation
- Call friends or family
- Make a grocery list
- Watch a TED.com talk

Section 6
Bonus How-To

• • •

CHAPTER 51

How to Sell to the Millennial B2B Buyer

• • •

IN 2014, GOOGLE REPORTED THAT 46 percent of potential buyers researching B2B products were Millennials, up from 27 percent in 2012. Today, 73 percent of Millennial workers are involved in decisions to purchase products or services for their companies or their own business, and 34 percent are the sole decision-makers regarding purchases.

As more and more Millennials begin controlling big budgets, it becomes increasingly critical for seasoned sellers to understand and connect with the Millennial B2B buyer.

BENEFITS OF SELLING TO MILLENNIAL B2B BUYERS

1. **Loyalty limbo.** Whether they are new to the buying role or looking to reevaluate any long-standing relationships or traditional processes, the window to win Millennial loyalty is open.
2. **Vast value.** Because Millennials are young in their careers, they inevitably carry a high lifetime value. Nurture the relationships to turn their inevitable job hops into new opportunities.

3. **Peer persuasion.** Millennials turn to their robust social networks to crowdsource decisions as well as recommend and refer business. Deliver exceptional value, and social sharing shall be your reward.

8 Keys to Positioning a Product or Service with the Millennial B2B Buyer

1. Know Millennials. Fifty-two percent of workers say they're least likely to get along with someone from another generation.

Millennials communicate, shop, make decisions, and buy differently than previous generations. A firm understanding of the behavior and values of Millennials is the first step in establishing common ground with a next-generation buyer.

Survey your current Millennial buyers—not by calling but with a mobile-friendly survey—and ask such questions as:

- How do you search for products/services?
- How do you prefer to communicate?
- What associations or social networks do you belong to?
- What would make our company more appealing to you?

Based on your survey data, create a detailed Millennial buyer persona, a semi-fictional representation of your ideal customers, that highlights demographics, motivations, what blogs they read, devices they use, podcasts or audiobooks they listen to, how they shop online, prefer to communicate with vendors, and so on.

2. Use their communication style. Millennials spend more than 3.5 times overall usage time in messaging apps than those over forty-five years old, with older users defaulting to apps that replicate desktop functions like e-mail and web browsers.

Evolving technologies have created a tangled web of varying communication preferences. The clashing of communication channels is at an all-time high in the workplace. Some folks want face-to-face; others want a phone call, an e-mail, a text, or message via the latest chat service. One thing is for certain: never leave a voice mail for a Millennial. (See chapter 47 for why Millennials won't answer your phone call.)

How sellers want to communicate is less important than how buyers want to communicate. Sellers should defer to the buyer's communication preferences. (See chapter 8 for more details on this.) For Millennial buyers, that may be texting, Slack, Skype, or some other innovative communication platform. Adjusting in real time to various communication channels is the new norm when selling to Millennials.

3. Attract instead of prospect. Millennial B2B buyers cited Internet search and vendors' websites as their two top means of researching products and services.

Historically, the sales process has been very linear—qualifying, educating, creating interest or need, and closing—but the Millennial B2B buyer prefers a different process. The Millennial B2B buyer gathers information up front by consuming information via social networks, videos, blogs, and such. As a result, sellers have to do much more work attracting versus prospecting.

What's the best way to attract the Millennial B2B buyer? Deliver valuable, compelling content where they are searching for that information. Uncover (via a survey) what topics or questions they are searching for online and create content that fills the need of the potential buyer. High-value content will also position you as an expert/authority that can be trusted.

Ensure that your content is plentiful and as digitally native as Millennials are so that the Millennial B2B buyer can easily beat a digital path to your front door.

4. Maintain an active web presence. Sixty-two percent of Millennials say that if a brand engages with them on social networks, they are more likely to become a loyal customer.

Millennials grew up on the web searching forums, reading blogs, evaluating Yelp reviews, Googling everything, and tweeting at brands as if they were personal friends. Millennials' buying behavior is different from that of previous generations because of their highly social and hyperconnected upbringing.

Millennials will make decisions about you or your product based on your digital presence or the lack thereof. Unlike with previous generations, a face-to-face meeting is not needed to build trust and will only support the relationship or impression that has already been established online. Millennials place a higher value on virtual.

Social media impacts industries differently. However, a vibrant social-media presence will only elevate your brand in the eye of a Millennial buyer. Make it easy for the Millennial B2B buyer to discover your products and services and to begin a conversation.

5. Provide proof. Eighty-four percent of Millennials report that user-generated content on company websites has at least some influence on what they buy.

Once he or she is attracted, how do you move the Millennial B2B buyer along in the buying process? Provide proof. For a generation that has been bombarded with ads their whole life, straightforward and honest proof is what demonstrates the most trust with Millennials.

Create a compelling story with real images of real customers getting real results. Use testimonials, case studies, white papers, infographics, before-and-after photos, and success stories. Leverage video when possible, as video is Millennials' preferred content format when researching a new business product and service.

Millennials are massively persuaded by peers and will lean into their massive online networks to gather peer reviews, recommendations, and referrals. Ask your current Millennial buyers to create proof-packed content. After a good or bad experience with companies, 70 percent of Millennials feel a responsibility to share feedback with them. Nurture Millennial influencers to provide proof and help promote your products and company story.

6. Routine buyer adaptation. Buyers are now as much as 57 percent of the way through the buying process before actually engaging with a seller.

The information age has shifted more power to the Millennial B2B buyer. In the past, sellers had to find buyers and convince them that they needed to buy. Today, sellers are interacting with educated buyers and must adapt to where the buyers are in their decision process. Sellers have to be able to qualify a lead when the lead comes to them with a lot of existing knowledge.

Sellers should listen to understand what the buyer already knows, ask questions to uncover what the buyer needs to know, and then demonstrate value for the buyer's need. Covering redundant info that is clearly displayed online will frustrate the Millennial B2B buyer.

7. Paint the big picture.

50Fifty percent of Millennials say they are more likely to buy a brand they know supports a cause. Ninety-one percent of Millennials would switch brands to one associated with a cause.

Millennials desire simplicity, authenticity, and social responsibility in the goods and services they buy at a personal consumer level. This buying lens is likely to be carried into the B2B buying role. Companies serious about corporate social responsibility will earn Millennial business.

Help the socially-minded Millennial B2B buyer to see the big picture behind the product. For example, Warby Parker stresses that it is the "only carbon-neutral eyewear brand in the world," which aligns with one of the company ground rules: "Green is good."

Paint the bigger picture behind your product and be rewarded with a Millennial purchase.

8. Swift mobile communications. Eighty-two percent of Millennial B2B buyers say that mobile devices are important when researching new products and services.

On-demand info gathering and mobility throughout the sales cycle is a Millennial expectation. Millennials grew up in a response-rich, mobile environment and now expect prompt responses and mobile-friendly communications at every crossroad.

Sellers must rethink their sales copy and all communications through the lens of mobile in order to connect with the Millennial B2B buyer.

Section 7
Conclusion

• • •

CHAPTER 52

How to Successfully Thrive through Change

• • •

THIS STORY POETICALLY HIGHLIGHTS HOW you can smash through stagnation. Unleash more opportunities, productivity, and creativity by mastering the five stages of change listed below.

The convergence of Millennials, technology, and the Internet have accelerated the rate of change and disruption that leaders and companies experience. The release of a single app can cripple an entire industry, alter employee expectations, or shift consumer behavior in the blink of an eye.

Considering all of the topics we've covered in this book and the ever-evolving times that lay ahead, it is critical that you become skilled in managing and thriving through change.

Change is no respecter of individuals or industries. Change is constant and gains momentum as more and more of the world comes online.

Thinking differently about a generation, adjusting your leadership or communications, or embracing a new way of working requires change. Agility has become our dearest friend in today's ready-fire-aim culture.

The popular American singer, songwriter, actress, and author Portia Nelson wrote a short story titled "Autobiography in Five Short Chapters." It poetically captures the stages of change and reveals the progression we must follow to successfully thrive through change.

Executing any of the chapters in this book takes change, so as you read the below, be mindful of which stage you are currently in and what it will take to move you to the next stage.

Chapter 1: *I walk down the street. There is a deep hole in the sidewalk. I fall in. I am lost. I am helpless. It isn't my fault. It takes forever to find a way out.*

STAGE 1 OF CHANGE: IGNORANCE

You are unaware that change is needed, because this is your first time encountering the issue. If you are in this stage, ask yourself or someone close to you: What needed change might I be ignorant of?

Chapter 2: *I walk down the same street. There is a deep hole in the sidewalk. I pretend I don't see it. I fall in again. I can't believe I am in the same place. But it isn't my fault. It still takes a long time to get out.*

STAGE 2 OF CHANGE: DENIAL

You are aware of the needed change but choose to ignore it. If you are in this stage, ask yourself: Why am I in denial over the needed change?

Chapter 3: *I walk down the same street. There is a deep hole in the sidewalk. I see it there. I still fall in...it's a habit...but, my eyes are open. I know where I am. It is my fault. I get out immediately.*

STAGE 3 OF CHANGE: RESPONSIBILITY

The habit of not changing your behavior becomes so detrimental that your eyes finally open and you see why and where the change must happen. This forces you to take responsibility for finding a swift solution. If you are in this stage, ask yourself: How can I take responsibility and champion change?

Chapter 4: I walk down the same street. There is a deep hole in the sidewalk. I walk around it.

STAGE 4 OF CHANGE: RESOLVE

Your awareness of the needed change enables you to take the necessary steps to resolve the issue. If you are in this stage, ask yourself: What change must happen to resolve this? And/or is the resolution working?

Chapter 5: I walk down another street.

STAGE 5 OF CHANGE: PROGRESS

You experience the exhilaration of discovering a new path and the excitement of what opportunities lay ahead. If you are in this stage, ask yourself: What opportunities are now available as a result of changing?

I believe Nelson chose the word "autobiography" intentionally for the title of this story because it's your story, it's my story—it's everyone's story. Cyclical change will forever be the narrative of the human race. May this serve as a simple manual for making change more manageable.

It's my sincere hope that after reading *The Millennial Manual*, you find your new street as it relates to leading, developing, and engaging the next generation, and you *choose* to walk boldly down it.

Good luck.

NOTES / REFERENCES

• • •

INTRODUCTION

- Crossman, David. "Simon Sinek on Millennials in the Workplace." Online video clip. YouTube. YouTube, 29 Oct. 2016.Web. 30 April 2017.
- Hoffer, Eric. BrainyQuote. https://www.brainyquote.com/quotes/quotes/e/erichoffer109153.html. Accessed 27 April 2017

CHAPTER 1

- Fottrel, Quentin. "Step Aside, Generation X- The Millennials Are Coming." *MarketWatch*, 30 May 2015, http://www.marketwatch.com/story/step-aside-generation-x-the-millennials-are-coming-2015-05-11. Accessed 27 April 2017.
- Clark, Jr., Yorton. "How to Effectively Manage a Multi-Generational Workplace." *MidAmerican Nazarene University*, 28 Jan. 2016, http://www.mnu.edu/newsroom/article/how-to-effectively-manage-a-multi-generational-workplace. Accessed 19 April 2017.

CHAPTER 3

1. Fry, Richard. "Millennials Overtake Baby Boomers as America's Largest Generation." *Pew Research Center,* 25 April 2016, http://www.pewresearch.org/fact-tank/2016/04/25/millennials-overtake-baby-boomers/. Accessed 19 April 2017.

2. Fry, Richard. "Millennials Surpass Gen Xers as the Largest Generation in U.S. Labor Force." *Pew Research Center,* 11 May 2015, http://www.pewresearch.org/fact-tank/2015/05/11/millennials-surpass-gen-xers-as-the-largest-generation-in-u-s-labor-force/. Accessed 19 April 2017.

3. "Pay Scale Study." *Millennial Branding: Navigating You to Future Success,* http://millennialbranding.com/case-studies/payscale-com-study/. Accessed 19 April 2017.

4. "Millennials Poised to Become Greatest Entrepreneurial Generation; Payscout's Global Capabilities." *Payscout,* 29 Dec. 2014, https://www.payscout.com/news/comments/press16. Accessed 19 April 2017.

5. "The 2017 Deloitte Millennial Survey- Apprehensive Millennials: Seeking Stability and Opportunities in an Uncertain World." *Deloitte,* 2017, https://www2.deloitte.com/content/dam/Deloitte/global/Documents/About-Deloitte/gx-deloitte-millennial-survey-2017-executive-summary.pdf. Accessed 19 April 2017.

6. Schawbel, Dan. "Millennial Branding and Beyond.com Survey Reveals The Rising Cost of Hiring Workers from the Millennial Generation." *Millennial Branding: Navigating You to Future Success,* 6 Aug. 2013, http://millennialbranding.com/2013/cost-millennial-retention-study/. Accessed 19 April 2017.

7. Twaronite, Karyn. "Global Generations: A Global Study on Work-Life Challenges Across Generations." *E&Y,* 2015, http://www.ey.com/Publication/vwLUAssets/EY-global-generations-a-global-study-on-work-life-challenges-across-generations/$FILE/EY-global-generations-a-

global-study-on-work-life-challenges-across-generations.pdf. Access 19 April 2017.

8. Donnelly, Christopher, and Renato Scaff. "Who Are the Millennial Shoppers? And What do They Really Want?" *Accenture*, https://www. accenture.com/us-en/insight-outlook-who-are-millennial-shoppers-what-do-they-really-want-retail. Accessed 19 April 2017.

9. Schawbel, Dan. "Hiring Managers Say Millennials Surpass Prior Generations in Several Key Business Skills, New Study Reveals." *Millennial Branding: Navigating You to Future Success*, 29 Oct, 2014, http://millennialbranding. com/2014/2015-millennial-majority-workforce-study/. Accessed 19 April 2017.

10. Mediakix Team. "How Snapchat Demographics Are Shifting in 2017." *Mediakix*, 2 June 2016, http://mediakix.com/2016/06/snapchat-demographics-infographic-statistics/#gs.null. Accessed 19 April 2017.

11. Hesseldahl, Arik. " Three Million People Now Use Slack Every Day." *Recode*, 25 May 2016, https://www.recode.net/2016/5/25/11772938/ slack-usage-numbers-scale. Accessed 19 April 2017.

CHAPTER 4

1. Daley, Jason. "The Future of Franchises: What's Next, and What's Still Needed- 3. Let the Games Begin." *Entrepreneur*, https://www. entrepreneur.com/slideshow/252649/3. Accessed 2 May 2017.

2. "Airbnb Chief Human Resource Officer Becomes Chief Employee Experience Officer." *Forbes*, 21 July 2015, https://www.forbes.com/ sites/jeannemeister/2015/07/21/airbnbs-chief-human-resource-officer-becomes-chief-employee-experience-officer/#7dc801cc7b64. Accessed 25 July 2015.

3. "Digital Leadership: An Interview with Angela Ahrendts CEO of Burberry." *Capgemini Consulting*, 2012, https://www.capgemini.com/

resource-file-access/resource/pdf/DIGITAL_LEADERSHIP__An_
interview_with_Angela_Ahrendts.pdf. Accessed 30 April 2017.

4. Morgan, Jacob. "Five Examples of Companies with Internal Innovation
Programs." *Huffpost*, 9 April 2015, http://www.huffingtonpost.com/
jacob-morgan/five-examples-of-companie_b_7023322.html. Accessed
2 May 2017.

5. Paynter, Ben. "How Charity: Water Uses Data to Connect Donors and
the People They're Helping." *Fast Company*, 20 Mar. 2017, https://www.
fastcompany.com/3068686/how-charity-water-uses-data-to-connect-
donors-and-the-people-theyre-hel. Accessed 30 Mar. 2017

6. Jenkins, Ryan. "17 Essential Elements of a Successful Millennial Recruiting
Video." *Talent Culture*, 24 Feb. 2015, https://www.talentculture.
com/2015/02/24/17-essential-elements-of-a-successful-millennial-
recruiting-video/. Accessed 2 May 2017.

7. Bercovici, Jeff. "Slack is Our Company of the Year. Here's Why
Everybody's Talking About It." *Inc.*, Dec. 2015/Jan. 2016, https://www.
inc.com/magazine/201512/jeff-bercovici/slack-company-of-the-
year-2015.html. Accessed 2 May 2017.

8. Morgan, Jacob. "How The Chief People Officer Of Taco Bell Creates
Great Employee Experiences." *Inc.com*, 25 Jul. 2016, https://www.
inc.com/jacob-morgan/how-taco-bell-thinks-about-developing-the-
employee-of-the-future.html

9. Jenkins, Ryan. "How Will Millennials Lead in the Workplace." *Ryan
Jenkins*, 14 Mar. 2016, http://www.ryan-jenkins.com/2016/03/14/how-
will-millennials-lead-in-the-workplace/. Accessed 2 May 2017.

10. Jenkins, Ryan. "How to Develop Millennial Leaders and Expand Your
Millennial Consumer Insights with Nim De Swardt." Audio blog
post. The Next Generation Catalyst Podcast. 6 June 2016. Web. 2
May 2017.

CHAPTER 5

1. Fottrel, Quentin. "Step Aside, Generation X- The Millennials Are Coming." *MarketWatch*, 30 May 2015, http://www.marketwatch.com/ story/step-aside-generation-x-the-millennials-are-coming-2015-05-11. Accessed 27 April 2017.
2. Park, Menlo. "Move Over Millennials - Here Comes Gen Z." *Central Valley Business Times*, 22 July 2015, http://www.centralvalleybusinesstimes. com/stories/001/?ID=28735. Accessed 20 April 2017.
3. Taylor, Evan. "How to Leverage Generational Diversity." *U.S. News*, 23 *Dec. 2013, http://money.usnews.com/money/careers/slideshows/how-to-leverage-generational-diversity. Accessed 30 April 2017.*

CHAPTER 6

1. "Big Demands and High Expectations: The Deloitte Millennial Survey." *Deloitte*, 2014, https://www2.deloitte.com/content/dam/Deloitte/ru/ Documents/Corporate_responsibility/ru_2014_MillennialSurvey_ ExecutiveSummary.pdf. Accessed 29 April 2017.
2. Jenkins, Ryan. "6 Millennial Motivators: A Guide to What Motivates Millennials at Work." *Ryan Jenkins*, 21 May 2015, http://www.ryan-jenkins.com/2015/05/21/6-millennial-motivators-a-guide-to-what-motivates-millennials-at-work/. Accessed 30 April 2017.
3. Boyd, Stowe. "Millennials and the Workplace." *Gigaom*, 26 Oct. 2016, https://gigaom.com/2016/10/26/millennials-and-the-workplace-2/. Accessed 20 April 2017.
4. "Top Attractors: Where Professionals Want to Work." *LinkedIn Lists*, https://lists.linkedin.com/2016/top-attractors/en/us/adobe. Accessed 30 April 2017.

5. "The Next Generation Worker: The Citizen Developer." *TrackVia*, 2014, http://d2z6avstustc5t.cloudfront.net/wp-content/uploads/2014/04/ The_next_generation_worker_Citizen_Developer_TrackVia_2014. pdf. Accessed 30 April 2017.

6. "The New Workplace Currency - It's Not Just Salary Anymore: Cisco Study Highlights New Rules for Attracting Young Talent Into the Workplace." *Cisco*, 2 Nov. 2011, http://www.cisco.com/c/dam/en/ us/solutions/enterprise/connected-world-technology-report/cisco_ connected_world_technology_report_chapter2_press_release.pdf. Accessed 20 April 2017.

7. Jenkins, Ryan. "10 Alarming Statistics that Expose Why Millennials Leave Organizations." *RyanJenkins*, 18 Feb. 2016, http://www.ryan-jenkins. com/2016/02/18/10-alarming-statistics-that-expose-why-millennials- leave-organizations/. Accessed 20 April 2017.

8. Benko, Cathy and Anne Weisberg. "Mass Career Customization: Building the Corporate Lattice Organization." *Deloitte University Press*, 1 Aug. 2008, https://dupress.deloitte.com/dup-us-en/deloitte-review/ issue-3/mass-career-customization-building-the-corporate-lattice- organization.html. Accessed 27 April 2017.

9. Fisher, Anne. "This Company Will Pay $1,200 a Year Toward Your Student Loans." *Fortune*, 23 Sept. 2015, http://fortune.com/2015/09/23/ pwc-student-loans/. Accessed 30 April 2017.

10. Harrington, Matthew. "Professional Growth and Development Number One Driver for Millennials in 2014 Employee Engagement Trends Report." *New Directions*, 21 Nov. 2014, http://www.newdirectionsconsulting. com/leadership-engagement/professional-growth-and-development- number-one-driver-for-millennials-in-2014-employee-engagement- trends-report/. Accessed 20 April 2017.

11. "The 2016 Deloitte Millennials Survey: Winning over the Next Generation of Leaders." *Deloitte*, 2016, https://www2.deloitte.com/content/dam/

Deloitte/global/Documents/About-Deloitte/gx-millenial-survey-2016-exec-summary.pdf. Accessed 25 April 2017.

12. "Millennials Report That the Biggest Shocker about the "Real World" Is Lack of Training at Work." *Mindflash*, 16 April 2015. https://www.mindflash. com/blog/pressrelease/millennials-report-that-the-biggest-shocker-about-the-real-world-is-lack-of-training-at-work/. Accessed 20 April 2017.

13. Jenkins, Ryan. "Zappos 11 Company Culture Aspects That Win over Millennials." *Ryan Jenkins*, 17 Jan. 2014, http://www.ryan-jenkins. com/2014/01/17/zappos-11-company-culture-aspects-that-win-over-millennials/. Accessed 30 April 2017.

14. Jenkins, Ryan. "How to Avoid the Top 2 Reasons Millennials Leave Companies." *Inc.*, 7 June 2016, https://www.inc.com/ryan-jenkins/ how-to-avoid-the-top-2-reasons-millennials-leave-companies.html. Accessed 21 April 2017.

15. Benson, Tracy. "Motivating Millennials Takes More than Flexible Work Policies." *Harvard Business Review*, 11 Feb. 2016, https://hbr. org/2016/02/motivating-millennials-takes-more-than-flexible-work-policies. Accessed 21 April 2017.

16. Peacock, Amelia. "Engage Millennial Employees with Feedback and Evaluation." *Clutch*, 7 Dec. 2016, https://clutch.co/hr/resources/engage-millennial-employees-feedback-evaluation. Accessed 21 April 2017.

17. Nisen, Max. "Why GE Had to Kill Its Annual Performance Reviews after More than Three Decades." *Quartz*, 13 Aug. 2015, https:// qz.com/428813/ge-performance-review-strategy-shift/. Accessed 30 April 2017.

18. "Millennials: Fueling the Experience Economy." *Eventbrite*, 2014, https:// eventbrite-s3.s3.amazonaws.com/marketing/Millennials_Research/ Gen_PR_Final.pdf. Accessed 21 April 2017.

19. "Company Benefits." *New Belgium*, http://www.newbelgium.com/ Brewery/company/benefits. Accessed 30 April 2017.

20. "Business Needs to Reset Its Purpose to Attract Millennials, According to Deloitte's Annual Survey." *Deloitte*, 2015, https://www2.deloitte.com/global/en/pages/about-deloitte/articles/2015-millennial-survey-press-release.html. Accessed 21 April 2017.

21. "5 Ways Millennials Are Changing the Workforce." *Bentley University*, 11 Dec. 2014, http://www.bentley.edu/prepared/5-ways-millennials-are-changing-workforce. Accessed 21 April 2017.

22. "The Millennial Survey 2011." *Georgetown University*, 1 Jan. 2012, https://berkleycenter.georgetown.edu/quotes/92-of-millennials-believe-that-success-in-business-should-be-measured-by-more-than-profit-deloitte-2012. Accessed on 30 April 2017.

23. Poswolsky, Adam Smiley. "What Millennial Employees Really Want." *Fast Company*, 4 June 2015, https://www.fastcompany.com/3046989/what-millennial-employees-really-want. Accessed 21 April 2017.

24. Gregoire, Carolyn. "This Man Faced Unimaginable Suffering, and then Wrote the Definitive Book about Happiness." *HuffPost*, 18 Aug. 2014, http://www.huffingtonpost.com/2014/02/04/this-book-youve-probably-_n_4705123.html. Accessed 30 April 2017.

25. Smith, Emily Esfahani and Jennifer L. Aker. "Millennials Searchers." *The New York Times*, 30 Nov. 2013, http://www.nytimes.com/2013/12/01/opinion/sunday/millennial-searchers.html?_r=0. Accessed 21 April 2017.

26. Charlton, Don. "5 Reasons You Struggle to Manage Millennials." *Inc.*, 29 Oct. 2015, https://www.inc.com/don-charlton/five-reasons-you-struggle-to-manage-millennials.html?cid=em01011week44day29a. Accessed April 21, 2017.

27. Jenkins, Ryan. "Create Enduring Millennial Motivation with "Why" Communication." *Ryan Jenkins*, 19 Nov. 2015, http://www.ryan-jenkins.com/2015/11/19/create-enduring-millennial-motivation-with-why-communication/. Accessed 30 April 2017.

CHAPTER 7

1. Clark, Kevin. "The NFL Team That is Solving Millennials." *The Wall Street Journal*, 16 June 2015, https://www.wsj.com/articles/the-nfl-team-that-is-solving-millennials-1434484144. Accessed 30 April 2017.
2. Elmore, Dr. Tim. "The New School Coach." *Growing Leaders*, Dec. 2015, https://growingleaders.com/wp-content/uploads/2015/12/TheNew SchoolCoach.pdf. Accessed 30 April 2017.
3. Manning, Peyton. Go All In! IASA 2015, IASA, 8 June 2015, Mandalay Bay, Las Vegas, NV. Keynote Address.
4. https://owl.english.purdue.edu/owl/resource/747/09/

CHAPTER 8

1. Jenkins, Ryan. "5 Ways Snapchat Will Redefine Workplace Communication." *Inc.*, 1 Feb. 2016, https://www.inc.com/ryan-jenkins/5-ways-snapchat-will-redefine-workplace-communication.html. Accessed 21 April 2017.
2. Brandon, John. "Here's Why Slack is Killing Email Once and for All." *Inc.*, 11 Nov. 2015, https://www.inc.com/john-brandon/here-s-why-slack-is-killing-email-once-and-for-all.html. Accessed 21 April 2017.
3. Newport, Frank. "The New Era of Communication among Americans." *Gallup*, 10 Nov. 2014, http://www.gallup.com/poll/179288/new-era-communication-americans.aspx. Accessed 21 April 2017.
4. Cummings, Carrie. "Infographic: How Mobile Use Varies across Generations." *Adweek*, 17 Aug. 2015, http://www.adweek.com/brand-marketing/infographic-how-mobile-use-varies-across-generations-166426/. Accessed 21 April 2017.

5. Jenkins, Ryan. "5 Reasons Millennials Aren't Answering Your Phone Call." *Inc.*, 17 Nov. 2015, https://www.inc.com/ryan-jenkins/5-reasons-millennials-aren-t-answering-your-phone-call.html. Accessed 21 April 2017.

6. Rampton, John. "The Future of Messaging: How to Text Without Data or Wi-fi." *Inc.*, 19 June 2015, https://www.inc.com/john-rampton/the-future-of-messaging-how-to-text-without-data-or-wifi.html. Accessed 21 April 2017.

CHAPTER 9

1. McChrystal, Stanley. "Listen, learn...then lead." *TED*, Mar. 2011, https://www.ted.com/talks/stanley_mcchrystal. Accessed 21 April 2017.

2. "The 2017 Deloitte Millennial Survey- Apprehensive Millennials: Seeking Stability and Opportunities in an Uncertain World." *Deloitte*, 2017, https://www2.deloitte.com/content/dam/Deloitte/global/Documents/About-Deloitte/gx-deloitte-millennial-survey-2017-executive-summary.pdf. Accessed 19 April 2017.

3. Schawbel, Dan. "Hiring Managers Say Millennials Surpass Prior Generations in Several Key Business Skills, New Study Reveals." *Millennial Branding: Navigating You to Future Success*, 29 Oct, 2014, http://millennialbranding.com/2014/2015-millennial-majority-workforce-study/. Accessed 19 April 2017.

4. "Reverse Mentoring - Investing in Tomorrow's Business Strategy." *Forbes*, 5 May 2015, https://www.forbes.com/sites/joshsteimle/2015/05/05/reverse-mentoring-investing-in-tomorrows-business-strategy/. Accessed 12 May 2015.

5. Koulopoulos, Tom and Dan Keldsen. *The Gen Z Effect: The Six Forces Shaping the Future of Business*. Routledge, 2016.

6. "Digital Leadership: An Interview with Angela Ahrendts CEO of Burberry." *Capgemini Consulting,* 2012, https://www.capgemini. com/resource-file-access/resource/pdf/DIGITAL_LEADERSHIP__ An_interview_with_Angela_Ahrendts.pdf. Accessed 30 April 2017.

7. "The Millennial Generation." *Lifecourse Associates,* April 2015, http:// conginst.org/wp-content/uploads/2015/04/CI-Millennials-Report-Complete-d2.pdf. Accessed 2 May 2017.

8. "The Most Innovative Companies of 2015." *Fast Company,* https:// www.fastcompany.com/most-innovative-companies/2015. Accessed 21 April 2017.

9. Elmore, Dr. Tim. "The New School Coach." *Growing Leaders,* Dec. 2015, https://growingleaders.com/wp-content/uploads/2015/12/ TheNewSchoolCoach.pdf. Accessed 30 April 2017.

10. Ha, Anthony. "Target Teams Up with Techstars to Create a Retail-Focused Startup Accelerator." *TechCrunch,* 18 Oct. 2015, https:// techcrunch.com/2015/10/18/target-retail-accelerator/. Accessed 2 May 2017.

11. "Simbioza." *Simbioza,* http://www.simbioza.eu/en/2016/about. Accessed 2 May 2017.

CHAPTER 10

1. Willyerd, Karie. "Millennials Want to be Coached at Work." *Harvard Business Review,* 27 Feb. 2015, https://hbr.org/2015/02/millennials-want-to-be-coached-at-work. Accessed 21 April 2017.

2. Elliott, Mark. Personal Interview. 16, Jan. 2016.

3. Jen Su, Amy. "The Questions Good Coaches Ask." *Harvard Business Review,* 12 Dec. 2014, https://hbr.org/2014/12/the-questions-good-coaches-ask. Accessed 2 May 2017.

CHAPTER 11

1. Lardinois, Frederic. "Study: 42% of Americans Check Their Email in the Loo." *TechCrunch*, 27 Aug. 2015, https://techcrunch.com/2015/08/27/study-42-of-americans-check-their-email-in-the-loo/. Accessed 25 April 2017.

2. van Rijn, Jordie. "The Ultimate Mobile Email Stats Overview." *EmailMonday*, http://www.emailmonday.com/mobile-email-usage-statistics. Accessed 2 May 2017.

3. "The New Workplace Currency - It's Not Just Salary Anymore: Cisco Study Highlights New Rules for Attracting Young Talent into the Workplace." *Cisco*, 2 Nov. 2011, http://www.cisco.com/c/dam/en/us/solutions/enterprise/connected-world-technology-report/cisco_connected_world_technology_report_chapter2_press_release.pdf. Accessed 20 April 2017.

4. Baskin, Elizabeth Cogswell. "Flexible Work Hours and Remote Work Can Increase Retention and Productivity." *Tribe*, 1 June 2015, http://blog.tribeinc.com/2015/06/01/flexible-work-hours-and-remote-work-can-increase-retention-and-productivity/. Accessed 2 May 2017.

5. Bercovici, Jeff. "Slack is Our Company of the Year. Here's Why Everybody's Talking about It." *Inc.*, https://www.inc.com/magazine/201512/jeff-bercovici/slack-company-of-the-year-2015.html. Accessed 25 April 2017.

CHAPTER 12

1. "The 2016 Deloitte Millennials Survey: Winning over the Next Generation of Leaders." *Deloitte*, 2016, https://www2.deloitte.com/content/dam/Deloitte/global/Documents/About-Deloitte/gx-millenial-survey-2016-exec-summary.pdf. Accessed 25 April 2017.

2. "Millennials Believe Business Can Do More." *Forbes*, 27 Jan. 2014, https://www.forbes.com/sites/joshbersin/2014/01/27/millenials-believe-business-can-do-more/. Accessed 15 Feb. 2014.

CHAPTER 13

1. Yaeger, Don. "Welcome to Krzyzewskiville." *Success Magazine*, 10 Aug. 2015, http://www.success.com/article/welcome-to-krzyzewskiville. Accessed 25 April 2017.

CHAPTER 14

1. "Latest Telecommuting Statistics." *Global Workplace Analytics*, Jan. 2016, http://globalworkplaceanalytics.com/telecommuting-statistics. Accessed 25 April 2017.
2. Reynolds, Brie. "FlexJobs Survey: Millennials More Interested in Travel, Work Flexibility than Gen X, Baby Boomers." *FlexJobs*, 30 Sept 2016, https://www.flexjobs.com/employer-blog/flexjobs-survey-millennials-interested-travel-work-flexibility/. Accessed 25 April 2017.
3. Knight, Rebecca. "How to Manage Remote Direct Reports." *Harvard Business Review*, 10 Feb. 2015, https://hbr.org/2015/02/how-to-manage-remote-direct-reports. Accessed 25 April 2017.
4. Griswold, Alison. "How to Keep Remote Workers from Screwing Up." *Bigness Insider*, 7 Oct. 2013, http://www.businessinsider.com/tips-for-managing-remote-workers-2013-9. Accessed 2 May 2017.
5. "Top 10 Companies Winning at Remote Work Culture and Their Secrets." *CloudPeeps*, 8 Sept. 2015, http://blog.cloudpeeps.com/top-10-companies-winning-at-remote-work-culture/. Accessed 2 May 2017.

CHAPTER 15

1. Abbot, Lydia. "New insights That May Make You Rethink How You Recruit Millennials." *LinkedIn Talent Blog*, 2 Aug. 2016, https://business.linkedin.com/talent-solutions/blog/hiring-millennials/2016/new-insights-that-may-make-you-rethink-how-you-recruit-millennials?utm_source=feedblitz&utm_medium=FeedBlitzEmail&utm_content=946764&utm_campaign=0. Accessed 25 April 2017.
2. Jedeikin, Jenny. "How SAP Revamped Its Employer Brand Strategy Attract Millennials." *LinkedIn Talent Blog*, 2 Sept. 2015, https://business.linkedin.com/talent-solutions/blog/2015/09/how-sap-revamped-its-employer-brand-strategy-to-attract-millennials. Accessed 2 May 2017.

CHAPTER 18

1. Maxwell, John. *The 5 Levels of Leadership: Proven Steps to Maximize Your Potential*. Hatchett Book Group, 2011, 207.
2. The John Maxwell Company. "4 Things to Look for When Hiring Millennials." *The John Maxwell Company*, 19 Oct. 2016, http://johnmaxwellcompany.com/blog/4-things-to-look-for-hiring-millennials. Accessed 25 April 2017.

CHAPTER 20

1. "CareerBuilder Survey Reveals This Year's Most Outrageous Employee Excuses for Being Late." *CareerBuilder*, 26 Jan. 2017, http://www.careerbuilder.com/share/aboutus/pressreleasesdetail.aspx?ed=12%2F31%2F2017&id=pr985&sd=1%2F26%2F2017. Accessed 25 April 2017.

2. Stanley. Andy. "Speaker Summary: Andy Stanley 2." *Catalyst*, 14 Oct. 2009, https://catalystleader.com/read/speaker-summary-andy-stanley-2. Accessed 2 May 2017.

3. DeLonzer. Diana. *Never Be Late Again*. Post Madison Pub, 2003.

4. Refinery 29. "Always Late? How to Be on Time — For Real." *Time*, 22 May 2014. http://time.com/106815/stop-being-late/. Accessed 2 May 2017.

5. Schocker, Laura. "This is Why You're Late All the Time (And What to Do about It)." *Huffpost*, 25 Nov. 2013, http://www.huffingtonpost.com/2013/11/07/psychology-lateness_n_4229057.html. Accessed 2 May 2017.

6. McCammon, Ross. "Time Management Tips: What to Do if You Are Always Late." *Entrepreneur*, 1 Mar. 2013, https://www.entrepreneur.com/video/225437. Accessed 2 May 2017.

7. Stevenson, Shawn. "Sleep Problems? Here's 21 Tips to Get the Best Sleep Ever." *The Model Health Show*, http://theshawnstevensonmodel.com/sleep-problems-tips/. Accessed 2 May 2017.

CHAPTER 21

1. "Bersin & Associates Unlocks the Secrets of Effective Employee Recognition." *Berlin by Deloitte*, 12 June 2012, https://www.bersin.com/News/Content.aspx?id=15543. Accessed 2 May 2017.

2. "New Research Unlocks the Secret of Employee Recognition." *Forbes*, 13 June 2012, https://www.forbes.com/sites/joshbersin/2012/06/13/new-research-unlocks-the-secret-of-employee-recognition/. Accessed 30 June 2012.

3. "The Effects of Employee Recognition and Appreciation." *Tiny Pulse*, https://www.tinypulse.com/hubfs/TINYpulse_Recognition_Report.pdf. Accessed 2 May 2017.

4. More than Half of Employees Would Stay Longer at Their Company if Bosses Showed More Appreciation, Glassdoor Survey." *Glassdoor*, 13 Nov. 2013, https://www.glassdoor.com/press/employees-stay-longer-company-bosses-showed-appreciation-glassdoor-survey/. Accessed 2 May 2017.
5. Starner, Tom. "Survey: Millennials Aren't on Board with Current Recognition Programs." *HRDive*, 5 May 2016, http://www.hrdive.com/news/survey-millennials-arent-on-board-with-current-recognition-programs/418650/. Accessed 27 April 2017.
6. "Millennial Employees Crave Recognition, Employer Reward Programs Miss the Mark." *Blackhawk Engagement Solutions*, 5 Aug. 2015, http://www.multivu.com/players/English/7590351-blackhawk-engagement-solutions-happy-millennials/. Accessed 27 April 2017.

CHAPTER 22

1. "Millennials Don't Want to Embrace Failure." *Forbes*, 11 Feb. 2015, https://www.forbes.com/sites/neilhowe/2015/02/11/millennials-dont-want-to-embrace-failure/. Accessed on 15 Mar. 2017.
2. "The Millennial Generation." *Lifecourse Associates*, April 2015, http://conginst.org/wp-content/uploads/2015/04/CI-Millennials-Report-Complete-d2.pdf. Accessed 2 May 2017.
3. Elmore, Dr. Tim. *12 Huge Mistakes Parents Can Avoid: Leading Your Kids to Succeed in Life*. Harvard House Publishers, 1 July 2014, 36.
4. Rosenbloom, Stephanie. "The World According to Time Ferriss." *The New York Times*, 25 Mar. 2011, http://www.nytimes.com/2011/03/27/fashion/27Ferris.html. Accessed 2 May 2017.

CHAPTER 23

1. Chester, Eric. "Our Approach." *The Center for Work Ethic Development,* 2016, https://workethic.org/our-approach/. Accessed 2 May 2017.

CHAPTER 24

1. Friedrich, Amy. "3 Reasons to Work for a Millennial." *Inc.,* 19 Feb. 2016, https://www.inc.com/amy-friedrich/three-reasons-to-work-for-a-millennial.html. Accessed 27 April 2017.

2. Cummings, Carrie. "Infographic: How Mobile Use Varies Across Generations." *Inc.,* 17 Aug. 2015, http://www.adweek.com/brand-marketing/infographic-how-mobile-use-varies-across-generations-166426/. Accessed 27 April 2017.

3. Jenkins. Ryan. "10 Alarming Statistics That Expose Why Millennials Leave Organizations." *Ryan Jenkins,* 18 Feb. 2016, http://www.ryan-jenkins.com/2016/02/18/10-alarming-statistics-that-expose-why-millennials-leave-organizations/. Accessed 27 April 2017.

4. Jenkins, Ryan. "The Top 8 Weaknesses and How to Overcome Them." *Ryan Jenkins,* 22 Aug. 2016, http://www.ryan-jenkins.com/2016/08/22/the-top-8-millennial-weaknesses-and-how-to-overcome-them/. Accessed 2 May 2017.

5. Willyerd, Karie. "Millennials Want to Be Coached at Work." *Harvard Business Review,* 27 Feb. 2015, https://hbr.org/2015/02/millennials-want-to-be-coached-at-work. Accessed 27 April 2017.

6. "Young, Underemployed and Optimistic: Coming of Age, Slowly, in a Tough Economy." *Pew Research Center,* 9 Feb. 2012, http://www.pewsocialtrends.org/files/2012/02/SDT-Youth-and-Economy.pdf. Accessed 27 April 2017.

7. Gillespie, Nick. "Millennials Are Selfish and Entitled, and Helicopter Parents Are to Blame." *Time*, 21 Aug. 2014, http://time.com/3154186/millennials-selfish-entitled-helicopter-parenting/. Accessed on 30 April 2017.

CHAPTER 25

1. Newport, Frank. "The New Era of Communication Among Americans." *Gallup*, 10 Nov. 2014, http://www.gallup.com/poll/179288/new-era-communication-americans.aspx. Accessed 27 April 2017

CHAPTER 26

1. "Deloitte: Future Leaders Say Business Must Encourage Innovation for Growth, to Retain Talent, and Positively Impact Society." *Deloitte*, 22 Jan. 2013, https://www2.deloitte.com/global/en/pages/about-deloitte/articles/business-must-encourage-innovation-for-growth.html. Accessed 2 May 2017.
2. "Millennials (Gen Y) Innovation Survey." *Deloitte*, April 2013, https://www2.deloitte.com/content/dam/Deloitte/global/Documents/About-Deloitte/dttl_Millennial_Innovation_Survey_LTAM_2013.pdf. Accessed 2 May 2017.
3. Jenkins, Ryan. "Hewlett Packard's Ex-CTO Shares How Millennials Should Execute Their Best Ideas." Audio blog post. The Next Generation Catalyst Podcast. 1 Feb. 2016. Web. 2 May 2017.

CHAPTER 27

1. "Big Demands and High Expectations: The Deloitte Millennial Survey." *Deloitte*, 2014, https://www2.deloitte.com/content/dam/Deloitte/ru/Documents/Corporate_responsibility/ru_2014_MillennialSurvey_ExecutiveSummary.pdf. Accessed 29 April 2017.

2. Jenkins, Ryan. "How to Develop Millennial Leaders and Expand Your Millennial Consumer Insights with Nim De Swardt." Audio blog post. The Next Generation Catalyst Podcast. 6 June 2016. Web. 2 May 2017.

3. "The 2016 Deloitte Millennials Survey: Winning over the Next Generation of Leaders." *Deloitte*, 2016, https://www2.deloitte.com/content/dam/Deloitte/global/Documents/About-Deloitte/gx-millenial-survey-2016-exec-summary.pdf. Accessed 25 April 2017.

4. Fottrel, Quentin. "Step Aside, Generation X- The Millennials Are Coming." *MarketWatch*, 30 May 2015, http://www.marketwatch.com/story/step-aside-generation-x-the-millennials-are-coming-2015-05-11. Accessed 27 April 2017.

5. Jenkins, Ryan. "22 Helpful Statistics for Recruiting and Engaging Millennials at Work." *Ryan Jenkins*, 25 Jan. 2016, http://www.ryan-jenkins.com/2016/01/25/22-helpful-statistics-for-recruiting-and-engaging-millennials-at-work/. Accessed 2 May 2017.

6. Jenkins, Ryan. "6 Millennials Motivators: A Guide to What Motivates Millennials at Work." *Ryan Jenkins*, 21 May 2015, http://www.ryan-jenkins.com/2015/05/21/6-millennial-motivators-a-guide-to-what-motivates-millennials-at-work/. Accessed 27 April 2017.

7. "The 2015 Millennial Majority Workforce: Study Results." *SlideShare*, 22 Oct. 2014, https://www.slideshare.net/oDesk/2015-millennial-majority-workforce. Accessed 27 April 2017.

CHAPTER 28

1. Jenkins, Ryan. "4 Signs That Games Will Usher in a New Era of Work (Book Review)." *Ryan Jenkins*, 6 Dec. 2013, http://www.ryan-jenkins. com/2013/12/06/4-signs-that-games-will-usher-in-a-new-era-of-work-book-review/. Access 27 April 2017.

2. Gladwell, Malcolm. "Complexity and the Ten-Thousand-Hour Rule." *The New Yorker*, 21 Aug. 2013, http://www.newyorker.com/news/ sporting-scene/complexity-and-the-ten-thousand-hour-rule. Accessed 2 May 2017.

3. "2015 Sales, Demographic and Usage Data." *Entertainment Software Association*, April 2015, http://www.theesa.com/wp-content/uploads/ 2015/04/ESA-Essential-Facts-2015.pdf. Accessed 27 April 2017.

4. Jenkins, Ryan. "12 Startling Gamification Stats." *Ryan Jenkins*,4 Mar. 2013, http://www.ryan-jenkins.com/2013/03/04/12-startling-gamification-stats/. Accessed 27 April 2017.

5. Mather, Katie. "Playing Video Games Actually Gives You One Major Advantage in Life." *Elite Daily*, 23 June 2016, http://elitedaily.com/news/ playing-video-games-major-advantage/1532644/. Accessed 27 April 2017.

6. Jayanth, Meg. "52% of Gamers are Women - But the Industry Doesn't Know It." *The Guardian*, 18 Sept. 2014, http://elitedaily.com/news/ playing-video-games-major-advantage/1532644/. Accessed 27 April 2017.

7. Weinberger, Matt. "Amazon's $970 Million Purchase of Twitch Makes So Much Sense Now: It's All about the Cloud." *Business Insider*, 16 Mar. 2016. http://www.businessinsider.com/amazons-970-million-purchase-of-twitch-makes-so-much-sense-now-its-all-about-the-cloud-2016-3. Accessed 27 April 2017.

8. Putterman, Alex. "Turner Sports Pleased with Rating of First Season of 'ELeague'." *Awful Announcing*, 29 July 2016, http://awfulannouncing.

com/2016/turner-sports-pleased-with-ratings-on-first-season-of-eleague.html. Accessed 27 April 2017.

9. Rigoni, Brandon and Bailey Nelson. "Few Millennials Are Engaged at Work." *Gallup*, 30 Aug. 2016, http://www.gallup.com/businessjournal/195209/few-millennials-engaged-work.aspx. Accessed 27 April 2017.

10. Rockwood, Kate. "The Best Bosses Watch These Numbers to Keep Employees Happy." *Inc.*, June 2016, https://www.inc.com/magazine/201606/kate-rockwood/monitoring-employee-engagement.html. Accessed 27 April 2017.

11. Benko, Cathy and Anne Weisberg. "Mass Career Customization: Building the Corporate Lattice Organization." *Deloitte University Press*, 1 Aug. 2008, https://dupress.deloitte.com/dup-us-en/deloitte-review/issue-3/mass-career-customization-building-the-corporate-lattice-organization.html. Accessed 27 April 2017.

12. "Getting into the Game." *D2L Corporation*, 2014, https://www.d2l.com/wp-content/uploads/2014/12/Getting-in-the-Game..pdf. Accessed 2 May 2017.

13. Estes, Wade. "Five Companies Successfully Targeting Millennials: Case Studies and Marketing Strategies." *Study Breaks Magazine*, 4 June 2014, http://studybreakscollegemedia.com/2014/five-companies-successfully-targeting-millennials-case-studies-and-marketing-strategies/. Accessed 2 May 2017.

CHAPTER 29

1. Chen, Ada. "Everwise Raises $8 Million in Series A Funding to Transform Career Development for Today's Workplace." *Modern Workforce*, 8 Dec. 2015, https://www.geteverwise.com/press-release/everwise-raises-8-million-in-series-a-funding-to-transform-career-development-for-todays-workforce/. Accessed 2 May 2017.

2. "How Dreamers become Doers." *Inc.*, Sept. 2016: 44-54. Print.

3. HeyTodd. "Meet the Modern Learner." *Slideshare*, 16 Dec. 2014, https://www.slideshare.net/heytodd/the-modern-learner-infographic-final-v4120414. Accessed 29 April 2017.

4. Jenkins, Ryan. "Train Millennials Using Microlearning to Score Their Attention and Retention." *Ryan Jenkins*, 3 Dec. 2015, http://www.ryan-jenkins.com/2015/12/03/train-millennials-using-microlearning-to-score-their-attention-and-retention/. Accessed 29 April 2017.

5. Von Ins, Clara. "Designing Learning for Tomorrow: A Millennials Perspective." *Association of Talent Development*, 31 Mar. 2016, https://www.td.org/Publications/Blogs/L-and-D-Blog/2016/03/Designing-Learning-for-Tomorrow-a-Millennial-Perspective. Accessed 29 April 2017.

6. "How the Workforce Learns in 2016." *Degreed*, 2016, http://get.degreed.com/hubfs/Degreed_How_the_Workforce_Learns_in_2016.pdf. Accessed on 29 April 2017.

7. "Management Matters." *Grovo*, https://www.grovo.com/management-matters. Accessed 29 April 2017.

8. "The 2016 Deloitte Millennials Survey: Winning over the Next Generation of Leaders." *Deloitte*, 2016, https://www2.deloitte.com/content/dam/Deloitte/global/Documents/About-Deloitte/gx-millenial-survey-2016-exec-summary.pdf. Accessed 25 April 2017.

9. "A Generation of Leaders." *The Hartford*, 2015, http://www.thehartford.com/sites/thehartford/files/millennial-leadership-2015.pdf. Accessed 29 April 2017.

10. Kessler, Glenn. "Do 10,000 Baby Boomers Retire Everyday?" *The Washington Post*, 24 July 2014, https://www.washingtonpost.com/news/fact-checker/wp/2014/07/24/do-10000-baby-boomers-retire-every-day/?utm_term=.793b1761adf6. Accessed 29 April 2017.

11. Bersin, Josh, et al. "Global Human Capital Trends 2016- The New Organization: Different by Region." *Deloitte*, 2016,

http://www.workdayrising.com/pdf/Deloitte_GlobalHumanCapital Trends_2016_3.pdf. Accessed 29 April 2017.

CHAPTER 30

1. "Employment Experience of Youths: Results from the Longitudinal Survey News Release." *United States Department of Labor*, 8 April 2016, https://www.bls.gov/news.release/nlsyth.htm. Accessed 30 April 2017.
2. Adkins, Amy. "Millennials: The Job Hopping Generation." *Gallup*, 12 May 2016, http://www.gallup.com/businessjournal/191459/millennials-job-hopping-generation.aspx. Accessed 30 April 2017.
3. Jenkins, Ryan. "10 Alarming Statistics That Expose Why Millennials Leave Organizations." *LinkedIn*, 3 May 2016, https://www.linkedin.com/pulse/10-alarming-statistics-expose-why-millennials-leave-ryan-jenkins. Accessed 30 April 2017.
4. "The 2016 Deloitte Millennials Survey: Winning over the Next Generation of Leaders." *Deloitte*, 2016, https://www2.deloitte.com/content/dam/Deloitte/global/Documents/About-Deloitte/gx-millenial-survey-2016-exec-summary.pdf. Accessed 25 April 2017.
5. Abbot, Lydia. "New Insights That May Make You Rethink How You Recruit Millennials." *LInkedIn Talent Blog*, 2 Aug. 2016, https://business.linkedin.com/talent-solutions/blog/hiring-millennials/2016/new-insights-that-may-make-you-rethink-how-you-recruit-millennials?utm_source=feedblitz&utm_medium=FeedBlitzEmail&utm_content=946764&utm_campaign=0. Accessed 30 April 2017.
6. Welch, Abby. "Is Job Hopping Losing Its Stigma?" *Accountemps*, 18 Dec. 2014, https://www.roberthalf.com/accountemps/blog/is-job-hopping-losing-its-stigma. Accessed 30 April 2016.
7. "Big Demands and High Expectations: The Deloitte Millennial Survey." *Deloitte*, 2014, https://www2.deloitte.com/content/dam/Deloitte/ru/

Documents/Corporate_responsibility/ru_2014_MillennialSurvey_ExecutiveSummary.pdf. Accessed on 29 April 2017.

8. Success Staff. "Introducing the YouEconomy." *Success*, 10 June 2016, http://www.success.com/article/introducing-the-youeconomy. Accessed on 30 April 2017.

9. "The 2015 Millennial Majority Workforce: Study Results." *SlideShare*, 22 Oct. 2014, https://www.slideshare.net/oDesk/2015-millennial-majority-workforce. Accessed on 27 April 2017.

10. Deal, Jennifer J. and Alec Levenson. "Millennials Are Ambitious and Crave Career Progression." *Training Journal*, 21 Jan. 2016, https://www.trainingjournal.com/articles/feature/millennials-are-ambitious-and-crave-career-progression. Accessed on 30 April 2017.

11. Morgan, Jacob. "How The Chief People Officer Of Taco Bell Creates Great Employee Experiences." *Inc.com*, 25 Jul. 2016, https://www.inc.com/jacob-morgan/how-taco-bell-thinks-about-developing-the-employee-of-the-future.html

12. Jenkins, Ryan. "Why Rookies Trump Veterans in the New Game of Work." *Ryan Jenkins*, 7 May 2015, http://www.ryan-jenkins.com/2015/05/07/why-rookies-trump-veterans-in-the-new-game-of-work/. Accessed 1 May 2017.

CHAPTER 31

1. Gillespie, Nick. "Millennials Are Selfish and Entitled, and Helicopter Parents Are to Blame." *Time*, 21 Aug. 2014, http://time.com/3154186/millennials-selfish-entitled-helicopter-parenting/. Accessed on 30 April 2017.

2. Townsend, Dr. John. "Dealing with Entitlement." *Dr. Townsend*, https://drtownsend.com/dealing-with-entitlement/. Accessed on 1 May 2017.

3. Kurzweil, Ryan. "The Law of Accelerating Times." *Essays-Kurzweil Accelerating Intelligence*, 7 Mar. 2001, http://www.kurzweilai.net/the-law-of-accelerating-returns. Accessed on 1 May 2017.

4. Snow, Shane. *Smartest: How Hackers, Innovators, and Icons Accelerate Success*. Harper Business, 9 Sept. 2014, 4

5. Moss, Erica. "How to Attract and Keep Millennials at Your Company." *Millennial Marketing*, Mar. 2015, http://www.millennialmarketing. com/2015/03/how-to-attract-and-keep-millennials-at-your-company/. Accessed on 30 April 2017.

6. Lemle, Dr. Russell B. "How Being Entitled to Our Way - Gets In the Way." *Psychology Today*, 21 Aug. 2011, https://www.psychologytoday. com/blog/me-first-we-first/201108/how-being-entitled-our-way-gets-in-the-way. Accessed on 1 May 2017.

7. Greenleaf, Robert K. *Robert K. Greenleaf Center for Servant Leader*. 2016 https://www.greenleaf.org/what-is-servant-leadership/. Accessed on 1 May 2017.

8. 99U. "SImon Sinek: Why Leaders Eat Last." Online video clip. YouTube. YouTube, 4 Dec. 2013.Web. 30 April 2017.

CHAPTER 32

1. Bersin, Josh, et al. "The Employee Experience: Culture, Engagement and Beyond." *Deloitte University Press*, 28 Feb. 2017, https://dupress. deloitte.com/dup-us-en/focus/human-capital-trends/2017/improving-the-employee-experience-culture-engagement.html?id=us:2ps:3gl:c onfidence:eng:cons:031616:em:dup1179:1PSBkNzx::184663656600:b: Human_Capital_Trends:Employee_Experience_BMM:nb%25250A. Accessed 30 April 2017.

2. Morgan, Jacob. *The Employee Experience Advantage: How to Win the War for Talent by Giving Employees the Workspaces They Want, the Tools They Need, and a Culture They Can Celebrate.* Wiley, 27 Mar. 2017, 1, 6, 9.

3. Donston-Miller, Debra. "Workforce2020: What You Need to Know Now." *Forbes*, 5 May 2016, https://www.forbes.com/sites/workday/2016/05/05/workforce-2020-what-you-need-to-know-now/#384ba8a12d63. Accessed 1 May 2017.

4. Kumar, Amit, et al. "Waiting for Merlot: Anticipatory Consumption of Experiential and Material Purchases." *Sage Journals*, 21 Aug. 2014, http://journals.sagepub.com/doi/abs/10.1177/0956797614546556?rss=1 &%2523aff-1=&. Accessed 30 April 2017.

5. Nuñez, Mario. "Does Money Buy Happiness? The Link Between Salary and Employee Satisfaction." *Glassdoor*, 18 June 2015, https://www.glassdoor.com/research/does-money-buy-happiness-the-link-between-salary-and-employee-satisfaction/. Accessed 30 April 2017.

6. "How HR Can Improve Employee Experience." *Blue Board*, 18 Aug. 2016, https://blog.blueboard.com/2016/08/how-hr-can-improve-employee-experience/. Accessed 30 April 2017.

7. "Millennials: Fueling the Experience Economy." *Eventbrite*, 2014, https://eventbrite-s3.s3.amazonaws.com/marketing/Millennials_Research/Gen_PR_Final.pdf. Accessed 21 April 2017.

8. Rigoni, Brandon and Bailey Nelson. "Few Millennials Are Engaged at Work." *Gallup*, 30 Aug. 2016, http://www.gallup.com/businessjournal/195209/few-millennials-engaged-work.aspx. Accessed 30 April 2017.

9. Kung, Xin Ni. "10 Workplace Trends You'll See in 2017." *The Young Professionals Group*, 16 Feb. 2017, http://theyoungprofessionalgroup.com/10-workplace-trends-youll-see-in-2017/. Accessed 1 May 2017.

10. "Airbnb Chief Human Resource Officer Becomes Chief Employee Experience Officer." *Forbes*, 21 July 2015, https://www.forbes.com/sites/jeannemeister/2015/07/21/airbnbs-chief-human-resource-officer-becomes-chief-employee-experience-officer/#7dc801cc7b64. Accessed 25 July 2015.

11. Morris, Donna. "Experience Matters." *Adobe*, 17 May 2016, https://blogs.adobe.com/conversations/2016/05/experience-matters.html. Accessed 1 May 2017.

12. "Rewriting the Rules for the Digital Age: 2017 Deloitte Global Human Capital Trends." *Deloitte University Press*, 2017, https://www2.deloitte.com/content/dam/Deloitte/be/Documents/human-capital/2017-Deloitte-Global-Human-Capital-Trends_web.pdf. Accessed 1 May 2017.

13. Shergill, Prithvi. "Employee Experience in the Time of Uncertainty." *The Economic Times*, 8 April 2016, http://economictimes.indiatimes.com/small-biz/hr-leadership/people/employee-experience-in-the-time-of-uncertainty/articleshow/51738217.cms. Accessed 1 May 2017.

CHAPTER 33

1. Economy, Peter. "9 Powerful Tips for Communicating Better with Millennials." *Inc.*, 24 Sept. 2015, https://www.inc.com/peter-economy/9-powerful-tips-for-communicating-better-with-millennials.html. Accessed 29 April 2017.

2. Brown, Molly. "Meet Yondr, The Company that Wants You to Put Your Phone Away and Enjoy the Show." *Geek Wire*, 2 Dec. 2015, https://www.geekwire.com/2015/meet-yondr-the-company-that-wants-you-to-put-your-phone-away-and-enjoy-the-show/. Accessed 29 April 2017.

CHAPTER 34

1. "The 2017 Deloitte Millennial Survey- Apprehensive Millennials: Seeking Stability and Opportunities in an Uncertain World." *Deloitte*, 2017, https://www2.deloitte.com/content/dam/Deloitte/global/Documents/About-Deloitte/gx-deloitte-millennial-survey-2017-executive-summary.pdf. Accessed 19 April 2017.

2. Jenkins, Ryan. "How to Attract Millennials Workers in 2 Simple Steps." *Ryan Jenkins*, 17 Oct. 2016, http://www.ryan-jenkins.com/2016/10/17/how-to-attract-millennial-workers-in-2-simple-steps/. Accessed 30 April 2017.

3. Stoked-Walker, Chris. "The New Standard for Keeping Millennials Happy at Work: Buying Employee Loyalty Can Be Easier That You Think." *Bloomberg*, 28 Oct. 2016, https://www.bloomberg.com/news/articles/2016-10-28/the-secret-to-a-happy-millennial-is-an-amazon-gift-card. Accessed 1 May 2017.

4. Inc. Staff. "The 50 Best Places to Work in 2016." *Inc.*, June 2016, https://www.inc.com/magazine/201606/inc-staff/best-workplaces-2016.html. Accessed 30 April 2017.

5. Mahoney, Sarah. "GenY Battling for Balance, Wellness and Less Tech." *MediaPost*, 16 Feb. 2015, https://www.mediapost.com/publications/article/243840/gen-y-battling-for-balance-wellness-and-less-tech.html. Accessed 30 April 2017.

6. Fried, Jason. "How to Change your Culture—In the Most Mildly Radical Way Possible." *Inc.*, Mar. 2016, https://www.inc.com/magazine/201603/jason-fried/new-employee-benefits-suggestions.html. Accessed 1 May 2017.

7. "These Companies Have Amazing Perks—You Need to Apply ASAP!" *Rate My Job*, http://www.ratemyjob.com/perks/20625/14-companies-with-amazing-perks-that-you-need-to-apply-to-asap. Accessed 1 May 2017.

8. Fast Company Staff. "Beyond Foosball: Office Perks That Employees Actually Want." *Fast Company*, 8 Aug. 2016, https://www.fastcompany.com/3062050/beyond-foosball-office-perks-that-employees-actually-want. Accessed 30 April 2017.

9. "Company Benefits." *New Belgium*, http://www.newbelgium.com/Brewery/company/benefits. Accessed 30 April 2017.

10. Helmrich, Brittney. "Think Freezing Eggs is Odd? Check Out These Strange Employee Benefits." *Business News Daily*, 20 Oct. 2014, http://www.businessnewsdaily.com/7321-strange-job-benefits.html. Accessed 1 May 2017

11. "Millennials: Fueling The Experience Economy." *Eventbrite*, 2014, https://eventbrite-s3.s3.amazonaws.com/marketing/Millennials_Research/Gen_PR_Final.pdf. Accessed 21 April 2017.

12. "New Survey Show Students Want Employers to Help Manage Student Loans." *Iontuition*, 1 Sept. 2015, https://blog.iontuition.com/new-survey-shows-students-want-employers-to-help-manage-student-loans/. Accessed 30 April 2017.

13. "CommonBond Launches Most Comprehensive Employee Student Loan Repayment Benefit in the U.S." *CommonBond*, 10 Dec. 2015, https://commonbond.co/commonbond-launches-most-comprehensive-employee-student-loan-repayment-benefit-in-the-us. Accessed 1 May 2017.

14. "Employee Benefits." *PriceWaterhouseCoopers*, https://www.pwc.com/us/en/careers/campus/why-pwc/employee-benefits.html. Accessed 1 May 2017.

15. Noguchi, Yuki. "Ship the Breast Milk for You? Companies Add Parent-Friendly Perks." *NPR*, 27 Mar. 2016, http://www.npr.org/sections/health-shots/2016/05/27/479323050/ship-that-breast-milk-for-you-companies-add-parent-friendly-perks. Accessed 1 May 2017.

16. Inc. Staff. "The 50 Best Places to Work in 2016." *Inc.*, June 2016, https://www.inc.com/magazine/201606/inc-staff/best-workplaces-2016.html. Accessed 1 May 2017.

17. Jenkins, Ryan. "How to Attract Millennials with the Right Company Perks." *Ryan Jenkins*, 23 Feb. 2017, http://www.ryan-jenkins.com/2017/02/23/how-to-attract-millennials-with-the-right-company-perks/. Accessed 20 Jan. 2017.

18. Giang, Vivian. "Netflix Culture Shaper Says Toss the Handbook, Stop Offering Ridulous Perks." *Chicago Tribune*, 1 Sept. 2016, http://www.chicagotribune.com/business/success/fastcompany/tca-netflix-culture-shaper-says-toss-the-handbook-stop-offering-ridiculous-perks-20160901-story.html. Accessed 1 May 2017.

19. "Zynga." *Get in Media*, http://getinmedia.com/employers/zynga. Accessed 1 May, 2017.

20. "18 of the Best Perks at Top Employers." *Business* Insider, 12 Feb. 2013, http://www.businessinsider.in/18-Of-The-Best-Perks-At-Top-Employers/Mattel-Inc-allows-its-employees-to-take-paid-time-off-for-their-kids-school-field-trips-/slideshow/21362481.cms. Accessed 1 May 2017.

21. Dishman, Lydia. "These Are the Best Employee Benefits and Perks." *Fast Company*, 3 Feb. 2016, https://www.fastcompany.com/3056205/these-are-the-best-employee-benefits-and-perks. Accessed 1 May 2017.

22. Petrone, Paul. "10 Unusual Company Perks (That Employees Can't Help but Tell Everyone About." *LinkedIn Talent Blog*, 13 May 2015, https://business.linkedin.com/talent-solutions/blog/2015/05/10-unusual-company-perks-that-employees-cant-help-but-tell-everybody-about. Accessed 1 May 2017.

23. Fast Company. "Perks that Work: Sandbox, Massages, Trips, Hiking Gear, Workshops." *Chicago Tribune*, 16 Aug. 2016, http://www.chicagotribune.com/business/success/fastcompany/tca-perks-

that-work-sandbox-massages-trips-hiking-gear-workshops-20160816-story.html. Accessed 1 May 2017.

24. "The 2016 Deloitte Millennials Survey: Winning Over the Next Generation of Leaders." *Deloitte*, 2016, https://www2.deloitte.com/content/dam/Deloitte/global/Documents/About-Deloitte/gx-millenial-survey-2016-exec-summary.pdf. Accessed 25 April 2017.

CHAPTER 35

1. "The 2016 Deloitte Millennials Survey: Winning Over the Next Generation of Leaders." *Deloitte*, 2016, https://www2.deloitte.com/content/dam/Deloitte/global/Documents/About-Deloitte/gx-millenial-survey-2016-exec-summary.pdf. Accessed 25 April 2017.

2. Jenkins, Ryan. "How to Brilliantly Manage Your Millennials Employees in 2016." *Inc.* 22 Dec. 2015, https://www.inc.com/ryan-jenkins/creative-effective-new-way-to-manage-millennials.html. Accessed 29 April 2017.

3. Buckley, Dr. Patricia, et al. "A New Understanding of Millennials: Generational Differences Reexamined." *Deloitte University Press*, 16 Oct. 2015, https://dupress.deloitte.com/dup-us-en/economy/issues-by-the-numbers/understanding-millennials-generational-differences.html. Accessed 29 April 2017.

4. Jenkins, Ryan. "How to Create a Successful Mentorship in the Digital Age." *Inc.*, 8 Feb. 2016, https://www.inc.com/ryan-jenkins/how-to-create-a-successful-mentorship-in-the-digital-age.html. Accessed 29 April 2017.

5. Jenkins, Ryan. "5 New GE Initiatives That Will Attract and Retain Millennials." *Inc.*, 10 Aug. 2015, https://www.inc.com/ryan-jenkins/5-new-ge-initiatives-that-will-attract-and-retain-millennials.html. Accessed 29 April 2017.

6. Willyerd, Karie. "Millennials Want to Be Coached at Work." *Harvard Business Review*, 27 Feb. 2015, https://hbr.org/2015/02/millennials-want-to-be-coached-at-work. Accessed 21 April 2017.

7. Jenkins. Ryan. "10 Alarming Statistics that Expose Why Millennials Leave Organizations." *Ryan Jenkins*, 18 Feb. 2016, http://www.ryan-jenkins.com/2016/02/18/10-alarming-statistics-that-expose-why-millennials-leave-organizations/. Accessed 27 April 2017.

8. Peters, Susan. "GE, for You." *LinkedIn*, 26 July 2016, https://www.linkedin.com/pulse/ge-you-susan-peters. Accessed 1 May 2017.

CHAPTER 36

1. Hillhouse, Alison. "Consumer Insights: MTV's 'No Collar Workers'." *Blog.Viacom*, 4 Oct. 2012, http://blog.viacom.com/2012/10/consumer-insights-mtvs-no-collar-workers/. Accessed 29 April 2017.

2. "The 2017 Deloitte Millennial Survey- Apprehensive Millennials: Seeking Stability and Opportunities in an Uncertain World." *Deloitte*, 2017, https://www2.deloitte.com/content/dam/Deloitte/global/Documents/About-Deloitte/gx-deloitte-millennial-survey-2017-executive-summary.pdf. Accessed 19 April 2017.

3. "2013 Millennial Workplace Trends Survey." *Sam Clar*, 2013, http://www.samclar.com/sitefiles/files/IdeaPaint-2013-Millennial-Survey.pdf. Accessed 29 April 2017.

CHAPTER 37

1. Reynolds, Brie. "FlexJobs Survey: Millennials More Interested in Travel, Work Flexibility Than Gen X, Baby Boomers." *FlexJobs*, 30

Sept 2016, https://www.flexjobs.com/employer-blog/flexjobs-survey-millennials-interested-travel-work-flexibility/. Accessed 25 April 2017.

2. Jenkins, Ryan. "How to Avoid the Top 2 Reasons Millennials Leave Companies." *Inc.*, 7 June 2016, https://www.inc.com/ryan-jenkins/how-to-avoid-the-top-2-reasons-millennials-leave-companies.html. Accessed 21 April 2017.

3. Jenkins, Ryan. "5 New GE Initiatives That Will Attract and Retain Millennials." *Inc.*, 10 AUg. 2015, https://www.inc.com/ryan-jenkins/5-new-ge-initiatives-that-will-attract-and-retain-millennials.html. Accessed 29 April 2017.

CHAPTER 38

1. Brandon, John. "Here's Why Your Definition of 'Work' is Driving Millennials Nuts." *Inc.*, 9 Oct. 2015, https://www.inc.com/john-brandon/here-s-why-your-definition-of-work-is-driving-millennials-nuts.html. Accessed 29 April 2017.

2. O'Donnell, J.T. "2 Ways Your Work Ethic Can Get You Fired." *Inc.*, 26 Aug. 2015, https://www.inc.com/jt-odonnell/2-ways-work-ethic-can-get-you-fired.html. Accessed 29 April 2017.

3. Snow, Shane. *Smartest: How Hackers, Innovators, and Icons Accelerate Success.* Harper Business, 9 Sept. 2014, 4

4. Jenkins, Ryan. "Narrow the Generational Gap by Understanding Each Generations Unique Perspective of Work." *Ryan Jenkins*, 27 April 2015. http://www.ryan-jenkins.com/2015/04/27/narrow-the-generational-gap-by-understanding-each-generations-unique-perspective-of-work/. Accessed 29 April 2017.

5. Kim, Leonard. "5 Ways You're Misunderstanding Millennial Employees." *Medium*, 4 May 2016, https://medium.com/@

mrleonardkim/5-ways-youre-misunderstanding-millennial-employees-d08184227ba6. Accessed 1 May 2017.

6. Burdett, Eliot. "Six Reasons to Hire That "Lazy" Millennial Today." *NYSAE*, http://www.nysaenet.org/resources1/inviewnewsletter/new-item2/june2016/inview512article-6-6-2016. Accessed 1 May 2017.

CHAPTER 39

1. Metz, Cade. "Facebook Moves into Its New Garden-Roofed Fantasyland." *Wired*, 30 Mar. 2015, https://www.wired.com/2015/03/facebook-moves-new-garden-roofed-fantasyland/. Accessed 29 April 2017.

2. "Apple's New 'Spaceship' HQ Set to Open." *Fox News Tech*, 22 Feb. 2017, http://www.foxnews.com/tech/2017/02/22/apples-new-spaceship-hq-set-to-open.html. Accessed 29 April 2017.

3. Vanhemert, Kyle. "Your First Look at Google's Reconfigurable, See-Through HQ." *Wired*, 27 Feb. 2015, https://www.wired.com/2015/02/first-look-googles-reconfigurable-see-thru-headquarters/. Accessed 29 April 2017.

4. "Big Demands and High Expectations: The Deloitte Millennial Survey." *Deloitte*, 2014, https://www2.deloitte.com/content/dam/Deloitte/ru/Documents/Corporate_responsibility/ru_2014_MillennialSurvey_ExecutiveSummary.pdf. Accessed 29 April 2017.

5. Jenkins, Ryan. "The Hard-to-Ignore and Compelling Compelling Case for Flexible Work." *Ryan Jenkins*, 29 June 2015, http://www.ryan-jenkins.com/2015/06/29/the-hard-to-ignore-and-compelling-case-for-flexible-work/. Accessed 29 April 2017.

6. "Enough with the Free Food Already, Millennials Want Opportunity and Fair Pay." Forbes, 11 Sept. 2014, https://www.forbes.com/

sites/datafreaks/2014/09/11/enough-with-the-free-food-already-millennials-want-opportunity-and-fair-pay/. Accessed 15 Jan. 2015.

7. Robot, Hunter D. "How the Future Workplace is Going to Look." *The Center for the Future of Work*, 3 April 2015, http://www.futureofwork. com/article/details/riding-the-exponential-curve-in-ais-tail. Accessed 29 April 2017.

8. "What Generation Y Wants from Business, Government, and the Future Workplace." *Deloitte*, 21 Jan. 2014, https://www2.deloitte.com/ za/en/pages/about-deloitte/articles/what-generation-y-wants.html#. Accessed 1 May 2017.

CHAPTER 40

1. Jenkins, Ryan. "Why Rookies Trump Veterans in the New Game of Work." *Ryan Jenkins*, 7 May 2015, http://www.ryan-jenkins.com/2015/05/07/ why-rookies-trump-veterans-in-the-new-game-of-work/. Accessed 1 May 2017.

CHAPTER 41

1. Lindegren, Rebecca. "Baby Boomer Brain Drain (Infographic). *UNC Kenan-Flagler Business School*, 28 April 2015, https://onlinemba.unc. edu/blog/baby-boomer-brain-drain-infographic/. Accessed 29 April 2017.

2. Green, Jeff. "As Boomers Retire, Companies Prepare Millennials for Leadership Roles." 21 Jan. 2016, https://www.bloomberg.com/news/ articles/2016-01-21/as-boomers-retire-companies-prepare-millennials-for-leadership-roles. Accessed 29 April 2017.

3. Kahler, James Patrick. "5 Stats on Talent Management and Succession Planning." *Hireology*, 27 Feb. 2015, http://www.hireology.com/blog/5-stats-on-talent-management-and-succession-planning. Accessed 29 April 2017.

4. Collinson, Catherine. "Baby Boomer Workers Are Revolutionizing Retirement: Are They and Their Employers Ready?". *Transamerica Center for Retirement Studies*, Dec. 2014, https://www.transamericacenter.org/docs/default-source/resources/center-research/tcrs2014_sr_baby_-boomers_and_employers.pdf. Accessed 29 April 2017.

5. Rigoni, Brandon and Bailey Nelson. "Few Millennials Are Engaged at Work." *Gallup*, 30 Aug. 2016, http://www.gallup.com/businessjournal/195209/few-millennials-engaged-work.aspx. Accessed 27 April 2017.

6. Donston-Miller, Debra. "Workforce2020: What You Need to Know Now." *Forbes*, 5 May 2016, https://www.forbes.com/sites/workday/2016/05/05/workforce-2020-what-you-need-to-know-now/#384ba8a12d63. Accessed 1 May 2017.

7. Shah, Vishal. "3 Ways to Rock at Millennial Succession Planning." *LearnCore*, 25 July 2016, https://learncore.com/3-ways-rock-millennial-succession-planning/. Accessed 29 April 2017.

8. "The 2016 Deloitte Millennials Survey: Winning over the Next Generation of Leaders." *Deloitte*, 2016, https://www2.deloitte.com/content/dam/Deloitte/global/Documents/About-Deloitte/gx-millenial-survey-2016-exec-summary.pdf. Accessed 25 April 2017.

CHAPTER 42

1. Son, Sabrina. "3 Must Have Tools to Foster a Culture of Collaboration." *Tiny Pulse*, 28 Oct. 2015, https://www.tinypulse.com/blog/sk-company-culture-of-collaboration. Accessed 29 April 2017.

2. "How to Hook & Keep Millennial Talent." *Rewardian*, 15 Sept 2016, http://rewardian.com/blog/2016/09/15/how-to-hook-keep-millennial-talent/wp-admin/setup-config.php. Accessed 30 Sept. 2016.

CHAPTER 43

1. "Engagement: Out of Office, but Not Away from Work." *Randstad*, 24 June 2014, https://www.randstadusa.com/workforce360/workforce-insights/engagement-out-of-office-but-not-away-from-work/199/. Accessed 29 April 2017.
2. "The 2016 Deloitte Millennials Survey: Winning Over the Next Generation of Leaders." *Deloitte*, 2016, https://www2.deloitte.com/content/dam/Deloitte/global/Documents/About-Deloitte/gx-millenial-survey-2016-exec-summary.pdf. Accessed 25 April 2017.
3. "Study Highlights: Work-Life is Harder Worldwide." *EY*, http://www.ey.com/us/en/about-us/our-people-and-culture/ey-study-highlights-work-life-is-harder-worldwide#.WQUwpRiZN3K. Accessed 29 April 2017.
4. "Study: Work-Life Challenges Across Generations: Millennials and Parents Hit Hardest." *EY*, 14 Jan. 2015, http://www.ey.com/us/en/about-us/our-people-and-culture/ey-work-life-challenges-across-generations-global-study. Accessed 29 April 2017.
5. Roth, Daniel. "Behind the Top Attractors: How We Discovered the World's Best Hirer's and Keepers of Talent." *LinkedIn*, 20 June 2016, https://www.linkedin.com/pulse/behind-top-attractors-how-we-discovered-worlds-best-hirers-roth. Accessed 29 April 2017.
6. "2016 Work and Well-Being Survey." *American Psychological Association*, 2016, https://simplyworkcomp.com/wp-content/uploads/2017/02/APA-2016-work-and-wellbeing-survey-results.pdf. Accessed 1 May 2017.

7. Coleman, Jackie and John Coleman. "The Upside of Downtime." *Harvard Business Review*, 6 Dec. 2012, https://hbr.org/2012/12/the-upside-of-downtime. Accessed 1 May 2017.

8. Schwartz, Tony. "Paradox: How Sony Pictures Gets More Out of People by Demanding Less." *Harvard Business Review*, June 2010, https://hbr.org/2010/06/the-productivity-paradox-how-sony-pictures-gets-more-out-of-people-by-demanding-less. Accessed 29 April 2017.

9. Goetz, Kaomi. "How 3M Gave Everyone Days Off and Created an Innovation Dynamo." *Fast Company*, 26 April, 1 Feb. 2011, https://www.fastcodesign.com/1663137/how-3m-gave-everyone-days-off-and-created-an-innovation-dynamo. Accessed 29 April 2017.

10. Jenkins, Ryan. "How Workplace Training can Attract, Retain, and Develop Millennials with Steve Cohen." Audio blog post. The Next Generation Catalyst Podcast. 1 May 2017. Web. 1 May 2017.

11. Thurmon, Dan. *Off Balance On Purpose: Embrace Uncertainty and Create a Life You Love.* Green leaf, 1 Oct. 2009.

12. Reuters. "J.P. Morgan Wants Its Employees to Stop Working on the Weekend." *Fortune*, 21 Jan. 2016, http://fortune.com/2016/01/21/jp-morgan-work-life-balance/. Accessed 29 April 2017.

13. Jeffries, Stuart. "Ten Tips for a Better Work-Life Balance." *The Guardian*, 7 Nov. 2014, https://www.theguardian.com/lifeandstyle/2014/nov/07/ten-tips-for-a-better-work-life-balance. Accessed 29 April 2017.

CHAPTER 44

1. Stanley, Andy. *Next Generation Leader: Five Essentials for Those who will Shape the Future.* Multnomah Books, 2003. P. 49.

2. Stanley, Andy. "Challenging Leadership." Audio blog post. The Andy Stanley Leadership Podcast. 6 May 2016. Web. 29 April 2017.

CHAPTER 46

1. Jenkins, Ryan. "5 Ways Snapchat Will Redefine Workplace Communication." *Inc.*, 1 Feb. 2016, https://www.inc.com/ryan-jenkins/5-ways-snapchat-will-redefine-workplace-communication.html. Accessed 21 April 2017.

2. Ovide, Shira and Rani Molla. "Five Charts Explaining Why Snapchat's Worth $25 Billion." *Blloberg Gadfly*, 7 Oct. 2016, https://www.bloomberg.com/gadfly/articles/2016-10-07/snapchat-ipo-5-charts-explaining-why-it-s-worth-25-billion. Accessed 29 April 2017.

3. Fontein, Dara. "The Top Snapchat Statistics You Need to Know for Business." *Hootsuite*, 14 Dec. 2016, https://blog.hootsuite.com/snapchat-statistics-for-business/. Accessed 29 April 2017.

4. Schonfeld, Erick. "Twitter Hits 50 Million Tweets Per Day." *TechCrunch*, 22 Feb. 2010, https://techcrunch.com/2010/02/22/twitter-50-million-tweets-day/. Accessed 29 April 2017.

5. Miller, Joshua. "We're on Snapchat: Add White House." *The White House*, 11 Jan. 2016, https://obamawhitehouse.archives.gov/blog/2016/01/11/whitehouse-joins-snapchat. Accessed 29 April 2017.

6. "Millennials at Work: Reshaping the Workplace." *PriceWaterhouseCoopers*, 2011, https://www.pwc.com/m1/en/services/consulting/documents/millennials-at-work.pdf. Accessed 29 April 2017.

7. "Cisco Visual Networking Index: Global Mobile Data Traffic Forecast Update, 2016-2021 White Paper." *Cisco*, 7 Feb. 2017, http://www.cisco.com/c/en/us/solutions/collateral/service-provider/visual-networking-index-vni/mobile-white-paper-c11-520862.html. Accessed 29 April 2017.

CHAPTER 47

1. Cummings, Carrie. "Infographic: How Mobile Use Varies Across Generations." *Inc.*, 17 Aug. 2015, http://www.adweek.com/brand-marketing/infographic-how-mobile-use-varies-across-generations-166426/. Accessed 27 April 2017.
2. Economy, Peter. "9 Powerful Tips for Communicating Better with Millennials." *Inc.*, 24 Sept. 2015, https://www.inc.com/peter-economy/9-powerful-tips-for-communicating-better-with-millennials.html. Accessed 29 April 2017.
3. Rampton, John. "The Future of Messaging: How to Text Without Data or Wi-fi." *Inc.*, 19 June 2015, https://www.inc.com/john-rampton/the-future-of-messaging-how-to-text-without-data-or-wifi.html. Accessed 21 April 2017.
4. HIckman, Greg. "23 Crazy Mobile Marketing Stats Show Mobile is a Must in Your Business." *Mobile Marketing Engine*, http://mobilemarketingengine.com/23-mobile-marketing-stats/. Accessed 29 April 2017.
5. Silverman, Rachel Emma. "Workplace Distractions: Here's Why You Won't Finish This Article." *The Wall Street Journal*, 11 Dec. 2012, https://www.wsj.com/articles/SB10001424127887324339204578173252223022388. Accessed 29 April 2017.

CHAPTER 48

1. "Is There Still Such a Thing as Standard Office Attire?" *Office Team*, 31 May 2016, https://www.roberthalf.com/officeteam/blog/is-there-still-such-a-thing-as-standard-office-attire. Accessed 29 April 2017.
2. Peltz, James F. "Why Office Dress Codes Keep Getting More Casual." *Los Angeles Times*, 16 June 2016, http://www.latimes.com/business/la-fi-qa-dress-codes-20160616-snap-story.html. Accessed 30 April 2017.

3. Jenkins, Ryan. "4 Obstacles Millennials Must Overcome to Execute Their Best Ideas." *Inc.*, 5 Jan. 2016, https://www.inc.com/ryan-jenkins/4-obstacles-millennial-innovators-face-how-to-beat-them.html. Accessed 29 April 2017.

4. Feloni, Richard. "How Levi's Made 'Business Causual' The Standard in American Workplaces." *Business Insider*, 12 Aug. 2014, http://www.businessinsider.com/levis-helped-define-business-casual-2014-8. Accessed 29 April 2017.

5. "Cracking the Dress Code Dilemma." *Salary.com*, http://business.salary.com/cracking-the-dress-code-dilemma/. Accessed 29 April 2017.

6. Green, Dennis. "JPMorgan Just Relaxed Its Office Dress Code in a Huge Way." *Business Insider*, 3 June 2016, http://www.businessinsider.com/jp-morgans-relaxed-dress-code-2016-6. Accessed 29 April 2017.

7. Fernandes, Deirdre. "MassMutual's Relaxed Dress Policy Aims to Appeal to Millennials." *Boston Globe*, 19 Jan. 2016, https://www.bostonglobe.com/business/2016/01/19/massmutual-more-relaxing-dress-policy/q4EKNkKpySJCAkbpnUuxTJ/story.html. Accessed 29 April 2017.

8. "What to Wear." *Crown Horwath*, 2016, https://www.crowehorwath.com/insights/asset/what-to-wear-video/. Accessed 29 April 2017.

9. "The 2017 Deloitte Millennial Survey- Apprehensive Millennials: Seeking Stability and Opportunities in an Uncertain World." *Deloitte*, 2017, https://www2.deloitte.com/content/dam/Deloitte/global/Documents/About-Deloitte/gx-deloitte-millennial-survey-2017-executive-summary.pdf. Accessed 19 April 2017.

10. Hinchliffe, Emma. "40% of Millennials Say Mark Zuckerberg is Their Business Role Model." *Mashable*, 20 Sept. 2016, http://mashable.com/2016/09/20/zuckerberg-millennials-role-model/#_IyByOPjnqqC. Accessed 29 April 2017.

11. Gross, Doug. "Zuckerberg's Hoodie Rankles Wall Street." *CNN*, 9 May 2012, http://www.cnn.com/2012/05/09/tech/social-media/zuckerberg-hoodie-wall-street/index.html. Accessed 29 April 2017.

12. Saul, Heather. "Why Mark Zuckerberg Wears the Same Clothes to Work Everyday." *Independent*, 26 Jan. 2016, http://www.independent. co.uk/news/people/why-mark-zuckerberg-wears-the-same-clothes-to-work-everyday-a6834161.html. Accessed 29 April 2017.

13. "Introducing the You Economy." *Success*, 10 June 2016, http://www.success. com/article/introducing-the-youeconomy. Accessed 29 April 2017.

14. "Deloitte's Commitment to Building The Next Generation of Global Leaders." *Universum*, http://universumglobal.com/insights/deloittes-commitment-building-next-generation-global-leaders/. Accessed 29 April 2017.

CHAPTER 49

1. Terdiman, Daniel. "VR and Augmented Reality Will Soon Be Worth $150 Billion. Here are the Major Players." *Fast Company*, 13 Oct. 2015, https:// www.fastcompany.com/3052209/tech-forecast/vr-and-augmented-reality-will-soon-be-worth-150-billion-here-are-the-major-pla. Accessed 29 April 2017.

2. Mosendz, Polly. "Middle-Aged American Beat Millennials in Time Spent on Social Media." *Bloomberg*, 25 Jan. 2017, https://www.bloomberg.com/news/articles/2017-01-25/middle-aged-americans-beat-millennials-in-time-spent-on-social-media. Accessed 29 April 2017.

3. Keller, Gary and Jay Papasan. *The One Thing: The Surprisingly Simple Truth Behind Extraordinary Results*. Bard Press, 1 April 2013.

CHAPTER 50

1. Jenkins, Ryan. "30 Bold Social Media Statements You Need to Hear [Book Review]." *Ryan Jenkins*, 27 Jan. 2014, http://www.ryan-jenkins.

com/2014/01/27/30-bold-social-media-statements-you-need-to-hear-book-review/. Accessed 30 April 2017.

2. "Millennials at Work: Reshaping the Workplace." *PriceWaterhouse Coopers,* 2011, https://www.pwc.com/m1/en/services/consulting/documents/millennials-at-work.pdf. Accessed 29 April 2017.

3. "Despite Higher Risks, Greater Percentage of Employees are Holiday Shopping at Work, Finds CareerBuilder Survey." *CareerBuilder,* 24 Nov. 2015, http://www.careerbuilder.com/share/aboutus/pressreleasesdetail.aspx?sd=11%2F24%2F2015&id=pr923&ed=12%2F31%2F2015. Accessed 29 April 2017.

CHAPTER 51

1. Kantrowitz, Alex. "Google Says Millennial Influence on the Rise in B2B Buying." *Advertising Age,* 12 Mar. 2015. http://adage.com/article/btob/google-millennial-influence-rise-b2b-buying/297552/. Accessed 29 April 2017.

2. Vasquez, Adam and Heather Wadlinger. "The Next Generation of B2B Buyers: How the Millennial Business Buyer is Changing B2B Sales & Marketing." *Sacunas,* Mar. 2016, http://sacunas.net/reports/Millennial-B2B-Report_Sacunas-web.pdf. Accessed 29 April 2017.

3. Fottrel, Quentin. "Step Aside, Generation X- The Millennials Are Coming." *MarketWatch,* 30 May 2015, http://www.marketwatch.com/story/step-aside-generation-x-the-millennials-are-coming-2015-05-11. Accessed 27 April 2017.

4. Perez, Sarah. "Email is Dying Among Mobile's Youngest Users." *TechCrunch,* 24 Mar. 2016, https://techcrunch.com/2016/03/24/email-is-dying-among-mobiles-youngest-users/. Accessed 29 April 2017.

5. Schawbel, Dan. "Elite Daily and Millennials Branding Release Landmark Study on the Millennials Consumer." *Millennial Branding,* 20 Jan. 2015,

http://millennialbranding.com/2015/millennial-consumer-study/. Accessed 29 April 2017.

6. "10 Stats That Show Why User-Generated Content Works." *DMN*, 16 Oct. 2015, http://www.dmnews.com/content-marketing/10-stats-that-show-why-user-generated-content-works/article/444872/. Accessed 29 April 2017.

7. "Who Are Millennials." *Millennial Marketing*, http://www.millennialmarketing.com/who-are-millennials/. Accessed 29 April 2017.

8. "The Digital Evolution of B2B Marketing." *CEB*, 2012, https://www.cebglobal.com/marketing-communications/digital-evolution.html. Accessed 29 April 2017.

9. "2015 Cone Communications Millennials CSR Study." *Cone Communication*, http://www.conecomm.com/research-blog/2015-cone-communications-millennial-csr-study#download-research. Accessed 29 April 2017.

10. "Millennials' Mobile Demands Shift the Travel Industry." *Digital Commerce 360*, 12 May 2015, https://www.digitalcommerce360.com/2015/05/12/millennials-mobile-demands-shift-travel-industry/. Accessed 29 April 2017.

. . .

LIVE PRESENTATIONS

WANT TO BRING THESE STRATEGIES to your organization?
Ryan is available for keynotes, workshops, and webinars.
Inquire at www.Ryan-Jenkins.com/contact or text/call 770-695-7204.

TRAINING FOR MILLENNIALS

Need a turnkey solution to train and develop your Millennials?

21Mill is an online microlearning platform built to help Millennials perform better at work. 21Mill's training consists of twenty-one ten-to-fifteen-minute micro modules centered around Millennial-specific training topics. The content can be accessed via mobile or desktop 24/7.

Topics include:

- Overcoming entitlement
- Achieving work-life harmony
- Developing a strong work ethic
- Creating strong connections with colleagues
- Receiving and delivering workplace feedback
- And more...

Visit www.21Mill.com to learn more or request a free demo.

FREE WEEKLY INSIGHTS

Want Ryan's latest generational insights, strategies, and research delivered weekly to your inbox?

Ryan shares free weekly content (articles, videos, and podcasts) that will continue to help you better lead, develop, and engage the emerging generations.

Visit www.Ryan-Jenkins.com/subscribe.

ACKNOWLEDGMENTS

• • •

THANK YOU, ASHLEY, FOR BEING a patient wife, enthusiastic partner, loving mother, and a grammatical ninja. From the very beginning, you have been steadfast. Your unwavering belief, love, and encouragement has given me the freedom and security to dream, create, and persevere. I treasure you.

Thank you, Ella. Your smile, laugh, and zest for life drive me to limits I never knew were possible.

Thank you, Mom and Dad, for your countless and continual sacrifices. Thanks for creating a childhood environment filled with unconditional love that made it easy to experiment, fail, and grow. Dad, thanks for encouraging me to drink deeply from great books, pushing me to be a leader, and showing me how to be a great dad. Mom, thanks for your endless belief and support, for insisting I choose to "dance," and for relentlessly helping me to discover what I was created to do.

Thank you, Jason, for being a fearless older brother who blazed the trail. Thanks for turning back to include me, prop me up, and pour into me. Your encouragement, admiration, and respect mean the world to me.

Thank you to all of my extended family for your direct or indirect support. Every generation stands on the shoulders of those that came before them, but I got lucky to stand on the shoulders of positive, smart, adventurous, loving, sometimes quirky, and beyond generous family giants. I am lucky and will never squander my luck.

Thank you, friends (you know who you are), for being on the receiving end of countless conversations, questions, doubts, frustrations, brainstorms, and fears. Thanks for challenging, advocating, and celebrating with me at every step.

Thank you, colleagues, mentors, and partners, for parting with your time, wisdom, and advice. Your examples continue to inspire me and elevate my vision of what's possible. Your contributions and hard work have opened doors I never could have.

> I cannot remember the books I've read any more than the meals I have eaten; even so, they have made me.
> ~Ralph Waldo Emerson

Thank you to the past, present, and future authors, speakers, leaders, actors, musicians, artists, and strangers who will continue to shape me for the better.

Last, but not least, thank you to my Heavenly Father, with whom all things are possible.

• • •

RYAN JENKINS IS AN INTERNATIONALLY recognized Millennial keynote speaker, generations expert, and Inc.com columnist. For over six years, Ryan has helped organizations lead, engage, develop, and sell to the emerging generations (Millennials and Generation Z). Some of Ryan's clients include Coca-Cola, John Deere, Wells Fargo, Aetna, and Delta Air Lines.

Ryan is a leading voice on Millennials and Generation Z in the workplace. His blog, podcast, and Inc.com column inspire and equip thousands of people every week around the world. Ryan's passion, experience as a Millennial himself, and his fresh and forward-thinking approach to generations have made him one of the most highly sought-after generational and future-of-work keynote speakers.

Ryan's top-ranked generational insights have been featured in *Forbes, Fast Company, Inc.,* and *SUCCESS* magazines, to name a few.

Ryan is also a partner at 21Mill.com, a microlearning platform dedicated to helping Millennials perform better at work.

Ryan lives in Atlanta, Georgia, with his wife, two children, and dog.

Interested to have Ryan speak at your organization or at your next event? Visit www.Ryan-Jenkins.com/contact or text/call 770-695-7204.